DONALD
SOPER

A Biography

Donald Soper

A Biography

DOUGLAS THOMPSON

DENHOLM HOUSE PRESS
Nutfield · Surrey

First published 1971

© 1971 DOUGLAS THOMPSON

ISBN 0 85213 044 9

Printed in Great Britain by
Cox & Wyman Ltd., London, Reading and Fakenham

CONTENTS

Illustrations
    appear opposite pages 32, 33, 64, 65, 128, 129, 160 and 161.

1.

The Formative Years

The traumatic experience of the Boer War came to its incon-
clusive end in 1902. King Edward VII was at last crowned and
more than sixty years of Victorian pressure on the life-style of the
nation came to an end. Lord Salisbury, the last of the great Whigs,
retired from office. If events can carry a meaning deeper than
their simple contemporary occurrence and become portents, then
these three events do so. They heralded a period in which un-
dreamt factors were to change the face of England, if not the
world. An empire was doomed, a cultural pattern was broken,
the processes of government were forced out into untrodden
paths.

The war which had begun cheerily as an adventure for gently
born officers and the brutal soldiery in a far-off place had proved
to be a costly, protracted and disgracefully mismanaged shambles
which drew into itself the whole life of the nation. The people
suffered an agony of blood-letting and the imperial image was
shattered. Imperialism itself was to be among the doomed, though
dying slowly, and so was the patrician assumption that Christianity was the by-product of English culture by which all the
processes of administration and national life were regulated. They
were replaced by a deep revulsion against military prowess and
adventure and by a care-free abandon which has become history
as 'the Edwardian period'. Peace broke out and none guessed for
how short a period it was to endure.

If this was a time of the death of many old assumptions it was
also a time of new births. In 1902 the State, under the Balfour Act,
took over responsibility for secondary school education and set up
the tough aged-10 examination to guard the entry to this new

7

people's education. That Act in itself carried the promise of a new day – the masters of Britain were to be products of the new schools; there was a new road to the top.

In 1899, in a battle in the Trade Union Congress, James Ramsay MacDonald fashioned a resolution which resulted in the formation of the Labour Representation Committee which had as its objective the representation of the working-classes (a phrase in itself now out of date) in Parliament. A new voice was heard. So it was that with the disappearance of the last Prime Minister to sit in the House of Lords and with a new Party within the Commons, England's story reached one of those brink-moments in which anything might happen.

Gone were the days when the labouring classes could be legislated for as though they were still rural people whose hearts were steeped in the feudalism of the centuries. The years hurried on to 1906 when in the great landslide election the Liberal victory revealed the change which had overtaken the nation. In that election, the Labour Representation Committee, now become the Labour Party, found itself with 50 seats in the Liberal-controlled House. The voice of the 'working classes' sounded nationally for the first time.

Compassionate legislation was creeping on to the Statute Book. The Unemployed Workmen's Act, 1905, required Local Authorities to keep a register of the unemployed and to raise charitable help to succour them. While this Act was intended to avoid giving State help to the victims of unemployment, it did provide a precedent for the later Unemployment Exchanges Act of 1909.

In the wider context of world affairs the same process of change was present. In 1902 there was formed the Anglo-Japanese Alliance. For the first time a European World Power treated an Asian Power as equal. This action released the floodgates of Asian revival, to lead on to the modern Asian drama, Turkey's revolution, China's revolution, the Russo-Japanese war and the French Alliance.

A strange balance of change was struck, within and without. Abroad, our fleets were reorganized into the shape in use until recent times – Mediterranean, Atlantic and Home Fleets, and the first dreadnoughts were built. On the other hand, pacifism was gaining ground in the Liberal Party as the people digested the facts of the importation into the Transvaal of Chinese coolie labour which was segregated into camps. Had a disastrous war been fought for the benefit of the mine owners of the Rand?

In such periods of change as this at the turn of the century there are always personalities which link the old and the new. Every new day has its harbingers. The old ark launches its dove into the air. There are persons who, reared in the old school, dream some of the features of the new. The process of change gathers its energy as the minds of such persons thrust out probes into the unknown and, there are bodies of ideas which support such lives. Not least among these is the force of ethical religion, which detects the flaws in the old and struggles to adjust to a new day in which the flaws are gone but the virtues of the old are preserved. Reform precedes revolution.

The Free Church Tradition was one of such bodies of ideas and the new age owed much to it. If the old type of formal Christianity gave way under the strain of the times the freer forms of that religion provided both personalities and ideas which bridged the gap between the old ways and the new. Gladstone, MacDonald and others were fired with a passion for reform which was firmly founded on ethical criticism of the times, a deep optimism about the future, and a strong puritan integrity which defied the rot of post-war decay, firmly believing in the possibility of a new age to come.

Within a family of just such qualities Donald Oliver Soper was born on January 31st, 1903, to Ernest and Caroline Soper. Ernest Soper was the epitome of the character pattern which abounded in the Free Church life of the times. Of high integrity, of inflexible purpose and stern, he was yet deeply concerned with the practical application of Christianity to the age in which he lived. It was such people who were the power behind the then influential 'Nonconformist Conscience', not without enough money to live graciously but deeply aware of the responsibility which station, education and true religion confer. Years afterwards a young undergraduate of the times remembers him as 'an awesome figure whom one could not but revere'.

Caroline Soper was the ideal mate for such a man of the times and herself a classical product of the late Victorian era. With a fine education she combined that cultivated charm which the Victorian era had laid down as the pattern for young wives and mothers yet she was headmistress of a London girls' school for years. Her inspiration unquestionably lay across the lives of her three children, who could bring their friends into the home and always know that their mother would be also mother to them, softening father's stern judgement but herself ruling by tenderness.

This pattern of the master of the house, the cultured wife and the children growing up in protected graciousness (perhaps, the finest product of the age which was dying) was strong enough to thrust its influence into the new century. It has given to our times a kind of person able to take the changing circumstances and create from them positive values. It was in such families that the new thought of the dying century was family table talk. The urge which could descend at its lowest to 'slumming' and reach at its highest to genuine social reform was the subject matter of their mealtime conversation.

It has been said that the Methodist Revival travelled from the Oxford Don and his cultured world through to the rural masses of England: that the real reforms of our society have always happened this way. At the end of the nineteenth century it could be argued that the same principle held. The cultivated sense of responsibility for the world about them gave to folk in this class an appreciation of the newly emerging factors facing them. To quote the doyen of West African aristocracy, the Asantahene of Ashanti, 'Every good new thing springs off an old root'. Beneath the new world which was emerging, the roots of this old family life searched forward and absorbed the nutrition from the world of tomorrow. Firm direction, gracious guidance, close ties with a brother and a sister made the family the formative world in which thinking was done. How far away such a civilization now appears to be. Nevertheless, many of the pioneers of the twentieth century are the products of that culture.

Donald Soper, born in Wandsworth but brought up principally in the Streatham home, was one such projection of the past into the suburban scene. He had one brother to whom he was deeply attached and whose early death from the complications of diabetes, then a medical puzzle, had a serious effect on Donald's life. Beside the two boys was one sister to make the home the thing it should be. In such a home music was a cultural obligation and Donald's brother showed great promise in this field. Donald himself fell under its spell and the foundations were laid in childhood of his love of both the piano and the penny whistle.

A story which comes from much later in his life, carries poignant remembrance of his home life, his love of his musical brother and the deep sense of responsibility these things bred in him. On one of the Mission Projects of the Order of Christian Witness there was found to be in the team a young lad aged sixteen who had taken to the saxophone. His playing of this instrument was so atrocious that the 'family' of missioners rejected him and he was sent to practise as far from the rest of the team as possible.

When Dr. Soper made his regular visit to the team to give them his day's leadership, the boy immediately, and to the embarrassment of the team, pounced on the doctor with, 'I play the saxophone, Doctor'. 'Do you?' was the reply. 'Let's have a go.' They went to the chapel piano and the boy, accompanied by the doctor, produced appalling noises on his instrument. The doctor blenched but then drew the boy nearer and said, 'Look, you're just not getting the best out of that thing. Listen.'

He carefully fingered out chords on the piano with the boy following, and for the first time in his life the lad played true music. Was the boy brother? Was the teacher mother? Was the gesture the inescapable response of the boy trained in the Streatham home? The staff and children of the National Children's Home, for whom Donald Soper has played penny whistle obligatos in their great rallies for years, might well think so. The Methodist minister and the parish priest of a church in which he fell upon the church piano and crashed out jazz music have other opinions.

All this was the regulation cultural drill in the kind of home into which this baby of 1903 was born. There were other kinds of home. There were children with bare feet running the streets; there were the scant amenities of the Durham villages; there were the beer-soaked homes of the great cities and towns. These, as we have seen, were not forgotten in the suburban Streatham home but were accepted as part of the burden of responsibility borne by the class into which Donald Soper was born. But that realization did not for one moment relieve the parents of the duty of affording the children of the middle class the education to which they were traditionally entitled. That education, at home and in school, was undoubtedly seen as the preparation for the service of the Country, the Empire and the labouring classes now emerging on to the stage of national life. Kipling's poetry was not a joke in the pre-1914 world.

Mrs. Soper's choice of school for her son as he grew up reflects the same care and idealistic dream, for she sent him to Aske's School, Hatcham, in the area known as New Cross, London. Such a school is of the neither too high nor too low category – neither an Eton nor a new-type secondary school under the recent act of Parliament. Such schools were to produce national leaders within a generation. A sound, university-aimed and relatively ancient foundation with a ball at the heart of it – such was the Aske's of the early twenties.

In Donald Soper's case the ball matched the learning and his parents, one imagines, would have been puzzled or shocked had it not done so. 'If it is round and bounces I can handle it', was the belief of the boys, and Donald was no exception. Hockey, tennis, soccer and cricket provide four kinds of ball which he handled with dexterity. To these sports he added swimming. When later he went up to Cambridge he gained colours in each of these. Years later when in high office in the Methodist Church and sitting on the platform of the national Conference of that Church, he was sometimes assumed by the members on the floor of the house to be deaf when in fact the long cord was the earpiece attachment of a transistor radio on which he was following the Test cricket score during the duller debates.

Such a boyhood leaves marks which can never be eradicated. It imprints a self-confidence which can become either arrogance or magnanimity. It can produce a tendency to follow the father of the family into some ancestral pursuit or contrariwise into a repudiation of the father's profession. It can produce an aloof, superior attitude to the mass of people, not unlike the regard a man might have for the horse in his stable. It certainly engenders in the grown man an awareness of wider affairs. When the parental image contains that streak of puritanism which was in the Soper parents, there is no escape from abiding concern for great issues of national importance. It is probable, in 90 per cent of cases, however, that the concern will express itself in traditional attachments to the methods of the ruling classes. Where this does not happen, some other influence has been brought to bear which modifies the old pattern and, while retaining the character qualities, carries the person out into new adventures.

There is, therefore, a knife-edge crisis in the scene at the breakfast table in Streatham when Donald Soper was thirteen years of age. With the marmalade and toast he announced to the family his intention for his career. In Dr. Soper's own words, that morning is remembered like this.

'I never wanted to do anything else, and I can remember at the breakfast table, when I was thirteen years of age, announcing to my father that I intended to become a Methodist Minister. This was, of course, childish impertinence, but through my parents I had come to love the Church and find myself in it.'

The boy was thirteen, the year 1916, that horrible year when the whole world expected Britain to lose a war – by 1917 German submarines were squatting in the entrances to British harbours, the nation on hard commons and men dying in their thousands in France. What was it which drew the young lad out of the traditional pathway to plan his life in the Ministry?

The Wesleyan Methodist Church of that time was a powerful organization. Its main strength then lay in the middle class stratum of society. In the dark war days its main churches and halls from Westminister to Newcastle-on-Tyne were crowded with people. It was the age of strong evening services when the preacher had before him large congregations. Many of the churches were very deeply engaged in social service to the Armed Forces through canteens and other forms of caring. At the great railway termini evening troop trains were leaving for France and the public was on the platforms to wave good-bye to the men. It was possible, and frequent, for the whole mass of people to raise a hymn and for a Wesleyan Minister to lead them in prayer. Death is a leveller and war is the handmaid of death. The classes were meeting as never before, the great unwashed and the gently born milled together on those platforms. The parson was in the midst.

Whereas in the pulpits of such churches as that at Streatham the old ban on politics in the pulpit was still strongly upheld, there were voices in Methodism which spoke fearlessly about the war itself and the social and international affairs which wracked the nation. Indeed, the rebel parson was a phenomenon which paid little regard to the denominational lines dividing the churches. The moral upheaval which the war precipitated was the subject of frequent condemnation. In this respect the Wesleyan pulpit was probably more influential than the Anglican. Dr. Henry Bett was at this time thundering an uncompromising pacifism at York (Wesley). Henry Carter was the mouthpiece of his church on the intemperance of war-time Britain. A galaxy of men was serving in the Forces as chaplains, not a few under the leadership of George Standing, himself a Primitive Methodist leader who had fought and won the battle for Free Church representation in the ranks of commissioned chaplains.

Within the inner life of the Wesleyan Methodist Church there was much to feed the mind of a growing boy. Its overseas mission was one of the greatest – indeed the largest missionary society in Europe. Mission education within the Church kept Methodist people in touch with the corners of the earth from China to Central America. There were missionaries with the Chinese Labour Force in France serving as linguistic officers. There were Wesleyan missionaries down the coast of Africa. There were men helping escapees from the tyranny of the Belgian Congo to find a home in Rhodesia, and Leslie Weatherhead was with the Indian Army. The Church's people had an ear open to the world and – consequently – a stake in great matters.

There was nothing remarkable, therefore, in a boy grown in the Church dreaming that his whole potential could be absorbed in being among the loved ministry of such a Church – for no ministry was ever loved like this by its people. The Methodist Church was a perfectly proper vehicle for all the boy could dream the man might put into his world. Irrelevance would be the last thought in choosing to serve this way.

In one particular, perhaps, Donald Soper's memory of that thirteen-year-old decision is mistaken. A 'childish impertinence' he called it. Was this so? At thirteen the majority of his contemporaries were within a year of leaving school and going out into the world to work in jobs from which they would not change. The Methodist ministry of the times would recruit many from among such, its principle being that no candidate should be refused on financial grounds alone. The Soper progress of grammar school to university and to theological training was then a minority story conditioned by the background at home from which he sprang. Perhaps the 'call' was the more remarkable for that.

It is equally remarkable that many of the men recruited from the boys then leaving school at fourteen would become conventional imitations of the people in the background of Donald Soper's life, while he would follow the lines which that conventional world laid down for him and arrive in the Lords on the Labour benches. It is important to understand that this development was not eccentric but sheer logic. The Soper of today is the product of the puritan of yesterday. The journey from *The Times* to the *Tribune* is a natural journey. Pulpit, platform, a champion of popular rights and a dignified Roman official are all tribunes. They are all 'Soper', too.

There is a striking similarity to the progression of the Founder of Methodism, born in 1703. John Wesley went from a family which preserved the best aristocratic traditions to Charterhouse and from there went on to Oxford to take holy orders. He lived to become the idol of the illiterate people of Britain.

In Donald Soper's case it was an easy transition to pass from Aske's School to St. Catherine's, Cambridge. Here he read history, threw himself into the sporting life of the university and gained his colours in hockey, tennis, cricket, soccer and swimming. The first example of his skill in repartee which he later perfected on Tower Hill belongs to this period in his judgement on rowing as a sport. 'It is stupid to find eight men pulling their guts out to go in a direction opposite to that in which they are looking.' The remark tells us more about Soper than it does about rowing.

Cambridge afforded excellent opportunities for his love of music. His piano work was well known and in demand. He sang in a distinguished tenor which the years on the open air platform have destroyed. Strangely enough there was in his student days an open-air speaker, to whom Donald was greatly attracted, who similarly lost a singing voice. It was a wasted warning.

The unrecorded sacrifices in a life are sometimes the greatest and for one whose chief joy has been music to lose a singing voice is great enough. Today one of his best friends describes his 'Monday morning voice' as the sound of a dying corncrake. The description fits, for the corncrake is a bird which industrial pollution has driven from England and it makes a good symbol of the things destroyed by the sins which Soper attacks. It was different, however, in those St. Catherine's days. He could then bring home hit songs from the theatre and with no trouble produce them in his friends' rooms note perfect.

During the 1926 General Strike (which occurred during his theological training) with his friend Joseph Webb, today a veteran minister of the South African Conference, he opened a centre for strikers, particularly railwaymen, in Romsey Town, on the outskirts of Cambridge, where the men could gather, drink tea and attend the concerts he provided. Joe Webb would play the cornet and strum the piano while Donald sang and entertained on his penny whistle. In this centre, often surrounded by keenly questioning men, he discovered the thing which he was later to call 'the fellowship of controversy'.

On one occasion a village chapel near Cambridge invited Donald Soper to dedicate a new organ. This he did by giving a recital which consisted of variations on the tune 'My sweet Hortense', then very popular, though hardly in the Wesleyan musical tradition. Parodies of this tune proliferated in the 1914–18 army. One of his items he introduced by saying, 'You know the Bach fugues – now listen to this!' He then laced Hortense with trimmings. After the performance a bearded gentleman questioned him about this item, saying that he had studied Bach for years but did not recall this fugue. Donald muttered something about having treated the music somewhat futuristically and made a swift retreat.

Pedantic criticisms still infuriate him in Hyde Park while a violent attack on his main theme stimulates him. The point in the chapel was that Hortense had dedicated an organ successfully – Bach could not have done better. It was not his fault that Bach had not thought of Hortense.

It was while reading at St. Catherine's, in 1924, that he fulfilled his unchanged determination of his thirteenth year and offered as a candidate for the Wesleyan Methodist ministry. In those days the number of candidates was high and the competition strong. But the number of men offering who had an academic background was quite small. It is perhaps no exaggeration to say that the number was not only small but that it was also suspect in the pews of the Church. While year by year John Wesley's ancient foundation, Kingswood School, sent forward candidates for the ministry with a public school background, they were somehow different, probably ministers' sons. Other candidates with first-class degrees or other academic advantages were thought to have skipped the rough and tumble of working life in business or factory and less likely to make efficient ministers in the Methodist tradition. In some circles even the theological training undertaken by all the candidates was thought to 'spoil the men'. These were strange convictions in a Church which owed its origin to a Fellow of Lincoln College, Oxford, but many influences had entered into the Church since that beginning.

In practice this feeling meant that men who were already graduates when they offered for the ministry were subjected to precisely the same disciplines of selection as the generality of candidates. They must have been Lay Preachers; they must have received the approval of a local church for their candidature; they must preach trial sermons, stand the test of written and oral examination before the regional synods of the Church and the Connexional Committee of the Conference before they were accepted or rejected by the Conference itself.

Under such a system it is clear that the temptation to enter one of the other, sister Churches which had a system of taking men straight from the universities into theological training and on into the ranks of their ministries has always been great. One degree in the humanities, one in divinity with ordination to follow is so much simpler, but it does not make a Methodist minister, and it was a Methodist minister which Donald Soper intended to be. That calling demanded the years of Local Preaching (as Methodism describes the conduct of services by laymen) before candidature and up to seven years of 'Probation' before ordination.

Donald Soper's entry into the Methodist ministry coincided with an attempt to find a new way of dealing with this problem of the better-trained candidate. In the upshot a compromise solution emerged which has stood the test of the years and brought great blessings to the Methodist movement.

It was arranged that a selection of men with pre-candidature degrees should be housed at Cambridge, teamed into the university registration system by the goodwill of Fitzwilliam House (now Fitzwilliam College), and read divinity for two years to obtain a Bachelor of Arts degree before going out into the work on an adjusted period of probation. Accommodation was built at Wesley House, Jesus Lane, Cambridge, for some twenty men. 'The House' opened during Soper's time under the direction of Dr. Maldwyn Hughes, known to the men as 'The Boss'. At the same time in other Methodist theological colleges arrangements were evolving which allowed men to read a first degree as internal or external students of certain universities. The majority of the men, however, continued to take the non-degree training and in the general colleges the majority point of view remained biased to that type of preparation, so that the Wesley House men have continued down the years to carry a distinctive mark which has singled them out. In fact when they have done well they have done extraordinarily well.

When he appeared before the team of examiners at the final tests, known in Methodism as 'the July Committee', Donald Soper had just sat for Part II of the Historical Tripos and, the examiner being Dr. Eric Waterhouse, he was grilled by him on the Council of Trent. Information poured out of him with such fluency that the other men in the seven-strong group of candidates sank into despair of their own chances of acceptance in the face of such competition.

Entering this new system from 1924 until 1926 Donald Soper, at first based on Cheshunt College while 'the House' was building, followed up his historical reading with what was then Section 5 of Part II of the Theological Tripos (now Part III) which involved advanced study of the philosophy of religion.

He attended lectures in the university including those of Dr. Tennant, and there laid a solid foundation for a ministry of Christian apologetics. In the Tripos lists of May 1926 Soper was placed in the First Class. This success was a great stimulus to Dr. Maldwyn Hughes and to the new foundation of Wesley House, for its members were well aware that the University was watching the House with a critical eye.

The men of his year in Wesley House knew that they had an unusual and colourful personality among them even when they fought with him. They were all of a generation of students who were troubled about the Call to the Ministry and some have since left it, but somehow they knew that Donald Soper would stay the course, if only because he was the most revolutionary of them all.

As a student he worked hard in spite of numerous other activities. His considerable scholarly gifts were eclipsed by his personal drive and assurance to such a degree that, although his academic record was fine, it is not for this that he is now remembered among his contemporaries. He set trends and blazed trails. When he gained his First, for example, 'The Boss' was heard to say of another man who had scored only a Second Class, 'He has more philosophy in his little finger than Donald has in his whole body'. As is often the case with such personalities, those who knew him best knew him least. His contacts with other lives were outgoings but rarely incomings into the depths of his own life and thought.

His friendship with Joseph Webb, his junior in Wesley House, is perhaps characteristic. Webb was over in this country from the Methodist Church in South Africa for training, and such 'exhibits' were rarer in that day than this. He still tells of how, arriving by grace of God and the aid of a taxi at his journey's end, he was wandering round the court of Cheshunt College feeling very far from the Rand and very lost when a loud voice hailed him, 'Watcheer cock!' It is as likely as not that Donald Soper, the hailer, saw something in the cut of Webb's clothes which made him sure this character was 'colonial'. He took the overseas student under his wing heartily until the South African zest for life returned to cope with both Cambridge and Soper.

Soper made an excellent guide to the weird ways of Cambridge, both as university and town, and there was much for a South African to learn about British Methodism which only an old addict such as Soper could impart. So as close a friendship sprang up as Soper ever had in his student days. Methodism had not at that time yet founded its famous International Houses for overseas students and at term-end no one except Donald remembered that this student had no home for the long vacation. He became part of the Streatham family.

During one period in Wesley House Soper and Webb 'kept' adjoining rooms in the new building and practised a Christian Communism which was not always independent of other people's belongings silently extracted from the cupboards in their 'gyp rooms'. Yet, strangely, no one seemed to mind. 'It appeared to us natural', recalls one of the victims. Whether it was that the South African, feeling the cold, burned his gas fire continually, or for some other unspoken reason, Donald Soper moved in on Webb lock, stock and barrel, only returning to his own room to sleep. This arrangement was stopped dead in its tracks when The Boss found out. It is worth remembering that this could happen; it occurred without explanation because Soper was just Soper.

In this period Donald needed friends to aid him. He developed trouble with his eyesight which almost completely blinded him for a period. In this predicament it was the South African who proved himself the saviour. Though reading languages and Old Testament himself, he propped up Donald in his work by reading his texts for him.

Joe Webb probably had his reward when Donald, running into a patch of heavy weather with the lady who was subsequently to be his wife, prevailed upon Webb to make a special journey to London to act as intermediary in straightening out the situation. A trip to the cinema during which the advocate did his best proved successful and the relationship went on. The confident assurance we have noted stands out in this story. A handsome rowing man with a romantic background and fetching South African accent might have appeared to a less confident person to be the last choice to go as a lover's pleader. It was not so to Soper. He was sure that no intermediary could or would compete, still less appear to be more desirable. He was right.

This was nothing so simple as the strong man using the weaker. The two were co-equal giants, as the years have demonstrated since. Dr. Joseph Webb is as famous in his own world of the Republic as Donald Soper in his and in the corridors of World Methodist power Webb probably excels him in reputation.

Years have rolled by since those days in the House during which these two men have probably espoused opposing causes more often than not, for the born South African may labour for equality among the races and yet appear to go a long way round to achieve it, while the outside observer can, to the native, seem to be rash and extremist. In those years Donald Soper and his wife have paid one visit to South Africa as Dr. Webb's guests. On his frequent visits to Britain Dr. Webb has always sought out Donald Soper, but the great issues between the two nations have never been discussed by them at depth.

How far the friendships of some men are encounters rather than sharing is a fascinating study. Does the spirit long for intimacies which prove to be impossible for men of this type? There is a strange hesitation on the brink of self-disclosure which suggests that emotional energy is so deep that the person intuitively draws back from releasing it, except in acts of 'instant compassion' and bursts of generosity. There is a fear of long-term involvement and deep-level sharing which for others would be the goal of friendship. 'He travels the fastest who travels alone.' But does he always want to?

2.

Soper Breaks Out

The Methodist Conference stations the ministers of the Church to their 'circuits' (i.e. groups of churches) in September of each year. Many of them were and still are invited by the various circuits under arrangements which the Conference confirms. Others are sent out to posts to which they had not thought to go and year by year there are ministers uprooted from places to which they had been invited because the Stationing Committee considers their gifts would better serve some circuit with special needs.

Under this system Donald Soper left the Cambridge environment which had been his home so long and was posted to Oakley Place, a mission-centre lying off the Old Kent Road in the heart of South London. Change could hardly be more violent than this, yet in many ways he was returning home. Streatham was just round the corner and St. Katharine Docks nearby to revive old memories or bring out the contrasts.

He went to the South London Mission as a probationer, that is a young, unordained minister. He was slim, boisterous, wearing the (then) universally accepted student symbol of the 'Oxford bags' – wide-legged trousers with room for two pairs of legs. The rest of his attire was that of the young layman of the times – sporty jacket, bow tie, and a slouch. The days of the cassock as day/night wear were yet to come.

It was the era of the Central Halls. Joseph Rank had put his mark on Methodism and was followed by his zealous son, J. Arthur Rank, now Lord Rank. Their thesis was that a type of building was needed which looked as little like a church as possible and in which the equipment approached the current standards of the cinema. Here men and women were to encounter the Gospel in a neutral setting. The primary object of the Central Hall programme was mass preaching in preaching halls unhampered by an ecclesiastical overtone. The social emphasis which became part of the programme was a later development. Soper was chosen as a preacher.

The complex problems of 'Mighty London' had also fixed themselves on the Methodist conscience in the nineteenth century and the Rank family was generous in support of a special London programme under the direction of a special committee, the London Mission and Extension Fund. This was the outreach into the poverty and 'rescue' of the people of inner London. The London Mission Centres were places of compassion and evangelism. Great reputations had been made in this work, Dr. Scott Lidgett, Lax of Poplar, J. E. Rattenbury among them, and the new boy entered 'on test'.

By 1926 the pattern of this London mission work was beginning to look dated. There was something of the smear of 'slumming' and do-gooding upon it. What had been un-political was beginning to feel the breeze rising from the working man's self-consciousness which demanded not charity but a new social order. January 1924 had seen the first Labour Government.

Were second-hand clothes for the poor, one-day summer outings for the old ladies and the children, meetings with cups of tea or sobering-up facilities for the drunks, enough in a changing world? Why were people poor? What made people drown life in drinking? The services offered really belonged to people who accepted their under-privileged status without question, but the day of questioning had come. How long could the Church be content to arrange for the sons of public schools to live in settlements among the poor and for the richer suburban churches to pay for work done by 'heroic' ministers and Wesley Deaconesses? The new question was, Why is there an East End or a South London ghetto?

Students coming fresh from the colleges were critical, sensitive, often orientated to the Left but deeply attracted by the still popular Central Hall preaching centres and the London Mission stations. It is unfair to no one to say that the most adventurous among the probationers were keen to get to the Central Hall rostrums in London, Manchester, Birmingham and the other industrial cities. Nor were men lacking to try again in the crowded tenements.

Of the men longing for a chance in such places there were two kinds. One was the straight evangelist in the Sankey–Moody or Henry Drummond tradition who wished to offer the traditional Gospel where the people divorced from the Churches now were. The other group was seething with social ideas, eager to go in and change things at the base. For them Christianity was taking on a new social meaning. The first group would continue the long line of powerful preaching and programmes of compassion. The second might do anything, including move from the Left to the far Right, under the pressure of the enormous social problems of Britain. To preach to great crowds, to enter the conflict of social change, were the twin aims of some magnificent young men of that generation.

There were risks either way; of becoming a mouthpiece only, of being bogged down in administration. Two similar strains of young men could be found offering for the overseas stations of the Church. The Chinese Church categorized them. One they called the 'Spiritualizers' and the other the 'Socializers'. That Church was wise enough to accept both. The British Methodist heirarchy shared that wisdom but it is doubtful if it knew which type it stationed on the Old Kent Road when it put Donald Soper there as a budding 'Central Mission man'.

The years have led people to imagine that if the mission ministers were to be categorized as in China Soper would certainly fall into the category of 'Socializer'. The truth is not so uncomplicated as this. There is no accounting for his ministry without realizing that there is a Drummond under the skin. Straight evangelism is a passion which runs beneath his work from beginning to end and it was no easy battle to pass from a highly conservative interpretation of preaching to the pattern which he came to adopt. His life was torn by a volcanic demand to present the Christian Faith with converting power in people's lives. Donald Soper the evangelist and Donald Soper the sacramentarian are basic to Soper the reforming socialist. He has wrestled with the conviction that the Christian Faith is basic to true living, built-in for all humanity, and to convince and convert is the determination underlying the social witness and the public image.

In the early twenties the quest for new, intelligible preaching was a keynote in the training colleges. Dr. Maldwyn Hughes was one of a galaxy of tutors dedicated to making cogent evangelists of the men in their charge. The apparent failure of the Churches to hold the people lay heavily on their hearts. Their reaction to it was the conviction that there was nothing dated about the Gospel nor was the man-in-the-street allergic to Christ. They were sure that communication had failed by an imperfect presentation of what Christianity is. Update the expression of the Faith, include the new phenomena of our times within the embrace of an adequate theology, teach that theology where people actually were, in language they commonly used, and the result would be a resurgence of Faith. They saw this as a natural sequence; they believed a reasoned faith stated reasonably to be irresistible. Perhaps it was not then seen how deeply Platonic this conviction was. It implied that man was good and, once guided to see the good, must capitulate to it. Dean Inge, the 'gloomy' Dean of St. Paul's, was in his hey-day and his approach to intellectual evangelism epitomized the thinking of his day profoundly. The thinking owed much to him, his work being widely read.

It took the tragic years of the Thirties and Forties to correct this 'Confucian' belief in man's basic goodness; the insights of the rising analytical psychologies revealed the brute resistances to the good when it is seen. Through all the devastation which was to follow, however, those who had been trained to examine, restate and proclaim the Gospel have not faltered in their struggle. The Soper preaching has not deviated from the attempt to convert by persuasion. The task of doing this lies behind the whole Soper social ministry.

In his book *Tower Hill, 12.30* Dr Soper writes, 'The underlying conviction which prompted me to adventure myself upon the Hill was the certainty that Christianity is the real focus-point of all our questioning and that in it can be found the answer to every problem that vexes human kind. It is the complete world view. For me the teaching of Jesus, that all peoples belong to the family of God, and all things become the furniture of God's home, is the truth which makes us free. In it the apparent antitheses are reconciled, purpose and significance are everywhere discoverable, and nothing is trivial. Moreover to believe, with Jesus, that it is in God that "we live and have our being" and that we depend on him, and by his grace alone are able to do or be anything, is the key to the powers and forces and tendencies which make up the current of our daily life. Above all this, however, is the experience, albeit fragmentary and spasmodic, that in this booming, buzzing confusion I can hold fellowship with God through Jesus Christ – that God has called even me into partnership with himself'.

It is Christianity as the 'complete world view' which is the root from which the whole of the world-famous socio-political Soper attitude derives. It is because the world is political, social, economic and filled with problems which can only have socio-political solutions that he, and other ministers of his generation, have struggled with world problems in social terms. An all-embracing God embraces social structures and cares about them.

Soper came down to London already wrestling with the social milieu in which he struggled to assert human sanity. He was of the Left, pacifist, and trained in objective analysis of the contemporary situation in terms of Jesus' message to men. He went in the early years in London to the London School of Economics and Political Science as part of his Christian reaction to God's call. When the Methodist Conference thrust him into the heart of London it really decided for him the course he would take. This was God's, this city, this nation. How could it be so unless God was on safari within a rebellious world?

In 1921 the miners had struck against reduced wages and longer hours and the strike had failed. The owners of the mines had cut wages savagely and refused the demand for the reorganization of what was even then a dying industry. There was deep poverty in the north of England.

Soper came to the South London Mission in the aftermath of the 1926 General Strike which arose from the mortal struggle of the miners to get some redress. The General Strike also failed, in part at least, because the Trades Union Council deserted the miners and left them to their fate – and what a fate it was. Victimization of miners by delayed re-engagement, at lower wages and with still longer hours, the Trade Disputes Act which declared strikes illegal, the levying of the political contribution made illegal except with the signed consent of the contributor – such were the terms. Union funds slumped and membership fell. The government proved too craven to demand reorganization of the coal industry. In that first Church year of Soper's ministry the nation was to all intents and purposes at war with itself, and it was a bad war which need not have happened.

Men and women in droves were drifting from the north to London seeking work and new homes. Colonies of them dotted the London scene as later Irish colonies and immigrant colonies were to do. These immigrants were the pick of the northern labour force. Behind them they left the rest, old, inarticulate, beaten. The working days lost in the year of 1926 numbered 162,233,000.

In truth it took the years from 1919 until the mid-twenties to feel the real impact of the devastating losses of the First World War. Governments assumed the war had stopped and the world and nation were as before the declaration of war. The early demise of the first Labour Administration and the return of the 'Safety First' type of Baldwin Government – which lasted the whole of Donald Soper's time as a probationer – made up but one wave of the surging forces which met and broke over the ruins of British society. The promise of a land fit for heroes to live in, accepted as a possible goal by millions, met the countervailing force of the nation's poverty and the exhaustion of its leadership. That exhaustion demonstrated its presence by the stupid quarrelling over 'reparations' from Germany and the demand for the containment of that nation.

The world was heaving with new forces liberated by the war and born, as is so often the case, out of the exhaustion of the principal world powers, of which Britain was first when the war began. In 1926 an Imperial Conference was compelled to record equal status between Britain and her Dominions. Germany had to be admitted to the League of Nations. Kemal Ataturk wrote his *New Turkey* in 1927. On the other side of the world the weakness of the Great Powers made it possible for China to repudiate the unequal treaties and General Chiang Kai-shek thrust north on his mission of liberation from the control of both Western Powers and war lords. Never again would a Chinese park display a notice reading 'No Chinese or dogs admitted'. Stalin at last overcame his enemies and emerged master of the Russias while Trotsky fled. Borodin manipulated the Chinese revolution and was then ignominiously dismissed by the Chinese government.

The young probationer minister in the London Mission was a student of these things, his faith and theology demanding that he should be, for this was the arena of his God's activity.

Contemplating it, there were some extraordinary factors to be reckoned with in the life of the Christian Church which appeared to be indications of the relevance of his Gospel.

The years which saw such world-wide political débâcle were proving to be fruitful and innovating years within the Christian community. While Soper was still up at Cambridge the Christian Conference on Politics, Economics and Citizenship took place in Birmingham and such voices as that of William Temple and G. Studdert Kennedy were carrying Christian insights into the nation's life. It was the first conspectus of social phenomena viewed from the Christian angle to take place in British Christianity. Its Reports were basic to a preacher's thinking in those probationary years. In 1927 serious attention was given to the body of Christians speaking out across the divisions of the Church in the Lausanne Conference on Faith and Order. In 1928, in Jerusalem of all places, and only possible there because of the results of the War, there met the International Missionary Conference, drawing together the historic Church in equal consultation with the newer Churches born of the century-long modern missionary movement. The principal message of this Conference was that young Churches and old, within new nations and old, constituted one world partnership in service to the whole of mankind. Within that bracket it laid down programmes for social reorganization, health and hygiene, universal literacy, and education at all levels. It asserted that this whole programme was the expression of the true mission of God to the world. It marked the point of the emergence of such figures as Daniel T. Niles, Toyohiko Kagawa – perhaps the 'Sopers' of the Asian world.

Under the violent stimuli of the contemporary world and with gleams of hope issuing from the Church's new insights, the men who began their ministry in 1926 were men to envy. They were to be envied chiefly because they faced a tough situation but believed they had the resources to meet it. In Soper's case, as in some others, preaching was among the trusty resources – they believed in it, and, as we have noted, it was undoubtedly as a preacher that Donald Soper was stationed to the London Mission.

In Cambridge he had already won a reputation as one who preached with contemporary language and ideas and was in demand by the churches round about for special preaching occasions. His was a style which, as early in his story as the

student days, had won life-coverage and brought fresh meaning
out of the Gospel for church-goers and non-church people alike.

His personal attitude to this work is recorded in his own words.
'If I take God's gifts of truth and love and make them my own, I
am doing something that has never been done before in quite the
same way, because there has never been anyone quite like me.
Better still, if I show forth these truths and that love in my own life
and in my own words, I am adding something which is unprecedented and unique to the store of human knowledge and understanding. The required qualifications are not special gifts, but
personal honesty and simplicity. If, without affectation or pre-
tence, I can be myself, then the Cross of Jesus can be reflected in
my life and transmitted by my words with new emphasis and
stresses, which may by his grace rebound to his glory and the
blessing of others. What therefore I cannot do out of my own
attainments, God can do through me, just as I am, provided that I
allow no smear of insincerity to stain his image.' (*All His Grace*.)

The eyes of those in authority in the Church were on him. It
was the effect his preaching had on one young man in his congregation which opened out the vein of witness which was in the
end to make Soper known to the whole of Britain.

He tells the crucial story in his own words. 'One day a young
fellow in my congregation who worked in the City came to me
much exercised in his mind. He went each dinner-time to Tower
Hill, and among the various speakers to whom he listened he was
as impressed by the incisive and measured arguments of the Catholic Evidence Guild as he was dissatisfied with the fatuous and
petulant explosions of many so-called Protestant advocates. Was
there not an intellectual case for the faith which he heard from the
Methodist pulpit Sunday by Sunday? Could we not defend the
things dear to us reasonably and persuasively? He was sure that he
spoke for many others who felt that much religious propaganda on
the Hill was a waste of time and most ineffectively done. All sorts
of charges and arguments were made against Christianity. The
critics were left unanswered, and yet surely there were answers,
probably convincing ones. It was most unsettling to hear the
cynics getting away with it week after week, bringing Christianity
into ridicule, revelling in the incompetent attempts of sincere but
illiterate believers to champion the faith. Would I have a go at it?
I readily agreed.' (*Tower Hill, 12.30*.)

This was the break-out. All that had happened since the days in the Streatham home, the thirteen-year-old's decision for the ministry, and the struggle to update the theology of the Church at Wesley House, thrust him into this moment of decision. Assurance, education, intellectual breadth, the things folk had liked in him and the things they had disliked were summed up in that phrase worthy of John Wesley's Journal, 'I readily agreed'. As it turned out even the physique which earned college colours was part of the pre-evangelism which made the Tower Hill protagonist.

Tower Hill is adjacent to the eastern rampart of the City of London and has a bloody record in Britain's history. There is a garden and by its side there runs a wall from which speakers can address the crowd at their feet. An audience of two thousand people can be dealt with here. The crowd for many years has been a very loyal one, attending as regularly at the site as any church-goer at his place of worship. Composed mostly of men, the range runs from office workers to dockers, seamen, people out of work and a good sprinkling of those who would love to hold an audience themselves and are always ready to take over that created by some more successful teacher.

This is in fact the dream audience of the men who trained to speak to the unchurched world in ways which suggest that Christianity is a new-born creed to be introduced to a waiting world; the Soper generation of ministers, in fact. 'I readily agreed.'

Donald Soper's first break-out into this adventure is too good a story not to be told in his own words. 'Clad in Oxford bags, I arrived at the Hill about 12.30. Many meetings were in swing. I was profoundly nervous, but I finally saw a friendly-looking fellow sitting on the wall. I asked him: "How do you start a meeting?"

"Get up on the wall," said the friendly cove. "They'll come."

I did so, but, apart from the casual interest of a few, nobody else came. Feeling even more scared, I asked: "What do you do now?"

"Clap your 'ands, governor."

I said: "Will you clap yours?"

He agreed. I turned to another. "Will you clap?"

"Yes," he said.

We had a few rounds of applause and the crowd was there. My memory is a blank after that, but I know that I began to speak about the faith of Jesus and how I had come to accept it and indicated that there would be neither hymn nor prayer, but I was ready to justify that faith reasonably.' (*Tower Hill, 12.30.*)

It was a lame start in terms of technique but clearly defined in its content and the task of justifying the faith led him out into a miscellany of interests which have often since been deeply mis-understood by Christian observers. The truth is that this open air ministry, first at Tower Hill and later in Hyde Park, has de-veloped into a pastoral ministry with its peculiar form and content which has endured from 1927, without serious interruption, to the present day.

It repays study as a thing in its own right – and in fact has been granted such by George G. Hunter III in a thesis pre-sented to the North Western University, U.S.A. The fascinating element is to discover how much the preaching stylist owes to the open-air advocate and how much the open-air advocate is the echo of the preacher and public speaker.

'To justify the faith' is the basic aim of this open-air work. The natural assumption is that the faith itself will be the subject of ordered exposition. In the upshot the Soper technique of open-air speaking has not matured along this line. What has happened is that the questions rising from the audience have become the theme of the discussion and the work of exposition has been sub-jected to them. This is, indeed, the only adequate method.

One of Dr. Soper's young men tells the story of his own early experience of the work. He was put up by the doctor to speak and launched out into a detailed exposition of one of the main themes of the Christian faith. He quickly became bogged down in the detailed explanation of his subject, lost his audience and came under a barrage of heckling. He tells how the doctor pulled him down from the rostrum and mounted it himself. Taking the same theme he stated pithily the heart of the matter. Immediately the atmosphere changed and the questions flowed which contained within themselves opportunities to fill in the details of a theme which, stated baldly in a long address, was unacceptable.

This method has become a principle of open-air work. Throw in the subject in tabloid form and depend on the hecklers and questioners to fish up the detail in the subsequent debate. Here lies the possibility, however, of the criticism which Christian people have often made of Soper's ministry. An aphorism can state the main theme. Taken by itself the statement may appear outrageous – it is intended to be. It is only, however, the symbol on which the discussion depends and for the true Soper view of the matter under discussion it would be necessary to collate the whole cut and thrust of the debate. The famous statement which critics often quote is an example. Dr. Soper did once say: 'Better be Red than dead'; but the subsequent debate included the attitude of Jesus to the Roman Empire; the weird twists in history whereby black facts become white ones within a couple of generations; the place of pacifism within Christian thinking; the aftermath of the Maccabean Sabbath – pacifism under Roman army attack in the Wars of the Jews. In a word the total debate contained a Way of Life: Jesus' way of life.

It has always been possible for the occasional listener to resort to Tower Hill or Speakers' Corner, hear a snatch of the proceedings and come away with the impression that Soper might be a wonderful open air worker but that he was speaking of anything but the Gospel. 'Just a Socialist', 'Probably a Communist', 'Never heard him get round to the Gospel' – these are some of the reactions of the casual hearer. He does not realize that the whole action is aimed not at the casual hearer but a regular audience which follows its 'guru' week after week. Casuals are the minority.

Personal relationships between the speaker and the members of the crowd spring up and in their own way the listeners forge links of affection and confidence much as do members of regular congregations in church. The crowd is, indeed, a congregation, a 'following', and probably has a better estimate of Donald Soper than has his church. When great issues emerge or some scandal breaks across the nation they will look forward to the Tower Hill session to hear the reactions of the person they trust. This guidance-ministry is integral to the process as is the pastoral comfort they obtain in their own personal problems.

Personal relationship has been the principal attraction to Dr. Soper himself through the years in which he has continued this ministry – he would be the first to say that this is the feature which has kept him loyal to a method which has cost him much in physical strength. It is one of the clues to truth that what the nation has regarded as a national witness really rests upon personal relationships. But is this not utterly true to the Way of Jesus?

Lord Soper as a child (top) with his brother and sister

At a school camp (second from left, middle row)

West London Mission

Wesley House Cambridge

West London Mission

In a Wesley House Grou
(Seated, fourth from righ
Dr. J. Webb is seated
extreme left

At his first appointment,
Oakley Place, Bermonds

National issues have, ever since the Hebrew idea of God and history were enshrined in the Bible, been personal reactions to the crises in our human story. 'The little child in the midst' has been the answer to Roman imperialism subjugating Israel or any other giant form of power gone mad.

In such work down go the labels by which men mark out each other, such as The Man In The Street, the Public School Type, The Proletariat. People carrying burdens, people with cares gnawing their hearts, people out of love with life stand revealed as 'the lost' to whom Jesus spoke his wayside stories. Some there are, too, who though unchurched stand out as the 'found', with rich experience of Christ and the universals by which Christians live.

In the ministry of a young man down from Cambridge and with a relatively sheltered background, there could have been no better training in the art which is superlatively the crown of a ministerial life than this discovery that mankind is only a generic term which at bottom has no meaning; that there are men but no mankind. The corrective for one gifted with the power of great preaching lies here also, a discipline to curb the tendency to declaim pronouncements which men must accept simply because they are preached. The sieve of challenge strains the declamation and the test is applied – is it true for this man whose wife is ill, that man whose life is narrowed by financial anxiety?

As bonds of sympathy are forged between speaker and hearer it is discovered that the question asked from the crowd is the question which covers a question. One question is always two questions. A man, for instance, will make a bitter comment on a social system which sounds like sheer anarchy and could be labelled as 'doctrinaire nonsense', but it is not. A probing answer will show that the man himself is divided within himself and his damnation of the social system is in fact his own personal yearning for a new wholeness in his own living. The dreadful challenge lies in the fact that he expects from the speaker the answer to his submerged question rather than his obvious one. The Soper ministry could not have survived the years had it not given those intimate answers more often than not.

The art of giving the meaningful answer is soundly based upon the deep faith which the speaker has in man. To quote Soper, 'The fact that I am ready to trust people, or that I believe that they are fundamentally spiritual beings, is not just a subjective fancy of mine but an energy which flows through me, communicates itself to others, and alters things. Faith not only changes my attitude to my neighbour; it establishes and maintains a spiritual environment in which he is likewise affected' (*Tower Hill 12.30*). Faith is a living, creative force. Without cant, this can be described as his discovery of the attitude of Jesus as he moved through Galilee. It is this which compels the worker to go on unquenched through years of effort. Who knows what man will turn up on the crowd's fringe tomorrow? Who knows what twist of divine grace will appear in a friendship with that newly found man which one had not expected or even imagined?

3.

Start with a Question

Take a man's question and find in it his creed – this was the technique which had its birth for Soper in 1927. If a man thinks a thing worth mentioning in a public debate; if he does not mind his own reputation being staked on the airing of a viewpoint, then that question is revealing. Here is where that man suffers; here is where that man dreams; here is where the gateway to his life stands open. Enter and what happens? The answer is that one encounters God at work in this particular life. If God is at work in that life at this point then something is added to life for all men. For this question-maker is unique, as are all men, and from his uniqueness flows a contribution to the lives of any others who care to observe.

Immediately there emerges a clinical test of the truth of the Christian Way and the open-air forum becomes a laboratory, with Christ himself on the bench under the microscope. If all things cohere in Christ (as Paul declared), then it must be true that one can begin at any point which itches in any mind, with a question which comes from any of the disciplines of human thinking, and end up in the Christ-centred pattern of all things. Does this happen? Soper was sure that it did.

This was the theological outlook, as we have seen, in which he was reared. War and peace, socialism and capitalism, sex and marriage, master and man, civic corruption and ecclesiastical snobberies, historic processes and contemporary news gossip – any of these may provide the question. From any one of them, or from the question that has never cropped up before, there runs a road clear and signposted to the heart of the Christian life-style.

There are two ways of preaching the Christian message. One, and that most commonly used, is to proceed from Jerusalem down to Jericho from the place and symbol of religious doctrine and observance to the arena of man's everyday life. The other is to go from Jericho to Jerusalem and the latter is that which men in fact most commonly accept. This Soper discovered – but he discovered only what Jesus had discovered before him.

For Jesus the gospel lay in a woman baking bread, a farmer scattering seed, a prince going to seek a kingdom, a slave master fiddling his accounts. These were the gossip points in Jesus' world where the 'Times' was the street corner. Tower Hill and Speakers' Corner in our day present parallels to the daily life of Jesus and Soper has uncovered the roads that lead from the General Strike of 1926, the drama of Dunkirk, the shambles of Korea or Vietnam to the City of God.

It is a strange and fascinating exercise to coax the world into leading on to the Creator's plan for his world – highly pragmatic, deeply suspected – but in fact there is no other way to revelation. The alternative is an ivory tower of theological and spiritual sterility which, followed by too many Christian exponents, has led to a decline in Christian mission. 'He spent all his time arguing about the Queen,' complains the listener newly come to the Hill. Did he? Is the Queen outside the economy of God's world? Does her life not somewhere root down in eternals? She means something to someone or she would not crop up in debate, and if she means something she is in God's Kingdom-plan.

A thing cannot be thought and have meaning without being part of the whole and the whole is in God's perfect goodness or else Christianity is nonsense. Follow the queenly concept and you will end in the presence of God. The same would be true if the questioner raised the problem of sweeping the professional prostitutes off London's streets. All journeys are one journey. The tragedy of life is when people squat in a puddle by the roadside forgetful, or unaware, that the road goes somewhere. Paul had the nerve to command his folk to imitate him; Donald Soper has had the nerve to invite his crowds to follow him from whatever point bogged them down to the goal in which he passionately believed. Nor has he had the temerity to think them incapable of following. The Methodist minister has remained true to the basic Methodist doctrine that salvation is not only available for every man but that every man is perfectible into the image of Christ. Love is the instrument of salvation and perfect love the goal of it.

However pragmatic the process of open air witness, for purposes of witness there has to be an under-structure of ordered thinking and belief in the mind which can enclose and order whatever springs up in the apparently casual debate. The bits are bits, but they must all fit into a pattern in his mind. Without this overall mental system the effort would disappear into the sands, leaving nothing behind. The strength of the Soper technique – and the trap for the conventionally Christian casual hearer – has always been that his mental pattern has been wider than the conventional. The Kingdom of God as he sees it is truly universal and in this he is right. It is impossible for any man to ask a question which does not have a reference to the plan of God's salvation. Were this not so, then monotheism would be demonstrably false and the world controlled by a multiplicity of forces defeating science or philosophy.

This being so, the Christian teacher has to be lively enough to thrust through the variety of questions with the elements of the plan he sees but which his hearer does not see. His mind must be busy like a filing clerk stowing the parts of the discussion into their proper places in his system. He must be like a Business Efficiency Specialist demonstrating where the bits fit in. In the upshot he displays a feasibility study causing the hearer to see that the whole does work when life is perceived as a God-adventure requiring human co-operation. If, as Donald Soper himself states, he has never seen a 'conversion' under his open-air ministry, there is no doubt at all that he has effected this enlightenment in many minds and in them the central feeling about life has shifted to centre upon God's rule. His Master, as reflected in the Gospels, appears to have been content to do just this.

The process of 'bringing every thought into captivity' is the reason for social theory looming so large in the Soper witness. The pragmatic approach quickly dredges up from the crowd mind evidences of other master-plans which challenge the Christian plan. These alternative plans are always social, often socialist and from the beginning of the Tower Hill ministry vociferously communist. The Cambridge Soper knew this before ever he was pressed out into the open-air forum. While still a probationer he was studying at the London School of Economics and Political

Science because Christian order seemed to him to demand a total social theory. His own intellectual probing into this field joined with his reaction to the crowd's questions to make him see that the communist life-theory was a major challenge to the faith he preached.

The Old Kent Road ministry after all was only a decade after the emergence of the new Russia, and the Chinese Communist Party dated back only to 1921. The Red world was young, younger than the preacher, its advocates as zealous as he. Like the young men of his generation whom the Church sent to the Far East, Soper believed that a new world-claiming religion had come to birth in Communism.

This system was not merely an evil thing challenging the old Western order and to be damned out of hand in consequence. It was life, thrill, creed for a world's youngsters. Like Mao Tse-tung they claimed that they both respected and rejected Christianity because, while lovely, it was far too slow to cleanse and transform the post-world-war world. Soper's training gave him the ability to distinguish between Russian Imperial dreams, lying like a national hangover from Katherine the Great upon the Russian scene, and the strategic millennial dream which was true Communism. Moscow had its Sun Yat-sen University and Cambridge its St. Catherine's. This was a world-wide confrontation of religions.

'Red under the bed' responses to the communist challenge were beneath contempt, anti-Christ condemnations of it irrelevant. He set himself to discover where the fundamental creeds of the two faiths clashed, treating the communist enthusiast as a man, like himself, thirsting for a new world-order. There is an immediate risk for anyone who comes at the problem from this angle of being classified as a 'fellow-traveller' and Donald Soper has not escaped this taunt.

Both his writings and his speaking have penetrated to the realities of the communist conviction of a millennial outcome to the natural processes of history. He has not missed the messianic element in this faith. He is among those in the West who have realized that in Lenin the world has one of this century's great men. The close resemblance between the communist trend to elevate people by a personality cult, demanding constant reductions of the latest hero back to the ranks to make room for a new one, is singularly like the Bible story of 'the Judges' or the main theme of the Old Testament. Perhaps above all else he has seen that the dream in Lenin's heart is one which demands good men, who naturally love good, in order to reach reality. Perhaps this is the place where his criticism of the system pierces most deeply.

The ferreting out of these parts of the communist creed confer a seriousness on the Christian controversy with Communism which cannot be met in public debate by wholesale condemnation or snide proddings at the behaviour of Russians or Chinese. One remembers the occasion when the Russian Fleet paid a courtesy visit to Portsmouth and a civic dignitary said to a young naval officer of the U.S.S.R., 'I suppose you have to be a Party member to get a commission.' The officer blushed and said, 'Party member! I hope some day by hard work or some military action, if I am lucky, to merit the honour but that is as far away from me as for you to be a Life Peer.' It is that real communist world that has to be dealt with and it contains 900,000,000 people within its orbit.

So, in the open air Soper has made his three-pronged analysis of the basic thought-world of Communism. He has noted the under-structure in the Marxist assertion of historical materialism – now more commonly spoken of as dialectical materialism, and not to be confused with the dialectic process itself. This simply states that material entities and pressures produce all that makes up our life. Mental and spiritual life, if the latter term can properly be used, are the product of matter. 'The brain secretes thought as the liver secretes bile.' Thinking is the steam over the cauldron of the material volcano and the important thing is the boiling material mass deep in the crater.

One necessary result of this approach to why things are is the death of freewill in man. But another is the reappearance of a Christian idea in a new form. If a naturally determined process explains life, then it explains among other things goodness, truth and beauty, society and order and, ultimately a lawless, classless Utopia. It assumes that this sort of world happening in this sort of way produces this sort of goal. In a word, mind is built into the mindless world and the mind is good enough to produce good. How can a mindless root of being create this universe in which mental values are of the greatest? On this theory man's thinking cannot be the origin of value and purpose; it is itself but an emanation of matter. But purpose and value, being discovered, must be inbuilt, and we are back with the Christian poet, 'I doubt not through the ages one increasing purpose runs': the 'divine event to which the whole creation moves'.

The second of Communism's assumptions to which Dr. Soper turned his mind is that the human story is the story of man's tools. It is earnestly thought that the Marx-Hegelian theory of the emergence of the ruling classes is a sound description. The theory holds that whatever state a group of men exhibits is the fruit of the tools they have in that condition. To quote Dr. Soper, 'The ideas, ideals, religion, laws are but the pale shadow of the anvil, the dynamo, or the cartel'. (*Tower Hill, 12.30.*)

From this doctrine springs the theory of class-struggle. He who has tools wins; he who has not tools struggles to wrench them from the hands of those who have. The materialist belief denies the possibility of man creating tools; he himself is determined into being and therefore cannot be an originator of anything, including tools. The tools emerge from one another by the decay of one type demanding the emergence of another – the dialectical process operating. When by this process the lowest and least privileged non-tool-owning class inevitably comes to possess tools, who is to wrench them from his hand? None is left to do so and a classless tranquillity must result. Such an argument is the justification for the class struggle – it is worth while in the name of all classes for the lowest class to enter quickly upon its tool-controlling destiny.

The deficiency of this theory stands out clearly in Dr. Soper's view. In the first place, were human history of this kind, Marx and Lenin would not have occurred in human history at all, for they were not of the lowest class. In the second place the proliferation of tools should have increased the pace of class war. In fact, the discovery (or emergence from matter) of television and the mass-produced car, alongside many other modern tools, has been a standardizing influence on our life rather than divisive. It is far more accurate to describe man's progress in terms of his dreams deliberately fulfilled. His spiritual life has commanded his material and economics have not been the decisive element. It is fairer to Lenin to describe him in Christian terms than communist.

The third deep strand in Communism is deeply moving for the Christian because it enshrines a hope which in every creed has never died, the hope of perfecting human society. The advanced civilizations are seen as inevitably reaching the plethora of tool-possession and therefore the major scene for the expropriation of the tool-owners by the lowest stratum of society. This in its turn by an equally inexorable development must lead to a world revolution which will catch other social systems up into the communist one and through that pass to the ultimate society when law, rule, struggle are known no more.

Wistfully the Christian realizes that Marx and the communist great ones have believed that moment to be at the very door with an intensity equal to that of some Christian sects predicting 'the end of the world' on a certain date.

History shows us that the Western, sophisticated nations were not those which first entered upon the communist way. As Dr. Soper points out, one of modern history's greatest revolutions was triggered off by that strangely idealistic man, the Mahatma Gandhi, whose mind lay nearer to the compassion of Jesus. There is a curious contradiction in a creed which trumpets these massive materialist inevitabilities while at the same time goading men into a well nigh frenetic campaign to make them happen.

More important in our human affairs is the daunting variability of the human personality: the quirks, inspirations and insights of ordinary men and women from whose ranks modern leadership so often springs, but for whom there is no place within communist philosophy. Tomorrow's future is today's dream, and it is the determination in some heart or hearts that makes the dream come true. Let any man document simple human stories – like that, for instance, of Dr. Kofi Busia, Kenneth Kaunda or Masaryk, and he will end joined to Buddha, Confucius, Plato and Christ rather than Marx.

Another of the never-absent themes of the open air is the criticism of the Church and the churches. It is one thing for Donald Soper to have a following which trusts him and who will openly or secretly take his advice. It is quite another to expect the same people to have a place in their lives for the churches. This problem has haunted the last half-century and no one has suffered more from it than Lord Soper.

He has always, from those probationary days onward, had a half-agreement with such critics – knowing the faults of the churches better than the hecklers. Often, however, he has had a sense of frustration with the actual criticisms levelled at the

Churches, because they have sprung from a deep ignorance of what the Churches are today. Hecklers are so often stuck a quarter or half a century behind the times when they lay their charges. It is commonly thought, for example, that the Churches are committed to believing that the Genesis creation story is to be preferred to any scientific theory of the world's origin. Many think that the Churches enthusiastically approve of bishops blessing battleships. They are convinced that Christianity is world-rejecting and believes only in a hasty transit through this life to a realm above the bright blue sky. They will use this idea to abuse churchmen who appear to enjoy this world more than a little.

History, particularly of the Middle Ages, seems to have become part of modern mental furniture. The Inquisition, Holy Wars, consent to the slave trade, none too moral Popes, are parts of the historical legacy which live on and crop up in debate. Certainly the war of the sects is real enough, and provides an armoury of weapons with which to attack the faith, though increasingly it is paralleled by the divided voices of the Left.

This stream of invective and criticism hurled at the Churches through nearly forty-five years is in fact one of the most encouraging things about Donald Soper's open-air ministry – or any other like it. The gravamen of the charges is that the Churches deny Jesus! Were it not for the towering figure of the Christ there would be no ground for complaint about ecclesiastical conduct. 'Jesus had no place to lay his head; bishops have x pounds a year and live in palaces.' 'Jesus was the Prince of Peace; the Church sends chaplains to wars.' 'Jesus' message was love and the denominations tear out each other's guts.' To a speaker who is more keen that people should catch the faith than that the Church should catch them, this Jesus-standard by which men judge provides evidence that there is a great deal more faith around than the life of the Churches would suggest. Beyond that elation the speaker is depressed, however, by his own acknowledgement that so much of the anti-church opposition is soundly based. Dr. Soper was not long in discovering he could be ashamed of Churches.

He remarks, 'It is never merely a logical comparison between two abstract theories of life; almost always when men condemn the Church they do so not because of any theoretical inconsistency but by the standard of the very Jesus who is its Head and whom often they profess to reject.' (*Tower Hill, 12.30.*)

Dr. Soper's personal pacifism has been another fruitful source of open-air controversy. He tells us that he cannot remember an occasion in the open air when the issues of war and peace have not arisen. His well known pacifist position has been and is the point at which he is most vulnerable.

The students of his day were almost entirely pacifist and though he was a member in school of the Army Cadet Force of the time (O.T.C) and learned to handle a rifle and bayonet, by the time he reached Cambridge this was bygone. In the early twenties it was the militant rather than the pacifist who was the martyr; it was an act of heroism to walk the streets of some towns in the Territorial Army uniform. There was the revulsion in the lives of the ex-war students and there was the incredulous reaction of those younger that anyone could permit Ypres, Paschendale, Hill 60, etc., ever to occur.

Social reform via national salvation through Left politics and pacifism were twins. To be in the one movement was to be in the other. Lip service to 'No More War' was compulsory for all who sought public approval. There were then plenty of pacifists.

Life, however, has a way of sorting the men from the boys and it happened in this issue as in others. Young people had to come to terms with the rise of revolution and the mounting pressures of fascism, the build-up to the Ethiopian conflict, the Franco rebellion in Spain, the Jap threat to the Chinese revolution. There emerged the beginnings of the conditions now well known. Aggression, tyranny and totalitarianism moved the Left to violence to combat violence, a new philosophy sprang up of violent resistance of which the International Brigade in Spain was the symbol.

What, then, was the modern young man to do? Could he be a social fighter and not fight? Could he be a pacifist and be a social fighter? The completely non-violent armies have melted away leaving a Gideon's army. The Metropolitan Police might well long for the days of popular pacifism as they deal with today's violent marchers.

Dr. Soper has remained rock-like in his pacifist position and has given offence by doing so to as many on the Left as on the political Right. He remained obdurate because his pacifist position rose from his basic faith rather than the post-war, pre-war moods of the nation. His interpretation of Jesus' teaching categorically forbids taking life or using violence to attain an end. No situation justifies violence, not even in the search for good. The civil forces of law and order he sees as permitted under the edict of God. 'Would I not forcibly pull a child back out of danger?'

War and peace is not for him an issue for debate – war is contrary to the will of God in Christ and there is no room for question. His difficulties at the beginning of the open-air ministry, however, lay round this 'fight or not fight' point. Nearer to our own times his battle has been different. Why, ask the socialist and other Left groups, is he not with us in our marches of protest, our sit-down operations, our police-baiting campaigns? He has the intellectual courage to apply his belief to causes he loves equally with the activities of those he opposes.

This ministry which began while he was a probationer was far from being the only activity of those days but was only one part of a busy London church life. He was studying for his doctorate in Philosophy which he gained with a thesis which was apparently as far removed from the debate of Tower Hill as could be. *Edmond Richer and the Revival of Gallicanism* (unpublished thesis, London University, 1929) is concerned with the principles upon which the Christian Church should be governed. Where lies authority? Is it in the Head of the Church on earth or is it diffused among the bishops in council? Is there such a thing as proper regional liberty and autonomy within the true system of ecclesiastical government?

It is tempting to think that the attraction of such a theme for one holding his views of society perhaps lay in the fact that there is in the communist world a parallel debate between the Leninist theory of solid unitary control and the Trotskyist point of view which stands for widely dispersed centres of communist power. However this may be, it is true that here we have one example of Dr. Soper's instinct for the issues of tomorrow. In recent years the Gallican issue has come prominently to the fore and writers of many denominations now debate it.

A busy church, a rising reputation as a preacher, the forum of Tower Hill and the struggles of thesis writing might have been enough but, like most Wesleyan probationers, he was attempting to keep intact the engagement to marry Miss Marie Dean and now without help from Joe Webb. The gruelling probationary period – in most cases four years – had to be fulfilled before young ministers could marry, a rule which applied to all who served overseas as well as to the men in Britain. Men develop, girls grow up; there are casualties. The girl watching the activity of her man now really in the work might well have second thoughts about sharing it with him.

Marie Dean, always beautiful, always cultured, demonstrated her courage by weathering those years and their wedding was one of the three events which made memorable the year 1929. Donald Soper was ordained into the 'Full Connexion' of Wesleyan ministers, he was granted his doctorate in Philosophy, and he was married. At the time of his marriage he informed the Church and Methodism generally that he was marrying a wife and not a curate. Most Methodist ministers have said something similar, few have found the division possible and some would be quite defeated in their work without a wife who is involved in the life of the Church.

The Soper marriage faced a ministry which had wide tracts in it which could not be shared. It has encountered journeys, weird hours of work, the problems of Central Mission staffing and a hundred other obstacles to the closely shared 'curacy' type of home-life. The courage which has forged a home out of this tempestuous life and included this unpredictable husband, is of the highest order. As one by one the four daughters of the marriage have come along, its depth of meaning has increased. A home is a haven and it is the stormy lives which need haven most. Donald Soper has had a haven marriage. Behind it has been that rare spirit which could realize that she must herself plan a life and without repining go steadily on to build it. To be near enough to the work to be respected in it, graciously not to be there when to be there was impossible, and to add a personal contribution to the partnership, has been a work of grace. As Dr. Leslie Weatherhead said years ago, 'He is wise and loving enough to encourage her to be herself – and a very sweet self it is.'

On completion of probation, Methodist ministers are moved to a new appointment – if only to get a manse to live in – though there are other reasons. So it was with the Sopers. He left the Old Kent Road and was sent to the Central London Mission to preach at the Islington Central Hall.

45

With this move to Central London, Dr. Soper was on the Methodist map and he was sent there to put this experimental hall on the map by his preaching gifts.

A better time for one with his gifts and his viewpoint to occupy a 'Hall rostrum' could hardly be imagined than the period from 1929 until 1936, when he left.

In international affairs the signing of the Kellogg Pact renouncing war gave a new vitality to the peace-war controversy which was underlined by the national rejoicing and special prayers which marked the event. European affairs at the time were tied in knots by the bitter debate about reparations and the occupation of the Rhineland and Ruhr by allied forces. The American economy went down in the famous Wall Street Crash and doubts swept across the world about the basic system on which Western civilization rested. In 1930 the German National Socialist Party gained 107 seats in the Reichstag, a German airship having circumnavigated the world in the year before. American loans to Europe were terminated. The U.S.S.R. development thrust forwards as Trotsky fled to Turkey. Not surprisingly, Sigmund Freud pin-pointed the world's disarray with the publication of *Civilisation and its discontents*.

British Imperial Power was fighting a dour rearguard action as the First Round Table Conference met in 1929 to discuss the future status of the Indian Empire. By 1930 Mahatma Gandhi had launched the Civil Disobedience Campaign. At home the Labour Party had come to power in 1929 with 287 seats in the House and Ramsay Macdonald headed the Government with Arthur Henderson, a Methodist, at the Foreign Office. Miss Margaret Bondfield became the first woman Privy Counsellor. The *Daily Worker* was born in 1930. J. M. Keynes wrote his *Treatise on Money* in the same year and Laski his *Liberty and the Modern State*.

These were not the only challenging signs and portents. Cultural events included James Jeans' *The Universe around us* which stimulated enormous debate among preachers and publicists; Robert Bridges' *Testament of Beauty* in contrast with Erich Remarque's *All Quiet on the Western Front*. Nor should it be forgotten that Don Bradman scored 334 runs in a Test Match at Leeds.

It was as though some universal war of the giants were in progress at all levels of the ancient cosmogony – thrones, principalities and powers – all on their own levels locked in death struggle. The League of Nations, ancient Imperial Orders, the body of Europe, were racked with pain, and within Britain, on everyman's doorstep, were the infamous 'thirties'.

In 1931 the number of unemployed in the country was 2,648,000 and the early thirties showed no improvement of this figure. It was at this time that the word 'dole' became a part of the national vocabulary. In 1932 the T.U.C. membership was about 4,500,000, half the 1920 figure, and was suffering from the blows received a few years earlier. Oswald Mosley broke away and formed the British Fascist Union, sensing that the struggle of Germany to grope her way out of her similar troubles might have thrown up the answer which he could copy.

The great depression in Britain was patchy in its impact, and was most vicious in South Wales, West Cumberland, the Tyne-Tees area and industrial Scotland. There were in 1932 men in the mining industry aged 21 years who had never worked a day in their lives but were actually studying for Mine Deputies Certificates in the blind hope that the industry some day would absorb them. There were men ageing but not yet pensionable who settled on their lees in idle villages within Durham, left to rot as truly as the pit heaps from which they grubbed fragments of coal to keep their cottages warm.

Probably the south of England never really knew the weight of this national débâcle. J. B. Priestley wrote at the time, 'If half London had been in the plight of these wretched towns in Durham, if every street in every direction from the Houses of Parliament and the Bank of England had been crowded with men who saw no hope of another job and women who had long stopped pawning things because the pawn shops were full, there would soon have been a plan'.[1] There was no plan – until European history thrust the plan of rearmament down the British nation's throat.

The drift to the South and to London was, nevertheless, colossal and Soper's Islington had plenty of evidence of it. Methodism's London Missions had their full share of trying to help the nation's wanderers.

[1] *Britain in the 20th Century*, Reynolds and Brasher, Cambridge University Press.

Historians may, perhaps, say in centuries to come that Britain's destiny was sealed in the 1930s and sealed by lethargy in authority. It was a 'moment' of crucial debate. Something had to take Britain out of the morass; was it to be Capitalism, Socialism, Fascism, Communism? Fascism was paying dividends on the Continent; in 1933 it gained a 92 per cent vote in the elections in Germany. There followed large-scale conflicts between fascist and anti-fascist parties in Hyde Park, London. The unemployed were tinder ready for any spark. Macdonald handed over power to Stanley Baldwin and the edict went forth to build up the Royal Air Force, accompanied by a thunderous Commons warning from Churchill of the danger of German air power. The looming of war on the one hand and the rage of George Lansbury about the Means Test at the beginning of the 1934 Session of the House bracket the period.

The times have made much that is Donald Soper, building up from the inherited facts of his life and the convictions which his faith produced in him. Seldom has he failed to mirror the concerns of the hour. Those Thirties years are him to an amazing degree. Men of the same period know why, while younger people wonder just what made him.

The age is gone, but the man remains, and with him remains the deep, scarifying knowledge that life can be again like it was then, brutal, tinny, dumb, strident, an affluent heaven and a poor man's hell. Some of his arrogance is the awareness that our civilization is always as horrible underneath; it is hatred of what hurts. An age which flocked to watch the theatrical show 'Cavalcade', cheeks wet with pride over England's glory, but left the pitman's wife without even the privilege of scrubbing her man's back; what could a prophet not say to it? Soper said most things.

It is an open question which of the great prophets of doom appealed to him in those years which cried out for – and found – their prophet. It could have been that the pulpit of Islington Hall shook to the thunder of a man possessed, 'Woe to the bloody city'. But it was not so. Notes in the Press of the period give us a picture of one who wooed and cajoled people into listening. We are told that his talk was 'full of homely humour', that his own family life often provided the illustrations, his speaking was 'earnest good sense'. 'A simple style like a friend chatting with his friends would suddenly blossom into grandeur.' The 'hourly issues' of the day were his material. A sermon was like 'a story with an epilogue'. Even then someone complained, 'You talk over the people's heads', to which he had the tart reply, 'I'd rather be over their heads than under their feet'. On the other hand one of the people who has over long years been a social worker in London tells how she heard from the suburbs that a man in London spoke about religion as though it could be understood, went and heard him and became a lifelong friend to broken people. There is something exhilarating in reading in the *British Weekly* of those times that Donald Soper's preaching depended on the world around him and what it was saying. The Central Hall rostrum becomes the Galilean sea-shore.

In 1932 when the Methodist Missionary Society arranged its annual May Meeting it was decided that an emphasis should be laid on Chinese affairs because the staff there had been through some difficult revolutionary times and it was felt that the Church should be told about them. The rally was booked to take place in Westminster Central Hall and the Hall would be full. A Mission House Secretary gathered together a team of missionaries on leave to brief them on their performance. There were three of them – all thoroughly 'blooded' in war, tumult and escapes during the last few years. The Secretary explained the drill – short, terse, pointed, evangelical, and on no account was any speech to take off into rhetoric because one of the 'well-known Home men' would be the last speaker. He would see to the rhetoric. One of the men on leave interjected, 'He picks up the bits?' A very sour 'Precisely' was the answer he got.

On the night the Hall was crowded and the subject seized the mind of the great congregation. The interjector was third to speak, and, fresh from central China, near the place where Mao Tse-tung was a young man growing up, he described the social work of the Church. Using the vocabulary of the Chinese times he called the Christian Movement 'The Fourth International'. Dr. Soper rose to speak – the Home man to supply the rhetoric. He picked up this phrase, which clearly excited him, and for twenty minutes wove it into a dazzling picture of a world movement outshining anything the World Council agencies have since accomplished. Later, in the Speakers' Room, he caught hold of the young missionary. 'Thanks,' he said. 'I hadn't an idea of what line to take when I came in.' The Acts of the Apostles tells us that the Athenian crowd called Paul 'a seedpicker' – he too picked up the bits. It is not given to many departmental secretaries to have this skill.

4.

The Flowering Years

In 1887 a Welsh, evangelistic, sacramentarian Wesleyan minister whose sacramentalism did not exclude the most extravagant methods of mission work known to his times, founded the West London Mission of the Wesleyan Methodist Church by beginning to preach in the St. James' Hall, Piccadilly. His name was Hugh Price Hughes.

His ambition is recorded in words characteristically portentous at the end of the nineteenth century. 'Let us, then, in the name of God and humanity combine heartily to abolish slavery, drunkenness, lust, gambling, ignorance, pauperism and war.' A man of restless and unpredictable energy, he gave himself to London with a devotion which never faltered and a zeal comparable with that of William Booth and other Free Church leaders at a time when the Nonconformist preacher was a power to be reckoned with. One of the hostels of the West London Mission is named after him to this day. The work of the Methodist Church in the West London world is his memorial.

In 1907 another great man came to the West London Mission who has left his mark on the story of his Church, John Ernest Rattenbury, grandson, son, brother and uncle of Wesleyan ministers. After founding mission work in northern England, Leicester and Nottingham, he was stationed to the work begun by Hugh Price Hughes. He preached first in the Lyceum Theatre and then moved to the newly-built Kingsway Hall, giving altogether eighteen years to the Mission.

He carried forward the same passionate blend of sacramentarian and evangelical religion which issued in a strong social ministry. Some would call him a 'High Wesleyan'. Many did not like his

51

approach. Moreover, he battled out the issue of Methodist Union on the 'wrong' side. He left the London Mission and Kingsway Hall to be minister at Trinity, Southport – church of the Methodist school for ministers' daughters. He was an architect of the National Free Church Council and became its President in 1936, after he had retired. In that year Donald Soper came to the Kingsway Hall as the youngest Superintendent of a Central Mission. In the same year Leslie D. Weatherhead left the great Brunswick Church at Leeds and came to the City Temple. An era began.

Dr. Weatherhead's appointment to the non-Methodist City Temple was a subject of controversy. Many thought that he should have been stationed at Wesley's Chapel, City Road, London and that he was denied that historic pulpit because his highly modern approach to life and religion was not thought suitable for such a church. There could be no controversy about Donald Soper's appointment. Hugh Price Hughes was preaching in the open air before he came to London and carried on that work in Hyde Park and other places in the West End. The emphasis on the Sacraments which had marked the great men of the Mission was Soper's also. His preaching ability was proven. In the Islington days he had begun social work for ex-prisoners and other casualties of central London. Dr. Rattenbury's scholarship had matched his evangelical gifts. The same was true, though in different disciplines, of Dr. Soper. The one anomaly was that the general rule stated that a Superintendent Minister in a Methodist Circuit should have 'travelled' twenty years; Donald Soper had travelled but eleven. This the Stationing Committee and the Conference waived.

When the new leader took over, the Mission had four social service items in its programe and they all reflected the original concern of Dr. Hughes' times, his interest in 'social purity' and the warping of young people's lives by the life of London. There were a Girls' Hostel, a hostel for syphilitic girls, a student hostel and the famous Creche, one of the first of its kind – infants and little children were hardly 'people' in those early years.

When his ministry opened in the Kingsway Hall, on September 17th, 1936, Donald Soper clearly felt that he needed strong backing and sought it at his welcome meeting and with his first sermon there. Significant of the times, his coming was covered by the Press in a way that has now long ceased to happen, and the reports were enthusiastic, similar to notes the Press made on his work at Islington. He might refer, they thought, to anything from 'the plough to the throne'. In fact, Londoner that he is through and through, the 'plough' was really not very likely to be mentioned. They remarked on the easy conversational style of his preaching, 'like a man talking to his friends'. They commented on his use of humour in the pulpit. 'Shrewd mother wit'.

This conversational style of preaching was coming in at the time, not only on Donald Soper's lips but among many of the younger ministers, and was as new and awakening then as the 'you' form of prayers has become in modern times. It was a reaction to the declamatory style of the great Victorian preachers who still had their disciples in some of the famous pulpits. It was soon being said that Weatherhead's style gently caressed his hearers while Soper's style was like bright chat over a cup of coffee, but both shared their attachment to this new 'I'm-alongside-you' type of address, even when the congregation ran to thousands of people.

As his work at Kingsway began, there is a strange, imperial mark on the story which was very much 1936. One of the newspapers records what a thrill it was to walk down the road past the Hall and see outside it a large archway inscribed with the words, 'To the friendship of the English-speaking world'. So the changes represented by the Imperial Conference and the sense of hope and faith in the links which still bound the nations of the old Empire, together with the realization of the significance of the United States, were part of the message of contemporary Christian witness. The archway was to give way later to the peace-dove motif.

There were crowds going to the Hall and they increased under the new preacher. People in that Britain needed voices to speak to them and they sought voices which bore the timbre of reality, the reality of the sort of Britain then struggling its way through a morass of problems. The Tower Hill exercise, the Press reporting and the grapevine of younger people who already frequented the Kingsway Hall, drew in many types of people. Would the man of Tower Hill preach as he talked in the open air? The answer to that question must have surprised many who went seeking it.

Dr. Soper laid a strong emphasis on conversion of the individual man to Christ and made it clear that he expected little without it from either man or the world. Speaking, for example, at a large London Mission Rally in the Hall near the beginning of his time there, he discussed with the young people – and they were 'insiders' of a great Church – the world fact of revolution and the ways by which various persons and groups tried to bring it about. 'There is no gradual process of passing from stage to stage until you are a fairly good man or this is a fairly good world. To say that it is possible to have such a reformation is no help to an ex-Pentonville prisoner or a man broken by life. Man is a sinner. He has got into a mess and he has no power of himself to change himself. But if we believe in the Lord Jesus Christ we shall be saved, because power will break through from him, changing us.'

This theme of the divine initiative in re-creating man and situations has defied theological fashion-changes and still forms part of his criticism of humanist and communist dreams of environmental transformation for man and society. The genius of the Christian way is this divine labour on man's life. Let reformers and revolutionaries like it or hate it there is, in Dr. Soper's view, this spiritual sub-structure beneath every social, political and charitable action. Man's effort is not a thing in itself; it is a dependent factor in a divine work.

There have been many men and women who, coming from different idealist groups, have companied with Donald Soper on the road to a better life order, and many still do, but sooner or later they find this element in his thinking. He is a 'supernaturalist', he expects the big thing to be done by God. Such people are then driven to judge for themselves the work he does as a clinical example of the things he believes. Like Jesus, God is needed to explain his actions.

The concept of God's grace ranks very high in his sermons and teaching. The only adequate explanation of how a day's work gets done shines through the Kingsway sermons. It is by the 'through-put' (to use the American business term) that a man experiences of God's ideas and actions passing through him – the responsive person – to their objectives in the world. The doctrine of the Holy Spirit, who chooses his man, trains his man, energizes life and get things done for humans through humans, is central.

It is, of course, a dangerous doctrine and has led many to the brink of disaster, because a man so easily slips into asserting his own will as the divine and, as a result, swells up in his own estimation until catastrophe ends the story. The safeguard is the concept of grace. If a man thinks himself by right inspired, he may end as another tyrant. If he expects to be guided by grace engendered in the heart of Jesus, he may become a saint.

Changes tumbled over themselves as Dr. Soper's hand fell on the work of the West London Mission. Each could have been an assertion of self-will, but neither he nor the people thought them to be so. They were, for them, changes caused by creative activities of the Holy Spirit working through a human agency, his divine radiance broken up into the peculiar spectrum of one human co-worker.

Perhaps this is the reason why one collection of his sermons is called, *All His Grace*. Can a man be proud of being an agent? Is it possible to be an aggressive, turbulent personality while acknowledging that one's status is slavery – and willing slavery at that? The answer is that pride and thrust properly belong to the slave. The man who believes that in himself he is self-made, self-sufficient and brilliantly gifted in his own right is not very likely to slog through an eighteen-hour day. He is too precious to waste – let others put in the overtime. It is a responsibility to be an asset. Such a man's contempt of the intellect of others would make controversy impossible. Controversy thrives for the man humble enough to believe that the Holy Spirit is just as likely to air some new factor in a situation through his opponent. The Volga, the Indus, Ganges and Yangtze are proud rivers, but what do they do but channel the floods from far away?

Any who imagined that the life of Kingsway Hall would now be like an Adult School or Labour Party Sunday School mixed with a heckling session were quite shocked by the actual nature of the worship which was most carefully liturgical, and by the preaching which was Bible-based. The attraction lay in these noble twins, worship and Word, being related to what was going on in the Commons or not going on in the mines and docks.

One of the first things to thrive was the Thursday evening devotional meeting which had a programme of straight Bible or theological teaching, prayer and meditation, and the Doctor usually led the meeting himself. People called it the 'Guild', though no one quite knew why. It began in the Little Chapel but as time went by it grew so steadily that it moved into one of the bigger rooms. Three years after Dr. Soper's appointment, at the beginning of the Second World War, it was the root from which other activities branched and the source from which volunteers could be taken for service projects. Before the meeting began there was always a state-of-the-mission discussion and a review of current needs. Bands of people volunteered as they felt called to do. At one point, for example, young people of the Guild staffed an open-air street corner meeting on Kingsway. Others visited lodging houses nearby where the men welcomed a Sunday afternoon service. Some of the volunteers moved on to preaching in other London churches and into social work.

The excitement his ministry caused at that time can be gathered from the recollections of the young people who shared his ministry or first awakened to their own at the time. The Rev. Leonard P. Barnett, B.D., whose own ministry has been brilliant and effective since its beginning in 1942, is as good a witness as possible to what happened to many.

There is something completely Methodist in the framework of his story. Here is a Connexional Church at its best, caring for its young people going up to the 'Great Smoke' and seeing that they are put into the 'right' setting for the test of living in the metropolis.

He writes, 'It was autumn 1936: I was a raw provincial recruit to the Civil Service in London, taken in hand by a veteran Methodist uncle who performed a far more vital service for me than he ever could have known. He escorted me on what was my first visit to the Capital, established me at Regnal House, and on Saturday night took me to Kingsway Hall for a Celebrity Concert.'

'Dear Octupus'! The godly relative, the Church's youth movement in the Regnal League which was then an active parallel movement to Toc H, and the Central Hall programme which included those fantastic concerts from which quite famous people made their break-in to the music hall and entertainment world. One tentacle was already round Len Barnett's life – he would not sink in London.

The story goes on. Uncle said, 'There's a minister here, recently arrived, who should go far: he ought to be just what you need.' Methodism's greatest compliment to its younger ministers – he should go far! There is no hierarchy in that Church and so it has always been a problem where, having gone far, the minister was to arrive, but that does not stop Methodists prophesying that even their Presidents will 'go far' someday, somewhere. Heaven is full of them, so the prophecy is probably accurate.

The minister was Donald Soper, so Len Barnett tells us, and Len's uncle spoke truly. 'Within my first month in London the Crystal Palace burned down and the King abdicated; but far more important in the unfolding pattern of my life was that introduction to the West London Mission at Kingsway.'

This young civil servant was out of a Christian home, he was a Local Preacher on Trial aiming for full status in that brotherhood, but he was struggling through the pains of rebellion against traditional fundamentalist thinking in which alone he had heard the Christian case stated. He needed just those things for which Soper stood – an intelligible, intellectually respectable and satisfying faith for a young man of 1936.

'Donald Soper, therefore, came as the perfect answer to my needs,' Len Barnett goes on. 'Urgent, dynamic, brilliant in relating his faith to the uneasy world in which we were living as the coming confrontation with Hitler's Germany drew inexorably closer. Sunday by Sunday and Wednesday by Wednesday at Tower Hill during those years I was inspired, nourished, mentally stretched, as I listened to the impassioned and yet always flawlessly argued case for Christianity. The texts changed; the substance not nearly so often. Again and again I sat enthralled and convinced afresh at Donald's exposition of the great overarching theme of the Kingdom of Christ, Prince of Peace and Love who alone could bespeak into the wilful hearts of men his power and purpose, and deliver them from the bondage of the sin which warped and wrecked their highest desires and dreams.

'Every Sunday they came in their hundreds, keen, younger generation worshippers, many beyond the reach of any conventional cleric. Kingsway was thronged. Methodists assessing the size of the congregations have been inclined to suffer from double vision ever since the days of Wesley, but I truly recall many Sundays on which the Hall was packed to capacity. There were latecomers sitting on the steps leading up to the massive rostrum on which Doctor Soper paced restlessly, his voice resonant, as he pleaded a Gospel based upon the love of God in Christ and related to our daunting world scene.

'In season and out of season he declared the unchanging basis of

Christian faith, the power of divine love, suffering, non-violent redemption, sacrificial, alone able to shake the gates of hell. Again and again we heard the argument and advocacy, unyielding, pertinent in a world prepared to unleash the most horrible violence ever witnessed in man's affairs. It was a time when anything save military might seemed a monstrous irrelevance.

'Yet the overall abiding impression of those years, oddly enough, is not the preaching of a pacifist Gospel as such, but a full-orbed Gospel of personal and social redemption. It spelled out clearly that to be a Christian meant personal commitment to Christ and the inescapable challenge to Christianize the environment at every point. It was the insight of the Bible as a whole and the life and teaching of Jesus Christ in particular, in the light of the week's headlines and the relationship between the two which came up week by week, freshly minted, vital, topical, to earn acceptance in the minds of the congregation – so many of whom in the years ahead, like me, were to be declared Christian Pacifists and appear before tribunals again and again.'

Dr. Soper's reputation was not only growing at the Kingsway Hall. He was getting round the Methodist Church for preaching engagements and for special missions to areas in the provinces – activity which was ultimately to be the seed of his organization of campaign preaching. In 1937 the news of his work was breaking across the Press. *Reynold's News* featured his work on Tower Hill and in the following year *The People* ran a feature 'If I had only one sermon to preach' in which Dr. Soper appeared with a sermon on the fact of God. In it he sounded his own authentic note, arguing that the intuitive appreciation of God enjoyed by the man of faith was an experience parallel to and as valid as any scientific experiment of the times for the man who enjoyed it and therefore the man with the experience had a perfect right to attempt to communicate it. It was a line of argument which was, at the time, being greatly employed by Methodist preachers, largely under the influence of Dr. Frederic Platt, whose Fernley Lecture (1915) *Immanence and Christian Thought*, was being taken up as a theological guide by students.

Involvement in the world's issues was also beginning to cluster round Kingsway, shifting, as it were, from the hustings at Tower Hill to practical expression in a localized church. In 1936 the Italians ended their imperialist war in Ethiopia and that country was annexed to the Italian Empire in May. In early January 1937 the *Daily Sketch* reported that the Emperor Haile Selassie opened an exhibition at Kingsway Hall called 'Conquest of Healing' in which the Hall was transformed into a world picture of need and answer to need in Indian, African and Japanese villages, seeking support for the medical missions of all the Churches. With the type of congregation now centred on Kingsway, the effect of such an exhibition was to be seen in personal response rather than money. The attraction for Dr. Soper in holding such an exhibition was that in the work of medical missions there was an outlet for the desire to serve in his pacifist young people – especially when the most recent victim of brutal war – and international duplicity – was there in the Hall singing hymns among the young people.

The Islington insights also began to effect the work at Kingsway and in June 1938 the *Daily Herald* picked up an exclusive report on the opening 'near the Strand' of a hostel for ex-prisoners, financed by a group of leading Methodists. The house was to begin with twelve residents; it was the only one of its kind in London. Dr. Soper pleaded for reticence about its place and character, fearing that publicity might ruin its work by frightening off the men for whom it was opened. This was, perhaps, the first variant from the social programme of the Hugh Price Hughes tradition which was based, as we have seen, on moral protest. The work for ex-prisoners is based upon a social protest which secures to men the right to a fresh beginning in a society loaded against them. The social service programme which began to change as early as this experiment ran into the debacle of war in 1939; this had to be met by an *ad hoc* wartime programme and the expansions had to wait until Hitler was out of the way.

The network widened in another direction when the *Newcastle Journal*, the most staid and respectable of Tyneside newspapers, reported a demonstration which was intended to focus attention on the needs of the millions of unemployed by a symbolic action in London. 'Workless dine at the Ritz'. Six unemployed, five men and one woman, were the guests of the Peace Pledge Union at a meal at the Ritz. The *Journal* remarked, 'They arrived in old clothes but armed with invitations to lunch. The lunch cost eight shillings and sixpence. The guests said, "Today we dined at the Ritz, our first square meal for months." '

There is in this story the indication that the Peace Pledge

Union, with the Methodist Peace Fellowship, found a home and keen support in Kingsway. The association gave Donald Soper a great number of headaches and he did not always agree with the Peace Pledge Union's attitudes or association. But at the time the leading Christian voices, including such others as Maud Royden, were deeply committed to the pacifist point of view and the Union seemed to them the natural way of expressing this fact in society.

Shortly after the beginning of the war a British Council for a stable Europe issued an appeal for the discontinuance of the war, to which twenty-eight leaders gave their signatures, including Dr. Soper and Dr. Royden. It then appeared that this document was used as propaganda in Europe and the two preachers had to withdraw their support, Dr. Soper declaring that 'Any statement which has a fascist or Marxist smell about it is not the kind of pacifism which I favour.' The forward positions taken by persons such as Maud Royden or Dr. Soper are exposed to this kind of exploitation again and again and it takes a very strong mind to continue to uphold the forward positions. 'Can you afford to be associated with . . .?' is the question with which critics are armed at every turn. This particular example of a signature to a document being collected for a purpose quite other than that which the signatory understood to be the case was reported in a Manchester newspaper – how can the denial ever catch up with the action which it denies? The publicist has to learn to be resigned to misrepresentation and go on taking the risk of being deceived. Misreporting is another business altogether; that he simply accepts as inevitable.

As the nation got round to the fateful 'appeasement' period of 1938, the staunch pacifism of the previous five or six years, characterized by the famous by-election at East Fulham (where a Conservative rearmament candidate was roundly defeated by a Labour pacifist – a 14,521 majority for the Conservative Party being transformed into a 4,840 Labour majority), was giving way to a lethargic programme of armament manufacture. For those early years of Soper's ministry Stanley Baldwin's verdict, given in 1935, was correct. Speaking after that by-election he said, 'What chance was there within the next year or two of that feeling being so changed that the country would give a mandate for rearmament? Supposing that I had gone to the country and said that

Germany was rearming and we must rearm, does anybody think that this pacifist democracy would have rallied to that cry at that moment? I cannot think of anything that would have made the loss of the election from my point of view more certain.' (*Britain Since 1918*, B. B. Gilbert, Batsford.)

Soper was so deeply involved in this pacifist movement, and his voice heard so widely, that it would be wrong to avoid pointing out this national reaction on the issue of peace versus war. Before the Czechoslovakian shambles the nation was with the pacifists. For a decade there was a 'pacifist democracy' in this country and Christian advocates were more responsible for its existence than anyone else. Right or wrong, the pacifists did sway the nation. Problem situations usually slot into each other and it is a matter for conjecture just how far the fact that rearmament took up some of the dreadful slack of unemployment in 1937–8 was responsible for the nation's mood changing to one accepting the inevitability of war.

Dr. Soper's pacifism was immune to the balances, counterchecks and dubieties of the political debate. Would Germany win a hegemony of Europe? Was the rape of Austria, Poland or Czechoslovakia enough to change his mind? These events were decisive factors in altering the view of some minds which had through the inter-war years held pacifist views; but not his. War is wrong, he argued; the consequences of its wrong will in themselves be other wrongs. The tomorrow of the British nation might be through the dark night of defeat and occupation but this, for him, did not affect the fact that war should not be. It is a total rejection regardless of consequences which makes the peace war issue, in his view. Such a road is not everyone's road and the burden of believing it made an additional sorrow for him as the war developed and the nation's mood changed. Perhaps the strange thing is that the people did not reject him in the years which were to follow.

The Methodist Church as an official body realized in its Conference that the peace/war problem divided sincere Christians, some taking up arms, some going to the tribunals claiming conscientious objections to service; and it instructed its ministry and members to care for both types. The chaplaincy service was manned to full capacity of the Methodist quota and ministers were also under obligation to appear before the tribunals to give evidence of sincerity in cases where an application was made. There was a welcome for the man in uniform at Kingsway: there were also many Methodists serving sentences for conscience' sake in Wormwood Scrubs and others on non-combatant tasks in London. Churches embrace mankind; sects exclude the variant types.

The crucial days of the latter half of the year 1938 in which the nation endured the deep sense of shame because of the Czech settlement and yet, strangely, the deep relief of the false hope that war was not to be, brought to Donald Soper his own personal crisis. The impetuous speed of his work since his first appointment caught up with him and when in August 1938 he went down with appendicitis and was hustled off for operation, he did not get out again and back to work for nearly six months. The *Sunday Referee* voiced the gladness at his return to work on March 12th, 1939 by covering the story of his re-appearance at Tower Hill, noting that the resumed meetings took him into the seventh hundred in the Tower Hill series.

It was an unpleasant period during which Dr. Soper was out of action. It began with the Munich Agreement of September 1938, in which the Czech nation was offered up as a sacrifice. As Jan Masaryk said, 'A sentence without right of appeal and without possibility of modification.' It continued with Britain's broken-winded attempts at rearmament in which the Government seemed to lack the nerve to take over the factories needed if the planes and tanks were to be hurried into existence. This tardy programme was balanced by the mad fact that the Agreement itself gave to Germany some of the finest armament factories in the world inside Czechoslovakia. Did Chamberlain not know they were there? As our 1937 armament programme faltered in execution, the unemployed numbered 1,791,000 and there were over a million people on public assistance. There is an historical crumb of significance in the fact that a Jew, Hore Belisha, was the person who gingered up the rearmament programme. A Jew, Disraeli, had troubled Bismark; another troubled Hitler.

In January 1939 the Spanish War ended, to all intents and purposes, with the fall of Barcelona to the Fascist forces. Britain recognized the Franco Government in February 1939 – and 6,000 battle-hardened German soldiers went home from Spain; another 20,000 Italian troops, perhaps battle-experienced, returned to

Italy. The union of Germany and Austria squeezed out thousands of Jews who fled to British mandated Palestine. Overtopping the quota of immigrants by thousands, they arrived in leaky ships, smuggled their way in, or died trying. Arab and Jew alike blamed the Mandatory Power, and the Coldstream Guards and other units policing Palestine were caught in the jaws of savage 'eye for an eye' retaliatory warfare.

The Prime Minister's message to the nation, however, informed the world that 'Europe is settling down to a period of tranquillity.' It is true that remnant Republicans in Spain, anti-Nazi Germans in Czechoslovakia, and Jews perishing in the Mediterranean found tranquillity. The Falange and Gestapo helped them. Lord Beaverbrook used the *Daily Express* to tell the nation, 'No war this year or next'. In the week that Donald Soper returned to the wall at Tower Hill – on March 14th – Hitler pounced and possessed himself of Czechoslovakia. With Hitler in Prague, Mr. Chamberlain speaking at Birmingham complained, 'Surely I was entitled to consultation!' It was enough to drive the dumb to shout in the streets. There were over a thousand people round Donald's pitch that day. He got back just in time to comment on Hitler's reprimand of Chamberlain for continuing a British rearmament programme after their amicable talks of 1938!

The young people, many with pacifist convictions, who thronged the Kingsway Hall during that shameful period of hesitant non-government in Britain, were the tough kind whose programme could not be deflected by the times but whose voices were heard alongside their leader's in the national debate. Thanks to the fellowship in the Hall, their faith, hopes and opinions had deeper roots than those possessed by the mass of the people. The absolute moral law of Jesus' second commandment drove them into action as well as protest and some of them made personal discoveries of inner resources.

Len Barnett's story continues in a typical example of this personal self-discovery. 'It was in Kingsway Hall, one Sunday night, as Donald was conducting worship, that without warning, I found the idea burgeoning, then captivating my mind that I, too, ought to be a minister. I came out of the service deeply shaken. I had no thoughts of the ministry before that moment save in close association with an attitude of repugnance. I thought ministers a queer breed: and still do.

'I had left school and decided against seeking a place at a university out of an impatience to earn my living. My old headmaster was disgusted with my lack of ambition; but I was insistent. To imagine myself now giving up all thoughts of progress in a Civil Service career and starting to tread unfamiliar and – if the truth be told – unwelcome fields of study, was something to which in the ordinary way I would not have given a second's thought. Yet, a sense of constraint gripped and held me; and within days I sought an interview with Dr. Soper and somewhat diffidently told him what had happened; that I felt I had received a "call" to the Ministry.

'His reaction was, looking back on it at the safe distance of over thirty years, typical. There was no look of delight and pleasure on his face. I might as well have told him I was fond of kippers for breakfast. He nodded calmly.

' "That's interesting," he said briskly. "I'm glad to hear of it. Well, time alone will tell whether your call is genuine, won't it?"

'And that was that. I retreated somewhat crestfallen. I didn't expect to be patted on the back and told what a splendid thing it was to be a minister. But I did long for a warm word of encouragement and some advice, at least, about the way ahead. Perhaps I got it and have forgotten. Perhaps he thought my call was hero worship thinly disguised and would freeze in the cold air of reality.'

Here again is that strange incapacity to draw closely alongside people which dogs the footsteps of the strong man in public service. That Donald Soper was proud of this Kingsway candidate is certified by his later association with his work, especially when Len Barnett was a secretary of Methodism's Youth Service, and still earlier, when Barnett did offer as a candidate for the ministry, it was Dr. Soper who, as his Superintendent Minister, nominated him in the District Synod.

But the encouragement and practical guidance which this candidate needed was given him by Miss Elaine Hammerton, one of the Methodist saints, who then ran the Methodist Study Centre which took up students at the point at which they were stuck, however high or low, and saw them through to their journey's end. Civil Service training had done enough for Len Barnett to make him able to track the right file when it was necessary. It is

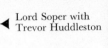

Lord Soper with
Trevor Huddleston

The Methodist Recorder

West London Mission

At the Methodist Universit
Tokyo (in the background
Toyohiko Kagawa)

In Ceylon in 1947

West London Mission

possible to speculate on how many women, in the Deaconess Order or in other professional capacities within the West London Mission and in Methodism generally, have given the personal caring to folk whose original movement towards a new life began with Donald Soper but who never made a personal relationship with him. Deaconess, warden, or secretary, these women have understood why one who loved people intensely needed this service done for him. It is their secret and they will keep it. Len Barnett does not recall Donald Soper ever talking with him about his studies beyond a cheery, 'Well, Len, how's it going?' when they chanced to meet in the Hall. Yet he has remained Dr. Soper's stout defender through all the years as have hundreds of others whose experience was similar.

By April 1939 the Kingsway programme was going fully again under the recovered minister, who took up once more his open-air work, his preaching and his work on radio, which was beginning to feature as a national highlight of the air. They were strange, breathless days. The nation was forever looking over its shoulder. What was to happen? The gas masks were already distributed, a trial children's evacuation of London had already been carried out in the autumn of the previous year. Young people in the congregation were caught in the internal debate, to object to national service or to accept it? Opening the morning paper was largely an exercise in looking for what new thing had gone wrong. When the war did come, it was felt almost as a relief – at least the nation knew where it was.

In the summer of that year, however, the Methodist Conference did a thing which it never likes doing. It shifted a young minister with only fourteen years' service in his record from a place where he was doing extremely well to another and more difficult post. When Dr. Leslie Weatherhead was taken from Leeds Brunswick Church in 1936 to serve the City Temple, a young minister with a gift for central missions was taken from Scarborough's Queen Street – a thriving preaching centre attracting many holidaymakers – and sent to take his place. On the eve of the war, after but three years in Brunswick, he was moved again, this time to Westminster Central Hall. Dr. W. Edwin Sangster came to London.

This appointment began what the work of the war was to cement, the near-legendary three-point ministry of Methodist star preachers in London. The veteran preacher at City Temple, Leslie Weatherhead, the wizard of Westminster, W. E. Sangster, and, junior member of the team, Donald Soper at Kingsway. They could hardly have been more different, yet in some way they made a unity which the whole Church appreciated.

Weatherhead had his deep interest in the pastoral psychology of the minister's work and followed his line with unremitting zeal. For years he was, and for many still is, the interpreter of the Faith from that angle. His preaching had the sweep of a great Palestinian dragnet so well known to the first apostles. He used it to net fish of all kinds into the consultations at pastoral level where the harvest of his preaching was gathered. The City Temple congregation was huge and the influence of that pulpit, through Weatherhead's writings and printed sermons, reached out over the world. He had a genius for the dramatic which was demonstrated in a quiet understatement and a very guileful simplicity. His services were wrapped in beautiful music and skilful lighting. His voice, with its whispering quality, made his hearers feel that this man's speech was a private word in every individual ear.

Some would say that his style and indeed his whole approach to the work was Greek in derivation. He sought with modern theory and brilliant, imaginative thought to make the story of Jesus acceptable to the young people of his time. If his work was 'emotional', and some said it was, it was the type of emotion to be met in Wordsworth's poetry, while his theology owed its appeal to some Browning-like quality which would not admit that there were mysteries which man was not intended to unravel. He might have had the motto, 'Come! I will lead you through.' Enemies he had; there were those whose idea of psychological work was coloured by a lurid travesty of Freud and they thought Weatherhead to be his London agent. Others there were who thought that there was a new gospel at the City Temple which derived from Emil F. Coué rather than Paul (between whom Dr. Weatherhead did once point out similarities). There were those who thanked their God that City Temple was not a Methodist Church – let the 'Congs' have him. But the world listened to his message. One very famous ex-missionary who had something to do with Leslie Weatherhead's beginnings in the ministry said, 'I can really explain his success – I told him to get a line, stick to it, and preach it until people were weary of hearing it. They would take notice then – and he did!'

Weatherhead sprang out of the First World War and an Indian background. His Madras ministry was his real beginning. Sangster sprang straight out of the same war but at a different level. One was combatant officer, with Indian service, then chaplain; Sangster was one of those who went into theological training from the Forces as so many sturdy men did, with a war-found or war-tested faith. He exchanged the Royal West Surrey Regiment for Handsworth and Richmond colleges.

Sangster's contemporaries in that time of college re-opening remember that the man whom the whole Church ultimately came to know was nascent in the student. He was serious, out of sympathy with the post-war high spirits of the majority of the men training with him. Introspective people and those more than a little shaken by the war gravitated to him. He had a formed prayer-life and an evangelical hold on the Faith.

In 1939 when he came to Westminster he was already well known throughout the Church and was known as one of the prophetic preachers. If anyone ever stood in the great Old Testament tradition and sweetened it with the love of Jesus, it was he. People in authority presumably expected the mantle of the great Dr. Dinsdale T. Young to fall upon the Westminster man – some still do – and they were not disappointed. He spoke with enormous power, a mighty voice and in terms of thunder. His message was the classical presentation of the Gospel salvation and he clothed it in language weighty with the King James version of the Bible. It was preaching in the grand manner. His vocabulary was so distinctive that his staff picked it up. It is said that one morning he spoke to the charlady who was washing the main steps into the Central Hall. 'How go your labours this morning, my dear?' It was not her best day and she replied, 'Toiling in rowing Doctor, toiling in rowing.' His own wit was like hers, clothed in scriptural phrases more often than not. He said to one person who complained that he was an adopted child and so not like other people, 'How lucky you are; many are called but few are chosen – you were both baptized into Christ and chosen into your family – thank God for it.'

Homespun, up from the people, captured by Christ, gifted with a fine physique and an organ of a voice, people adored him or were suffocated by the style of piety he represented. Someone called it 'overpowering but genuine sanctity'. Saint he certainly was and a preaching-engine! To sit near him as he preached was an extraordinary experience. One could hear his breath come up, as it were, from his heels, expand that mighty chest and issue forth as modulated sound, now a whisper, now a roar. One could feel his pauses sink into his hearers and know that every pause was a carefully timed action, not timed by his brain but by the machine itself working subconsciously to serve his theme. The head held high, the mouth controlled by strong muscles, one knew that this speech was this organism's proper conduct. Speech was never done better, it could even make a London dialect musical.

Then there was Donald. Three men in a city: the other two more often than not thought him the 'bad boy' whose pranks could embarrass them at any moment. They had no conventional link between their spheres of work, and each was busy enough to exhaust all the time available. Sangster gave much time to the life of Methodism generally, Weatherhead had his own ecumenical world, Soper always lived in tension with the general Methodist hierarchical structure. But as the three ministries developed, from time to time they would meet to attempt some sort of co-ordination in their preaching at critical hours in the Church or national life. None could have done the work done by the other two; each had his own specialized following in consequence; but they made a proud trinity of brilliance, in the mind of the Church and of visitors to London.

A mythology grew up round their relationships and contrasts, 'I am of Leslie; I of Donald and I of the "Dear Doctor".' (As the years rolled by, some brother-ministers were to call Sangster 'Will', but his following never thought of him but with an awe which prevented such familiarity.)

Stories sprang up round the three men and their styles. 'Sangster loves his Lord; Weatherhead loves his people: Soper loves an argument' is a typical example. It is said that the Dean of Westminster Abbey, passing the end of the Central Hall queue on his way to take evening service, overheard two young office girls speculating on whether they would get into the Hall. 'If we can't get in, it's too late to nip over to Kingsway, but we can always slip into the Abbey; there won't be a crush there.' 'City Temple for popsies; Kingsway for Bolshies and Central Hall for saints.' This one was hardly fair to Dr. Weatherhead – his congregation was as mixed as the merchandise at nearby Gamages.

The growth of a folk-lore about a person is a sure sign that dynamic power possesses him. It occurs in all religions and in no religion. Dr. Weatherhead would be the first to tell us that it is a purely psychological phenomenon and, like the 'odic force' with which he deals in his thinking on healing, is not due to divine selection of the person concerned. Nevertheless, when people con-stellate round one person in this way and foe as well as friend create stories about him, if the personality himself has a demon-strable faith there is an exhilarating Gospel triumph.

It was more grace than Methodism deserved to have these three such persons in full career simultaneously when the Second World War crashed down on Britain. Nor can it be said that after Sang-ster's death and Weatherhead's retirement it has happened again. Soper remains – though but three years younger than Sang-ster – to soldier on (if the metaphor be allowed!) into the years which pay little heed to great preaching. He not only lives on but must make the adjustments that change requires.

5.

Soper in Wartime

Within the hour of Britain and France declaring war on Germany on September 3rd, 1939, the air-raid sirens sounded through the churches of southern England. It was a false alarm, as false as the expectations of the public who believed that one horrific blow would be struck at London, Portsmouth and other strategic southern centres. The real blow fell on a thousand programmes in a thousand churches and it destroyed the personal plans of millions. Nothing happened, but everything happened.

Until the invasion of Holland in May 1940 the general public thought there was little to remark about in the war they called 'the phoney war'. It had not bitten into the daily life of the people. Yet on the day the war began *Athenia* was sunk off the Irish coast, by the end of the month H.M.S. *Courageous* was at the bottom of the sea, in October H.M.S. *Royal Oak* was sunk in its own harbour at Scapa Flow and by the end of November 60,000 tons of shipping were sunk inside one week round the east coast of Britain. Scientific warfare was with us, the magnetic mine, which had such signal results, being the first to demonstrate its power. The public had thought it would be seen in the air, or in gas warfare.

The Military Training Bill introduced in the April before the declaration of war called up men between the ages of eighteen and forty-one years of age and this was the first item in the war scene to get inside the Kingsway Hall and other churches, but particularly into Kingsway with its strong pacifist following. There were some agonizing decisions to be made by large numbers of the young people in the congregation. The first months of the war reduced congregations in London churches dramatically, including Kingsway and Westminster Central Hall, and the regular programmes of the churches ran down. The 'phoney war' period, however, was long enough for Londoners to get their breath. Evacuees returned, people took up again their old habits and church congregations revived with surprising numbers, which included people the war had brought to London. Tower Hill, and, now, Speakers' Corner, picked up and Dr. Soper was plunged into controversy, now that his pacifism was confronted with the actuality of conflict.

He was also deeply committed on the air with the B.B.C. and by March 1940 the Press was thanking the B.B.C. for the insight which arranged the religious broadcasts Dr. Soper made, which were described in the Press as one of the nation's wartime assets.

Wartime London soon found its life-style and presented its own new problems, and not least among them was the use of the Underground railway stations as deep air-raid shelters. Kingsway Hall is within a very short distance of the Holborn Underground station which possesses a maze of deep tunnels, and in consequence the London authorities pressed its platforms into use as a day/night shelter for the local people or such of the commuter population as stayed in town. Night by night they took their bedding and comforts with them down below. Some left them on the platforms all day, and made themselves as happy as they could sleeping cheek by jowl on the platforms. Within all the deep stations during any night there must have been thousands of people coming and going, sleeping, playing cards, sharing vacuum flasks, listening to impromptu concerts or speakers. The most difficult thing to do was to thread a way through the platforms to catch a train.

By December 1940 Kingsway had reacted to this challenge on the doorstep by opening a Rest and Feeding Centre in the depths below the Hall. A news reporter ending his night prowl at six o'clock one morning at Holborn Station asked a Jew at the station entrance, 'Any chance of a cup of tea round here?' The Jew told him to get along to the Kingsway Hall for an 'honest cup' and 'you'll get a shave and a wash there too', he added. 'They'll set you up for work down there.' The reporter found all he wanted and the place full of people, with Dr. Soper serving the tables alongside his volunteers. The breakfast count was 700 meals a week, 36,000 in the year.

August of 1940 had seen the Londoner's war begin in earnest
with the 'blitz' but by this time the city was full of people again
and more than full, for the war brought masses of people to the
capital. It was on August 15th that the Luftwaffe, loosing 180
planes in a night, switched from its attempts to neutralize the
British airfields and began its attack on the whole population of
London; the first all-night raid began on the 23rd of that month.
It is hard to realize at this distance that the programmes of such
places as Kingsway grew and deepened under this assault. Fire-
fighting on buildings, care of people, the younger people roaming
the night streets, the life of the shelters, the cussed reactions of
the office workers to be at work 'in spite of Hitler', all amounted to
a heady state of excitement which increased rather than depressed
the social service programme of the halls. That the November
raids on Britain killed 4,558 persons was a fact that stimulated the
workers. To see a train, darkened and strangely sinister, pull out of
King's Cross railway station in the middle of the night, with
bombs crumping round the area, the sky above flashing with anti-
aircraft fire, while soldiers who had been on leave in the stricken
city sprinted to get into the moving train to avoid discipline for a
late return, was to realize that the nation was at war and somehow
didn't mind.

It was a German error on the grand scale. The R.A.F. was
about at its last gasp for supplies and a continuance of the anti-
military German attack could have paid off had they but known.
The civilian attack was counter-productive in the highest degree.
Londoners did not appreciate this attempt to destroy their city:
they refused to be destroyed. Wars are won by enemy mistakes
more often than by good planning.

In the city's reaction to the bombing the halls of London, and
its churches, took their part, and pacifist people at Kingsway
fought a war they deplored simply by continuing the work under
new conditions. The Youth Club, for example, was a hundred
times harder to handle, with the laxities which the atmosphere of
those days promoted. Boys of sixteen were turning up drunk; girls
were excited into a psychological drunkenness which increased the
difficulties of those caring for them. On the other hand, a quite
different, suburban type of youngster burst into lively intellectual
activity, demanding to know what the war would do to our civilization.

The Churches as a group were involved deeply in this latter effort to interpret the contemporary tragedy in terms of Christian social planning. Issues raised by William Temple and Studdert Kennedy in Soper's youth returned, with the old questions re-pointed. The Archbishops of Canterbury and York, with Cardinal Hinsley and the Moderator of the Free Church Council, produced a Five Point Statement of War Aims for Peace.

The Points were obvious enough. (1) The abolition of extreme inequalities of wealth. (2) Equal opportunity for every child in education and development. (3) The preservation of the family as a basic social unit. (4) The restoration of the sense of divine vocation in daily work. (5) The fair distribution of the riches of the earth to all.

The programme was debated up and down the country in grammar schools and wider rallies of young people and Dr. Soper went about the suburbs through the 'blitz' as a member of a Brains Trust. Sometimes his own position made the rally as, for instance, in one meeting in Essex where the young people, perhaps realizing the shaky state of the political parties when the war began, proposed the formation of a Christian Political Party in the House of Commons and he was landed with the lonely task of demonstrating why the Labour Party would do.

Now and again he would foray further afield as far as the Potteries or the North in the same cause, always linking the visits with some event in the life of the Churches as he went.

The pacifist campaign in the nation, which drew together many strange allies, ran on into the second year of the war and in 1941 there was a joint plan to publish a manifesto calling a People's Convention for Peace with a view to ending the war by negotiation with Germany which collected Dr. Soper's name to its proposals. Subsequently, the document was converted into a weapon of war to strengthen the enemy. He saw the distinction between this and the preaching of Christian pacifism coupled with his own belief that the nation should not have gone to war, and thereupon disclaimed the manifesto, withdrawing his signature. Always there is this loading in activities on the fringe of the debate and it becomes extremely difficult to steer a Christian course between the conflicting issues when parties each wish to make capital out of the association with a powerful person.

By the end of 1941 this campaign had cost Dr. Soper the freedom of the air which he had so long enjoyed. The B.B.C. banned
from its programmes the three principal Christian pacifist
speakers, Dr. George McLeod, Canon Charles Raven – Regius
Professor of Divinity in Cambridge – and Soper. The ban was
complete and he dryly observed, when asked by the Press, 'It is the
public rather than the preachers who suffer.'

Issues of the moment cropped up to complicate work on the
wider problems. The *Eastbourne Chronicle*, for example, records
Dr. Soper's indignation with the type of religious group in the
Free Churches and other places which opposed the opening of
cinemas on Sundays in places where there were enormous forces of
the army on coastal defence. 'It is strange reasoning which ap-
proves of a boy of eighteen years of age being compelled to fight
and to kill, but denies him a refuge in a cinema from the drab
Sunday streets.'

The Soper–Kingsway programme of those hectic years is not
unlike the reformation which overtook the nation's living standards. In June 1941 the Government rationed clothes and introduced the 'Utility' scheme which set a wartime standard for most
kinds of goods; furniture, utensils, bedding, clothes and right
across the board to hot-water-bottles. The nation moaned until it
discovered that the standard was extremely high and that a 'utility
model' could be thoroughly reliable and also cut out the 'snob
value' of the most expensive things. Hardware went classless! So it
was with the Church programme of those years, the trimmings
were off, the voices of prejudice muted, and people discovered a
new zest for work.

This sense of release bred by the communal life of the air-raid
shelters threw up an idea in the Guild at Kingsway which
was to be, perhaps, the war's greatest product in the life of the
Mission.

Late in 1941, to quote from the Rev. Albert G. Errey in his
work, *Experiment in Witness,* a private publication, 'Here was a
group of young people, with a strong sense of the relevance of the
Gospel to the war-torn world of that day, and with a real desire to
contribute to the task of making that Gospel known; already alive
to the value of taking that Gospel out of the Church to the places
where people were to be found; already aware in a dim way of the
possibility of preaching beyond the limits of their own church;

above all led by a greatly loved and respected man who was well known as an aggressive open-air evangelist.

'The next step was inevitable, though, as so often, it is only looking back that we can see how inevitable it was. "What do you think of sending out small groups of people from Kingsway into Essex and other places around London on preaching campaigns?" About a couple of dozen young people thought it a wonderfully exciting prospect and gladly volunteered for the experiment, though how it was to be worked out none had any but the vaguest notions.'

How it worked out in the long run is the story of the famous Order of Christian Witness, probably the product of his ministry which gave and gives to Donald Soper the greatest satisfaction of all the things he has done. It was the first attempt, and a successful one, to take the system of trek preaching, 'mission programmes', and use it for a modern approach to Christian evangelism.

The early months of 1942 were enlivened by the preparations for the work. A name had to be found for the Team and the work and the group elected to call themselves 'The Kingsway Preachers'. This established, they met at regular periods through the next few months for instruction by Dr. Soper in the art of preaching. Trained at last, where should the work begin?

The first place selected itself by one of those events which are common in the tight mesh of the Methodist Connexional system. At Dorking in Surrey, a dormitory town of London, there was a group of young people who had organized, as their reaction to the wartime atmosphere, an interdenominational group called Dorking Christian Youth, and it was their ambition to hold a week of mission to the town but they had no mission team to help them. The minister then stationed at Dorking was the Rev. Erastus Evans, M.A., whose ministry might well be described as a cross between that of Dr. Soper and Dr. Weatherhead. He relayed the Dorking need to the team at Kingsway and the deal was on: Kingsway Preachers, first encounter, Dorking.

Three teams were formed and with the bright-eyed optimism of the new preacher they began to outline carefully courses of addresses of what they wished to say to the people of Dorking. They hoped to speak for half an hour and then answer questions. One can only surmise that the Doctor let them do this knowing it would do their personal thinking a little good; he must have known it would do nothing for their open-air witness. They learned that quickly once they began. A few of the really keen did a dummy-run by trying out their material on a June Sunday afternoon at Marble Arch and found the experience rougher than they had imagined. The trouble about being the disciples of a really competent operator is that imitating him looks easy.

Snags cropped up in the preparation. At that time the churches across the country were operating a national programme called Religion and Life Campaign. This was using outstanding Christian experts in its work and it transpired that the Dorking people thought of their campaign as part of this prestigious movement. Erastus Evans had not bothered to tell the Team that; he just wanted the Team.

Dorking church life had its supply of traditionalists – after all it was in the 'bank manager belt' round London – and some of them awakened to the fact that this team from Kingsway was predominantly composed of pacifists and conscientious objectors! In the upshot one of the impressive evidences of the divine control of the campaign was that the outré views of some campaigners and the almost complete acceptance of pacifism among them did not destroy the campaign when it did take place.

During all that period of preparation the war had been in the worst fettle from the British point of view. Rommel was loose in the Western Desert, the Free French forces had capitulated at Bir Hakeim, the Western Desert Force had lost 230 tanks on the desert in North Africa on a day in June and our forces had retreated to just in front of the El Alamein line, held by British, Indian, South African and New Zealand forces. In London an enormous rally had demanded a second front be opened to aid the hard-pressed Russian forces. The German troops were romping over the northern Caucasus. The fiasco of the Canadian raid on Dieppe had thrown British prisoners of war in Germany into handcuffs, and out in the Middle East General Auchinleck fell from grace and was replaced by Alexander, just as Zuchov replaced Timoshenko in command of the defeated Russian armies of the southern front. The Royal Navy was not spared, H.M.S. *Eagle* and H.M.S. *Manchester* went down, running the Malta blockade.

The newspapers in the hands of the Dorking commuters as the event began can be imagined. The campaign began the day after

German forces reached Stalingrad, August 27th, 1942. Pacifist preachers have their own brand of courage! The most significant bit of news was probably that which the Dorking folk noticed least – American Forces landed that month on the Guadalcanal; that day the United States of America inherited world-wide responsibilities.

The Kingsway Preachers launched themselves into the onslaught on Dorking and, unlike later campaigns, the whole venture was staged outside the churches and, indeed, almost entirely in the open air. Three strategic spots on the main High Street were occupied by the preachers and Dr. Soper was with them in overall control of the programme. One night the work got all tangled up with a Civil Defence exercise; another night a thunderstorm broke across the town; but these contributed to the gaiety which possessed the Team. Living together and sharing meals, many of the members travelling up to the City after an alfresco breakfast to get on with their own work and returning at night in time for the forum in the streets, the days flew by. St. Ninian, that most humorous of British saints, would have been at home, for hilarity was the hallmark. Someone discovered Dr. Soper's passion for what was then a new product born of war, processed cheese. Secular songs replaced hymns round the schoolroom piano and people discovered that joy and evangelism belong together. It was out of that discovery that the appeal of the movement sprang.

Errey remarks, 'It was hardly surprising after all, for it was nothing more than a continuation of the ethos of the West London Mission into a new field.' There were some little habits of the Doctor's which contributed more than people realized. One campaigner remembers how, when he arrived at the church-base, he found Donald Soper packing straw into mattress covers for the 'family' to sleep on, and how he felt that this must be a terrific event if 'the Boss' shared in it like this. One early campaigner who is now a Chairman of a Methodist District with his own significant place in the Church writes, 'Who else of his standing would have given up a week in August year after year to lead, live with and sleep among a crowd of young people?' It is a good question, except that this sort of action *was* his 'standing'. He would have been someone quite different and without any peculiar significance had he not been just that way.

The astonishing thing to some observers is how, year after year, he who was such a master of the open-air forum tolerated the attempts of the young learners to do the same work and, tolerating it, did not diminish their impact on the crowds who listened. It has been said that with the Kingsway Preachers he began a process which pre-dated almost all which has since been done in 'lay training'. His 'in-service', apprenticeship type of training was an unexpected product for a man whose own preparation was so different. It might be said that the Church at the time possessed no form of training which he would have thought suitable to the purpose. There were Gospel Schools, Bible Colleges, summer courses, but some he suspected of a wrong biblical viewpoint, some were locked in archaic language, some would not share the unity of social and theological thinking which he believed essential, and no doubt there were some who would not have accepted a Soper-commended man in any case.

'From the start,' writes Mr. Errey, 'one of the features of the Campaigns of the Kingsway Preachers had been their communism. Week by week as Campaigns were in preparation, a more or less conical wooden money-box, painted white, stood on the table at the Guild and into the white box were put contributions to expenses according to means. For the most part it was the Campaigners who paid up, but sometimes others who could not go would slip something in.'

There is nothing remarkable in a money-box? Perhaps not, but the story goes on to tell that, once a Campaign began, every expense of each Campaigner was taken from this collection, whether the collection was enough or too little. Even when someone could well pay for this or that personal expense privately, he was not to do so. All came out of the common fund. This was no quaint regulation but part of the theological and spiritual basis of the Campaign. 'From each according to his ability, to each according to his need.' It is surprising what such a rule can do to a man's needs! It is more surprising what it can do to the fellowship of the Team. The system was responsible for a great deal in the intimate experience of brotherhood which flared up from the first. From the morning and evening prayers in the schoolroom of some chapel, to the number of slices of bread eaten by Doctor Soper – with cheese – one spirit prevailed. 'All things in common' really was *all things*.

A tiny scrap of press publicity of the Dorking Campaign resulted in a second, week-end, campaign in Bishop's Stortford, but the movement really got going when Mr. Stanley Sowton, the much loved Financial Secretary of the Methodist Missionary Society, invited the Kingsway Preachers down to his home ground round Rilla Mill, Liskeard, Callington and Launceston in Cornwall. This Campaign arranged for August 1943 was the first fully residential event; the Campaigners were together all the time instead of coming to the job from their daily work.

This was the real test – they were off the London scene and tackling the country mood of Cornwall. Living together all the time demanded a richer endowment of grace, but their 'guru' was with them. It was an excited Team which got off the crowded wartime train from Paddington and stepped into a steady drizzle. No civic or church welcome party awaited them. They went straight into the wet open air. The audience was a small group of loyal Methodist people doing the West Country honours.

It spoke much for the local church people that with Donald Soper preaching at Wesley Church on the Sunday, congregations were found for the surrounding churches where inexperienced campaigners were holding forth – and at that time, because of their inexperience, holding forth with set-piece sermons! Any man can compete with Donald Soper if he will give just his own freely-spoken story of his daily religion. As Soper himself has said, each man's experience of God is uniquely an instrument of the Spirit.

The team settled down to live in a tiny schoolroom of the church at Rilla Mill village, where the men's sleeping space looked out on the graveyard and the butter was kept cool under a gravestone. A drill evolved as they tackled the surrounding villages, the day being spent in 'knocking up' the village in house-to-house visitation – a programme which produced a minimum of adults and a plethora of children at evening open-air meetings. They discovered their own limitations in this setting, finding it very hard to make real contact with the thinking of the village people for whom London and even the war itself were very remote. It was exhausting.

In consequence they discovered of necessity the need for a 'day-off' to get their breath back. A couple of lorries were going off across the famous Bodmin Moor to fetch sand from the beautiful Camel Estuary and they hitched a lift out on these and returned

79

sitting on the sand. The moor gave them a new dimension and this system of a midway holiday became part of the planning of the Preachers. Dr. Soper remarked that 'By Tuesday the girls have hysterics and the men have become atheists.' If the Campaign had no dramatic results, it did provide one incident which attracted the Press.

The *Cambridge Railway News* carried an item headed, 'After you, Padre'. The paragraph told of the arrival of Dr. Soper in the main square of Launceston to find the open-air cinema van of the War Savings Movement esconced on his site. The two campaigns, both well advertised, had collided. 'After you, Padre' was the War Savings offer and Dr. Soper, using the van's amplification system, took precedence of the 'War Savings Chief' in speaking to a large audience. The evening Brain's Trust gained by the accident in timing but the rural blackout completely foxed the driver going back and he just could not find Rilla Mill.

During 1943 a young Canadian pacifist turned up in London who had been drafted for his war-service to the Canadian Fire Service and posted to its overseas headquarters at Wimbledon. His name was Keith Woollard. The Soper reputation attracted him to Kingsway and the Preacher project fascinated him with its possibilities. He threw in his lot with the Team. Two earlier Campaigns that year had revealed new difficulties, both of which emphasized the need for some overall management which Dr. Soper could not give. A Campaign at Harpenden – one more of the 'bank manager belt' suburbs of London – bumped into a local ecclesiastical arrangement that no church would go it alone in the area, and the Campaigners on this long-week-end campaign were all very Methodist. (Was this the real reason or was it an allergy to the Soper emphasis?) An attempt at Feltham, another rim-of-London situation, was frustrated by the sudden arrival of Hitler's flying bombs. As with bombs, two 'duds' in a row is depressing.

The big event of the Team was a Campaign planned for Barnstaple in August – now the chosen month for the work – 1944 and Woollard turned his attention to the organization problems of this campaign. Here for the first time a team effort of two or three persons giving a snappy address was substituted for the sermon technique of the earlier days. The three speakers fixed a common thought and came at it from three angles. Returning from this campaign it was Keith Woollard who said, 'Why don't we get more people to join us and make a really big thing of it?'

The grim winter of 1944 supervened; Germany was now the nation with its back to the wall. The Allied Forces were in Italy, the bloody battle for Monte Cassino was over, the Italian line of German resistance went down, the Russians had regained the upper hand and at Minsk had captured 100,000 German prisoners. Calais had fallen to the Canadian troops, Brussels was free. The German response to this situation was not unlike the defensive method of the skunk which turns its back on its enemy and squirts foul-smelling liquid. The first V Bomb landed in the London area on September 8th, 1944, and the second battle of London, the battle of civilian terror, was on. In sheer devastation and terror-making it surpassed the first great blitz and ended only when the victorious Allied Forces overran the launching sites in northern Germany. It has been said that not the Ardennes 'Battle of the Bulge' in which the German Forces failed to stem the Allied advance, but this new-weapon attack on London might have turned the war in Germany's favour – as Hitler believed it could. Montgomery racing up through Hamburg and on to Luneberg extinguished the menace. This time land forces saved England – and London.

The Team members of Kingsway Preachers, therefore, all during that black winter, retracted on London and served in the wartime programme there, their preaching being confined to lodging houses and street corners in town, with sporadic appointments in churches round London on Sundays. But Dr. Soper at Christmas 1944 wrote a letter to all the London Districts of the Methodist Church inviting delegates to a conference at Kingsway Hall to discuss the evangelical methods of the Kingsway Preachers and plan the expansion of their work. Three Campaigners were briefed to tell the story to whoever came to the meeting. It is said by his Teams that this was the only time they ever saw Dr. Soper really nervous. 'I just don't know what to expect,' he kept saying.

In the upshot the meeting was well attended, a large Campaign including new volunteers was planned for the August of 1945 and this Campaign was to be directed by Dr. Soper with the assistance of Keith Woollard and another seasoned Campaigner, Max Parker, who later became the General Secretary of the Fellowship of Reconciliation – the pacifist organization for peace. The war ended with the dramatic flash of Hiroshima and demobilization began. Woollard, whose Fire Service folded up, was seconded by his Church, the United Church of Canada, to remain a student in Britain and plans began for a large effort in the cathedral city of Salisbury.

The campaigners, now ecumenical in church loyalty, were put into training throughout the summer, the organizers visiting the outside groups. All studied the Bishop of Bradford's *What the Church teaches* and the Church of England Report *Towards the Conversion of England*, both of which were recent publications. The enterprise was given a new name to meet the influx of members from places other than Kingsway, and prepared to take to the hustings as The London Christian Campaigners. Two trial campaigns were undertaken, one in Melton Mowbray and another in the heart of Lincolnshire – the latter at last discovering that the best 'stand' for an open-air meeting in a village is outside the public house at closing time – a surprisingly late revelation! Other sections of the future team tried their skills in their own districts – including the large group at London's East Ham Central Hall, and Dr. Weatherhead's City Templars!

The Salisbury campaign dawned at last, after incredibly earnest preparation, and 130 young campaigners found themselves billeted in one place, with the wartime British Restaurant offering breakfasts and the Campaign cooks rustling up other meals. Dealing with 130 proved very different from the original 30 of the Dorking or Liskeard campaigns, but somehow they managed.

The beautiful cathedral city of Salisbury is also an important market town with a market square just made for open air speaking and this was the centre of the work. Day by day from midday the stand was manned by relays of speakers until well after dusk, each team doing an hour. The Team for the first time stumbled upon a technique which became a regular feature of the work. This was called 'infiltration', which is the deliberate stimulation of conversations between individual campaigners and members of the crowd. Against the background of the talks going on from the stand this is both easy to begin and very useful. One atheist thumbed a gesture at the speaker and said to his campaigner, 'He'd better not come back here.' Another said he didn't believe a word of it but that somebody must, to take such trouble to do it!

Even Dr. Soper learned something. One night he had been standing on a chair addressing the crowd, came to the end of his talk and expected the crowd, which had appeared to be listening intently, to drift off. Some did, but a large number carried on in the little groups round the individual campaigners, as though Donald Soper never existed.

How to draw in the net of people whose minds had been opened and hearts touched constituted a problem. The classical evangelical groups of the Victorian pattern had called for decisions on the spot – as Dr. Graham still does – but this did not commend itself to the team. Cards on which to register decision could be used and indeed were provided in the Salisbury campaign. But the team were not too happy about this and no public appeals for decisions were used. It was when in 1946 the operation was repeated in Plymouth on an even larger scale that the answer was found which appealed to most of the campaigners. The final rally of that Campaign took place in the great Plymouth Central Hall which was packed with people, there being standing room only for late arrivals. Here the Doctor used the Holy Communion as the token of loyalty to Christ – perhaps following the pattern of his radio-banned contemporary, Dr. George McLeod, who was doing just this among Scottish young people – and this habit has persisted in the work. So the two sides of Soper became impressed upon this movement; his skilled open-air evangelism and his basic sacramentarian conviction.

The Plymouth Team numbered 250! They were divided into 30 teams but even then presented too large an administrative problem and created too great a distance between the members and the leadership. It was tolerable when a Soper was present behind the divisional leaders, but good organization does not plan for one charismatic person to be the cohesive force in such a work as this. Some relief was found in arranging the campaigners according to what number could be slept in one place and putting that number under a 'commandant' who was separated to the work of seeing that things went smoothly. In this way the campaigning principle of working and living in 'families' emerged.

The work grew. It stretched beyond London, first in the south, but soon the great industrial cities were calling for campaigns.

'London Christian Campaigners' would no longer serve as a title. At a small meeting of leaders shortly after Plymouth the new title emerged, 'Order of Christian Witness'. Tower Hill and Hyde Park had given birth to a national movement.

6.

The Christian Socialist

1946 was Britain's first post-war year; Kingsway had survived a war, battered like most of Britain, and in the process Donald Soper had been formed into the man the country knew, or thought it knew. Weatherhead's City Temple was down, a wartime casualty of fire raids and he was preaching in a borrowed church. Across the way from Westminster Central Hall the Houses of Parliament had suffered bombing but the Central Hall was still there at the heart of the nation. All three preachers were in their pulpits to meet the new day – if it should turn out to be new.

What the arduous wartime road did to people is of the utmost interest and significance, not only to the person himself but to the world in which he offered himself as a contribution to the new stretch of road that lay beyond the war. Sangster emerged from his blitz flat one of the best known men in Britain, looked to by the newspapers for rich devotional work suited to the man who reads the *Daily Express* or *Daily Mail*. To the people on the fringe of Methodism who belonged to the traditional school, he was the one man whose image helped them to feel that the old Gospel was still honoured in the Methodist world. His field of influence was the Class (the Methodist fellowship group), the Bible Study, the Prayer Meeting, the tried ways of his mother-church. His was a militant Christianity. He wanted campaign and re-interpretation of the Faith, but above all a recall to the rock from which a Christian England had been hewn.

Leslie Weatherhead came to his borrowed pulpit better known than most men. In 1946 he published his twenty-third book – *A Plain Man looks at the Cross* – and his impact on the world was as much through his writing as in his church. The way in which the war had thrust his interests deeper and deeper into the individual's personal conflict can be traced in his writing as it moved through the valley of human suffering towards his great thesis of 1950, *Psychology, Religion and Healing*. In the 1946 book he does refer to the world about him and its misunderstanding of the value of Jesus for its social condition, but as he unfolds his argument through the book his diagnosis is the personal one of re-formed human lives being the most significant social step there is to take.

The closing words of *A Plain Man looks at the Cross* are in fact Weatherhead's greeting to the post-war world and to read them is to see what the war had done in him. 'So in Africa, so in London, so with the outcaste, so with the educated and civilized: so with men in olden days, so with modern men and women who are willing to be quiet and to consider; His words are true and they are only true of Him: 'I, if I be lifted up from the earth, will draw all men unto Me.' And when, bound to His Cross, He is lifted up before men's eyes, by some strange power which defies analysis, He, dying, brings them life; bound, He brings them liberty; suffering, He redeems them from the greatest anguish the soul can know, the agony of hopeless despair; and everlastingly loving, He challenges them, and claims them, and will never let them go, until He makes them His for ever.' This is the authentic word of one whose primary interest is the pinpoint of divinity in man, and it can be said that Dr. Weatherhead's post-war ministry was a dedicated attempt to mirror Christ's compassion.

And the 'tom-boy' of the Methodist London trinity, what of him? The youngest of the three, he who had the deepest personal views at the onset of war and those least adapted to a wartime scene, he surely had to develop most. In truth, change would be hard to identify. He came through on Victory in Europe Day with the same passionate faith which possessed him on September 3rd, 1939. He was, if anything, more committed to the pacifist position than in 1939, having the shambles which followed the war as evidence of his rightness.

He had flexed his muscles and gained strength. Tower Hill Soper was now also Speakers' Corner Soper and world famous; his radio work was regained and nationally appreciated. His following was not now the relatively lone young man who moved him out to Tower Hill but the host of young people of the campaigns, to whom he was supreme. He had gained the administrative expertise needed in Central Mission administration; for his preaching, the Hall was crowded, but now the provincial crowds wanted their Soper too.

He was the vocal social leader. Head had grown no less than heart. The six or seven contrasting types of manhood locked inside that one frame had each developed – this surely was the Soper miracle. One or two should surely have died to make room for the growth of the others, but it was not so. By a quaint wartime process, to find parallels to his growth it was necessary to look among the ex-Servicemen coming back from prison camps. For them also the whole self had grown and a man emerged – 'iron dug from central gloom'.

It was not possible to say that Donald Soper ended the war a better preacher or broadcaster. He ended the war more Donald Soper; that was all, but enough. Too much for his enemies, who were numerous; sufficient for his followers; he remained his own strangely isolated self, enigmatic in himself, crystal clear in his professional work.

When, therefore, the 'blue birds' swooped down at last 'over the white cliffs of Dover' and the men of war began to come home, grade by grade, from the oldest to the youngest for demobilization only to find that there was little food, few cigarettes, clothes rationing and an almighty political muddle about what to do next, Soper was poised for the changes to come. It was the 'red-tie' period of his life – he would turn up at the Methodist Conference wearing one, and speaking 'red-tie', too. At the peak of his strength, voice gaining rather than losing by his open-air work at this time, his ready smile greeting his public's criticisms with confident assurance that his answers were correct, or stamping up and down the Kingsway rostrum on a Sunday evening, quick-firing pertinent asides, he was assurance writ large.

Nationally, everything was going his way and a change in his work can be dated from that time, as the pacifist issue dropped out of the national debate, smothered by the dreadful blast of the Hiroshima bomb and over-smothered again by the Nagasaki blast which obliterated a city just to demonstrate that Bomb One was no freak. It was not yet time for 'Ban the Bomb', for possession of it was the monopoly of one end of the post-war world, what people called 'the right end'. But as the pacifist cause went into eclipse behind the terror screen of atom war, the day dawned for radical changes in the nation's own structure and they were changes which chimed with the Soper mind.

Changes which men imprisoned in Germany towards the end of the war knew all about were coming over the world scene. They had discovered their officer-captors suddenly friendly and expansive. 'Why does not Britain make peace with us and turn to fight Russia while there is time?' This was the question such officers asked in various differing forms. They would come to bid farewell to their captives before they went to the Russian Front and in saying good-bye declare they were going to die for England. They certainly died, as Russia revenged the inroads into her territories and the duplicity of the broken treaties of the earlier days of Hitler's war. On the other hand, young Britons would say they were Russia's friends for life.

Sure enough, the war ended with the rush across Europe of American tank formations attempting to forestall the Russian onward sweep, Patton and 'Monty' in headlong competition. The German officers' prognostications were cynically worked through and the shape of modern Europe emerged with the grim picture of both 'associate' armies panting on the rubble of Berlin; both home! To many this looked like the world's new ogre rearing itself before the wretched corpse of the last had been identified in its 'bunker refuge'.

The League of Nations finally died in April 1946 and in the same year the eastern section of Germany leaned away to the Left. In 1946 the United Nations Organization assembled in New York and the 21-nation Peace Conference was scheduled for Paris. By 1947 the Foreign Ministers' Conference in Moscow broke down arguing about the future of Germany and in 1948, while sixteen nations met to carve up Marshall Aid, the U.S.S.R. walked out of the Allied Control Commission which administered the defeated territories. So came the 'Berlin Airlift' with its 277,264 provisioning flights as the pressure of the U.S.S.R. was felt in strength, and in the politest of 'wars' the Western Powers called checkmate, or at least check. But 1949 produced East Germany.

Europe for some five years could be seen crystallizing into its new shape. Communist rule came to Bulgaria, to Yugoslavia and, last in the queue, Czechoslovakia. In the wider world the Chinese

Peoples' Democracy came to birth contemporaneously with the new Czechoslovakian State, after the long struggle in which U.S.S.R. moves in Manchuria and General Chiang's attack on the Fourth Route Army of Mao Tse-tung petered out.

Ravaged, filled with displaced persons, disorganized and looking across the Atlantic for the one part or up at its Russian occupation forces on the other, Europe lay in worse ruin than it had ever known. For all the damage sustained by Britain in London, Coventry, the South Coast towns and spattered over many other cities here it was somehow different. There was still an imperial 'feel' about the war-won situation, and the true damage to this country was to take more years to reveal itself than mere bomb-sites indicated. Bankruptcy is harder to detect than war damage. The nation was in debt to the U.S.A. to the tune of $3.75 billion, and was soon to need more.

Incredibly, Britain launched itself upon a course of action which in a decade was to change things so much that British national life contrasted with the life of both the newly emerged super-powers, being neither communist nor free-mercantile but a mixed economy of a kind which had not previously existed. This change went on, much of the time beneath the skin of the nation's daily life, as the problems of a battered world one after another beat down upon these islands, as they beat upon every place.

With greatly reduced power in the world but, in notion at least, an atomic power, this country became a diminutive third-type structure differing from North America and Russia alike. Spinning off colonies like Guy Fawkes fire-crackers, patching up old buildings at home, enduring penury, fending off 'take-overs' and striving, though threadbare, to keep up its perfect gentleman pose in a world in which gentry were now very scarce, it was made for the Sopers, for the whole nation was a debating society.

Who will ever know why Winston Churchill fell from power in 1945, especially as it was he who dictated that all Conservative parliamentary candidates should study Soper techniques on Tower Hill and Hyde Park! The landslide into a Labour Administration gave that Party a bumper 412 seats to the Conservative 213 and Liberal 12. Clement Atlee became Prime Minister with Ernest Bevin as Foreign Secretary and Hugh Dalton as Chancellor of the Exchequer. Post-war reconstruction, then, in its first phase, occurred under the imprint of this Party's ideology.

The Trade Disputes and Trade Unions Act 1927 was repealed, giving back certain rights to Unions and workers in relation to strikes; the Bank of England was nationalized; the National Insurance Bill was introduced, bringing social services into a new codification and this was followed by the National Health Act, and by 1948 national transport and steel were nationalized, just a year after the mines.

It was an enormous programme of deliberate change in the national shape. It was conducted to the accompaniment of world quarrels on reparations and aid, as well as shifts in power and world impoverishment. These were due to new lines of international trade not yet having established themselves in a world short of ships as well as cargoes. At home there was a fuel crisis, there was a bread crisis, there was conscription and there were corruption charges.

As the prophet is unintelligible out of his temporal setting, so Dr. Soper's ministry after the war cannot be understood without this background. In the years before the war broke on the world he was approved, disliked or wavered over on the grounds of his peace campaign. Now, with the war gone and his own chosen party in power and trying an at least partly socialist programme, he was branded by the world as a Socialist advocate who made a prime target for those who feared the Left, or wished to purvey a Christianity unlike his.

Challenged about his socialism in 1946, he told the *Staffordshire Evening Sentinel* after a rally that, 'The meaning of socialism is only to be seen when it is realized that the basis of society is not the competitive market but the family table. If we believe in the Sermon on the Mount, then the obvious consequence is that whether a man is good, bad or indifferent you cannot starve him. Socialism is the political and economic expression of human solidarity. We are all members of the same family and every man is our brother. I want a world in which it is tolerably possible for ordinary, decent people to live to the fullest extent of which they are capable.'

This quotation catches admirably the feeling in the heart of the mass of the British population at the war's end. Dr. Soper did it again when he took such a message to the country. Once more he caught the emotion in the common man, expressed it and in expressing it gave it clarity and, much more important, also gave it roots in philosophy and religion. As in the case of pacifism he used his faith to interpret what many people groped after and within the faith he found the tap root off which the public actions and choices grew. Christian Faith is a key which opens a thousand locks and if one has the courage to believe this and, more, the courage to enter the door when the lock is conquered, it is quite remarkable how often it is discovered that popular moods, vague feelings, catch-phrases of the times are emanations from deep-level wisdom.

The daily newspaper headlines are a vapour rising from profound human yearnings. They can pass with the day, their deeper meaning un-noted; but when the man of faith is on hand they become significant. The man-in-the-crowd is not a fool except when he damps down the rising surge of humanity itself which seeks expression through him. This is part of the reality of Soper's 'one family' and also of the thought of Carl Jung whose work was then coming to English thinkers. Soper has often been Man for men as they struggled to speak a mind deeper than their own. There have been many Tories among the men. He, however, has stayed Left and for theological reasons which he tirelessly deploys. All of which can be written off as obstinate obscurantism by people who do not like the Left or this particular man of faith.

It has been said by one who shared radio work with him that his habit of prefacing his answers to questions with the words, 'Speaking as a Christian Socialist' was quite infuriating. Many listeners would agree with this verdict, but the habit is part of the man who, in so speaking, did not intend disparagement either of the non-christian or the non-socialist, but intended the words to mean 'What I say has roots'.

The post-war Labour Administration's massive programme of nationalization and social welfare – a twin structure both parts of which were intended to support the other – was enacted under unrelenting opposition right through the Government's period of office. It had no powerful Press; it ran counter to inherited assumptions galore, and vested interests had to fight their rear-guard action. Great changes, in total a minor revolution, took place without any congratulations for their originators.

Under the battery of opposition, Dr. Soper shared the ignominy which was the lot of the Administration and was glad to do so, because he saw that much of what was being done was done once and for all. He has seen that some things done cannot be undone however much succeeding governments wish to undo them. More significant still, he has realized that 'capitalist society has itself so changed as to demand checks and balances in order to keep itself going'.

It has been a battle in which 'fellow-traveller', 'Red-cleric', 'no true Believer' have been some of the shot fired, but if one's convictions are founded in one's basic faith, what is there to do but bear the onslaught and, if possible, take advantage of it? It has been Dr. Soper's firm opinion that all forms of government or social policy which exalt the possession against the man or exalt a 'herren volk' over the 'ordinary, decent man' are policies which dig their own grave – the world is not so constructed as to allow them to succeed. This is as truly Old Testament belief as some of Karl Marx's convictions.

His work as a Methodist minister in charge of a large social service institution has been particularly relevant during the debate on social patterns at the point where the Welfare State has been accused of providing the chance for shiftless people to batten on the nation. The demand to 'deal with the scroungers' so often made in political rallies of his opponents has met with the scorn which alone an active worker in the field could supply. The implication that a whole section of the public, the working people, is irresponsible and lazy he described as 'impudent nonsense' and he has held that in the cases he has discovered, a handful in years, there has been as much that arose from medical as moral cause.

Politically, Dr. Soper's life has been lived in a two-pole tension between his convinced socialism and his membership of the Labour Party. He joined the Christian Socialist Movement and became its President. This movement has explored the theological and religious grounds for socialism as a practical economic way of life which mirrors the Christian faith. It contains within it a number of well-known Labour Party figures, with others. Mr. Harold Wilson is a member. Meetings have been held in the House of Commons for study of papers on the socialist case and it certainly has helped to keep the fires of idealism burning in all the political rough and tumble.

The other pole of his life is the Labour Party, which he resolutely cleaves to through thick and thin. He clings to it, not because it is the epitome of political rectitude, which he is sure it is not, nor because it is the only home of idealists, but because it does view the nation whole and plans for all sorts and conditions of men. It is common for the Conservative Party and Press to refer to the Labour Party as the Socialist Party – presumably lest it should be thought that the Tory world does not contain labouring men. This Dr. Soper has always resented. 'It is not a socialist party,' he roundly declares. 'I wish it were.'

Like his own Church into which were fed several streams of religious societies, ranging from the high churchmanship of Wesley to the democratic convictions of Bible Christians and the social emphasis of the Primitive Methodists, the Labour Party has a multiplicity of origins, only some of which were socialist in any true sense. It is an easy party in which to plan what is now called a 'mixed economy' which contains a rationalized capitalism, and in its days in office this has been its chief tendency. It is the voice of an enormous industrial movement, the Trade Unions. But it is not their party. They are its people. It is the home of the heart for intellectuals, who dream a utopian world and can find no other political resting place. It has an element of earnest Christians who wish to express their Christian social concern, but it is not religious. It has a number of humanists for whom the Party is the substitute for the Christian faith they have abandoned. Not all the Party likes Donald Soper, but it would be hard to find a section which is not glad to have him.

His closest associations within the Party have grown within the group which seeks a thoroughgoing socialist revolution within the nation – the Left Group in which Michael Foot is a vocal leader. Some of his closest associates he has discovered among the humanist section. Such men as Ted (Lord) Willis stand high in his regard. There are some who have never quite got over their astonishment at their affection for a parson. There are other Free Churchmen and Methodists who think they have quite got over their affection for this particular parson. One might wonder whether some of the non-Christian friends he possesses in the movement realize that he considers the public service they perform to be the activity of the Holy Spirit at work in them; he sees the Palace of Westminster as God's workshop equally with the Abbey nearby.

One of the media which helped to make him a nationwide

figure in the post-war years was the weekly review *Tribune* with which Michael Foot is closely identified. With occasional contributions in the earlier years, since 1953 his column has appeared regularly, either under the caption 'Personally Speaking' or headed up for some special purpose. *Tribune* is a well-to-the-Left publication which calls itself *Labour's Independent Weekly*. It presents good reviews and some poetry, organizes seminars and reading groups and struggles for a living. Down the years it has become identified as the socialist pressure group which criticizes the Labour Party itself when it strays into non-socialist lines of policy, equally with the opposite Party. It carries much Trade Union advertisement – and little other. It backs most of the demonstrations of the hour and a world policy which looks to the economic redemption of the Third World.

In such a publication there is plenty of room for someone to write third party comment on almost anything, provided it is angled the way the paper is going and this angle Donald Soper would wish to follow. The Labour Party Conference, the Tory Conference too; comments on American affairs and comments on U.S.S.R. run side by side. Now and again a religious thrust reminds readers of the Christian doctrine of the Kingdom of God, dreams of which began so much of revolution.

The contemporary linkage is not always there, the writer occasionally starting his own hare and chasing it.

'When it comes to self-criticism, conscious or unconscious, the Americans are gluttons for punishment. Believe it or not, last Friday's edition of the leading Louisiana daily paper ran a column on the present industrial trends and requirements. Immediately under it was the text for the day, for New Orleans is a pious city, and the text was Ecclesiastes 3.20: "All go unto one place, all are of dust and all to dust turn again."

'Well! well! There are not a few on both sides of the Atlantic who are convinced that this "dusty answer" of the Preacher (which is the other title of Ecclesiastes) is in fact applicable to the affairs of America, whether the Louisiana press intended it or not. They point to the decline in the gross national product, the average 15 per cent "hike" in wage settlements, the continued mood of recession, but above all to the sense of impotence that the war in Vietnam has produced.'

The article goes on to talk of the terrible psychological wounds which the Indo-Chinese conflict has inflicted upon the American self-image, reducing a confident and eager people to angry frustration.

'Now at last the illusion that links war with success is being destroyed. Thank God for that. It is humiliating for the citizens of America to discover that the most powerful, sophisticated war machine the world has known can win battle after battle in Vietnam against a comparatively weak enemy and at the same time totally fail to conquer this enemy or bring him to his knees, or stop the drain of American blood, or halt the flow of deserting soldiers, or abate the growing cynicism of American people and politicians alike.'

After discussing the monopoly control the arms industry has had upon the American economy for so long that an economy without it looks impossible, and the dilemma which ensues when it is evident that the war must end and disarmament follow, he diagnoses the fear and the recession to sheer bewilderment of this apparently insoluble problem. Is the mass violence which is growing the devilish economic salvation of a system which has thrived on armaments and victory so long? 'Guns for Gangs.' Is this the advertising slogan of tomorrow?

'Somewhere in this modern world these sombre discoveries had to be made. That they should have been made in America may seem intolerable to many Americans or at least most uncomfortable for them. Nevertheless I do not share the view of Ecclesiastes. America is perhaps a country that has still enough of its original drive both to learn this lesson, and to teach the rest of the world how to put its message into effect.'

A Methodist minister can hardly get farther out from the main stream of public life than to write in *The Tribune* for it is not the everyday reading of the Methodist public and this, without doubt, was one of the reasons why Donald Soper began to write in it and continues to do so. The shock effect of doing so, however, was much greater in 1946–56 than it would be today. Within the confines of his own Church's official life his position, even now when he was in the senior ranks of the ministry (which period begins at the twentieth year of a minister's career), was curious. A scrutiny of the lists of members of influential committees of the Church does not reveal his name very frequently – it is surprising what names it does reveal!

His own mixed attitude to great conferences and to committee work was undoubtedly one factor in his scanty record in them at that time. None could be keener than he in the creation and fighting through debate of resolutions on important issues, of which there were plenty in those early post-war years. Sometimes, however, he could be scathing about the impotence of high-sounding memoranda addressed to government departments or the world in general. The Church's reaction to his position on public affairs was equally mixed.

The Methodist Conference is a great assembly of well over 600 representatives – not delegates, for they are there in council and not as retailers of group or party opinions. Half of this representation is ministerial but in a Church so large it is not easy for a minister to be present often in Conference. Dr. Soper was, therefore, not always present in those years when great debates took place. When he was, the whole Conference was in attendance to hear him and friend and foe alike simply had to take notice. A tired Conference would fill up quickly, emptying the tea rooms and lounges when it was known he had intervened in a discussion, and the sudden access of Press men at the Press tables bordered on the absurd. There have never lacked those who said that he was sensitively aware of that full Press Table, but the insinuation that he 'fed' the Press material they could use for his own ends was, and still is, far from the truth. He is simply conscious that the Press matters and that if a thing is worth saying to the Church's courts, it is worth telling the nation.

Conference is addressed by representatives, when called by the President, from a tribune – a fact which the wags never forgot when Donald Soper mounted it to speak. It is the same tribune year after year, ported from town to town. Some have said that Dr. Soper's main themes likewise remained the same.

Red-tied, dressed in a modern lounge suit in those days, he had regular gambits with which he opened. If he were introducing a new piece of business and wished to get it on the conference map, it might well be that he would gentle the Conference.

'Mr. President, Members of Conference, I have no wish to bore the Conference (guaranteed laughter) but I am afraid I shall have to, as there is something of no little importance on my mind – a thing which some say I have not – but as someone said to me on Tower Hill the other day, "If you get it off your mind you might shut up." I will and I will.' In the forties there was no time limit on speeches and from this point on he might settle down to lead a very willing audience whither he would.

Intervening in a debate he would tackle it differently. He might pounce arrogantly. 'Mr. President, I would not wish to call the speaker's remarks stuff and nonsense but I would be glad if somebody would.' At other times when the debate had been inaugurated by some Connexional Secretary speaking for the Department for which he was responsible to Conference – and all the business of Conference is introduced in this way – his technique would vary. 'We are grateful for the leadership we get from our Departmental Secretaries. They are in a position to view things from the heights. May I, however, as one who simply works in the field, as it were, meeting simple men most of my time, make one minor contribution which can perhaps only be offered from that position.' At the beginning of such a preamble it is certain that the Secretary concerned would have whistled up his colleagues and committee members to support him. The door stewards would also be standing inside the doors they guarded.

One other type of intervention stands out and it was when some socially important issue became bogged down during debate in a procedural wilderness. The resultant speech could then be dreadful and fascinating. Like some knight in armour he would deal blows with the mace, sweeps of the great sword, wicked little jabs of the dagger, apparently revelling in the cruelty of carving up the 'establishment'. It says something for the Methodist Conference that it has not always fallen for this one.

One of the Departments of the Methodist Church which grew and thrived in the post-war years was known then as the Temperance and Social Welfare Department – later re-named the

Christian Citizenship Department. The mandate of the Department had a coverage almost as wide as life.

> 'The responsibility of the Temperance and Social Welfare Department shall be the effective presentation of the Christian social witness. The subjects within its purview, in addition to the Temperance Movement, shall embrace social questions, including Industrial Welfare, Gambling, Public Health and Social Purity, the Christian Observance of Sunday, World Peace and International Relationships, the preparation for and practice of Christian Citizenship, and the maintenance of the Christian ideal in social life' (*Minutes of the Methodist Conference*, 1947).

With this enormous responsibility the Department was in the care of well-known and respected men, Rev. Clifford Urwin being the General Secretary and Rev. Dr. Maldwyn Edwards his cosecretary. The Committee is studded with names which subsequently became widely known – Dr. David Mace, for example, the father of the Marriage Guidance movement, Henry Carter, whose name was respected right across the spectrum of Churches, Dr. Benson Perkins, whom it is ignorance not to know – but there is no Donald Soper!

In the post-war years this Department had its hands full. In 1946 the Conference adopted a *Call to World Peace* which was sent to U.N.O., His Majesty's Government and to other Churches. It ran to enormous length and dealt with the, then, secret power of the atomic weapon, the responsibility of the developed nations and the programme of 'noble' policies set out in the U.N.O. Charter. 'Conference solemnly adjures the Governments of the United Nations not to come short of the high purposes to which they are pledged; and in the name of God and His Christ, the Conference calls on all the peoples of the world to make these aims their own and to undertake the holy crusade of establishing peace on earth.'

There is enough in this Declaration to keep Dr. Soper on his feet for a whole Conference and the wide generality of the terms, together with the unreal assumption that the Methodist Conference in the United Kingdom had the influence to sway the addressees, is characteristic of the style which he attacked again and again. 'A Resolution, even if unanimously adopted, is never an end in itself.'

National developments feature in the Resolutions of the same year and one on Social Legislation has a prophetic ring to it which the years endorsed.

'The Conference notes with profound interest the changes in the social life of the people of Britain that are foreshadowed by the raising of the school age, the provision of family allowances and measures before Parliament dealing with National Insurance, and National Health and the direction of industry. The Conference is glad to recognize that these proposals go far to embody the principles and aims set out in the Declaration of Conference on the Christian View of Industry in relation to the Social Order. So far as these measures lift the standard of life of the people and help to remove the shadows of ignorance, poverty and disease, the Conference believes they should be welcomed by all Christian citizens.

'The Conference, however, is concerned with the spirit which must inform the life of the people if these measures are to achieve their desired end. The Conference believes that they call for a deepened sense of corporate responsibility, a willingness to work together for the common good and for quickened industrial effort if the means to achieve these ends are to be forthcoming. A profligate temper in the community would imperil the national well-being.

'The Conference believes that the Christian principle of mutual responsibility is of urgent application to the present situation in national affairs, and calls on the Methodist people to witness to it, as they share in the upbuilding of the New Order in national life' (*Minutes of the Methodist Conference, 1946*).

This is an example of the triumph of the Soper point of view in those years and the sort of debate which gave him opportunity to hammer home the social meaning of the Faith. Here a Church high court is underwriting the Labour Party's plans for Britain and in face of opposition in much of the Press and, for example, within the medical profession itself, comes out for the New Order on Christian principles. The solemn warning of the later paragraphs show how clearly the Christian socialist, in counsel with his Conservative brethren in a Church assembly, could foresee the need for a change of heart in the mass of people if the new things were not to be ruin rather than salvation.

There are resolutions on Housing, Conscription, Gambling, the legislation setting up New Towns, venereal disease in the British Army of the Rhine, the European Refugee problem of the late 1940s – in which the Department is authorized to spend the Church's money in help. As 1948 arrived, the picture of Britain's depressed economy, and the anxieties about the international situation, is clear in the Resolutions.

> 'It (the Conference) now recalls that three years after the cessation of hostilities no peace treaty has been made with Germany, Austria or Japan, that grim tragedy has fallen upon Palestine and that the world, despite the existence of the United Nations Organization, threatens to divide into hostile camps, separated by differences which have so far proved irreconcilable.'

This discreet summary conceals the Cold War's beginning, the disappointment of the nation at the slow economic recovery, which proved far harder than any could have guessed, and the weariness of the nation. Like other similar bodies the Conference lashed the weary horse of British life with whips of words. Their significance now is the revelation of how dated were the remedies recommended, how wrong the estimate of the Church's position in the new Britain, and how Imperial thinking remained after the crash of Europe.

> 'The Conference believes that especial responsibility rests on Great Britain to supply leadership to the peoples of Western Europe, and to maintain the British Commonwealth as an instrument of freedom and peace of nations.'

This resolution goes on to urge the complete destruction of all atomic weapons and a system of invigilation to prevent their reappearance.

The Soper point of view in such a mental climate, in relation to

East–West relationships in particular, was away out ahead of his Church's insight. His estimate of the Russian emergence in post-war Europe was realistic and a true forecast of what was to come in the world. From about 1948 on into the beginning of the fifties, his position among his fellow ministers and in the religious Press was insecure because he appeared to be 'fellow-travelling' (a term then coming into use). He could see ahead to the first Russian atomic bomb tests which took place in 1949. He did not share the dismay caused by America ceasing to be unique in atomic power simply because he knew the information leakage must come or the scientists in the East catch up. The view (which he shared) that scientific discoveries will always universalize themselves whatever is done to prevent it torpedoed much disarmament talk.

Nevertheless, being pacifist in such depth, this did not for him mean an arms race but a neutralist national position. Being a Christian believer to him meant that history was God-controlled and even the submergence of Britain under the tide of Communist expansion would not prove the end of anything; it was a stage in history. While there is life there is evolution. Where there is death there is nothing but silence. He acquired a reputation at this time, therefore, as pro-Russian or at least anti-Western. It was a time when the Tower Hill and Speakers' Corner audiences understood him better than his fellow-churchmen. His dream of a Britain which would repudiate atomic weapons for itself with disdain, standing stripped of protection between the two giant powers which he knew would never discard them, might have been a foolish dream or a mistaken one, but it was within the bounds of possibility if the nation's people could be persuaded. It was worth marching for. His demand that diplomatic and cultural relationships should be as keenly fostered with the East as with the American continent in the end became policy in spite of jingo protests.

7.

Founding an Order

Man of controversy, Dr. Soper was now in the public eye because of his professional life as a speaker in his own Hall and through the country; he was preaching his minority views of world affairs in the open air; the news reporters were never far from his tail; and as the B.B.C. opened its famous 'Any Questions' programme, it forgave him and he appeared on it from the second show onwards. This amounted to pretty nearly total exposure and was bound to bring maximum reactions. He was a national figure. At this juncture he might have 'taken off' and become a personal star, guru, B.B.C. pundit and generally affluent Contemporary Person. Others have done so.

Instead he founded the Order of Christian Witness from the sprouting life of the Kingsway Preachers. The inaugural Conference of the Order took place on Saturday, November 16th, 1946. A letter was sent out over the signature of Dr. Soper tracing the way the group had been led over four years. He wrote,

> 'Fundamental to the idea is the conviction so clearly stated in the Church of England report *Toward the Conversion of England*, that even as the clergy are ordained to the ministry of preaching, so is every church member ordained to the ministry of witness. Here I am persuaded is the open secret of revival.
>
> 'The Conference is open to all who are concerned to further the witness of the whole Church with particular emphasis on campaigning in the open air. Membership in the Order will involve:

1. The recognition by the individual church member of his or her responsibility to witness not only by their life but also by their words.

2. Further, the recognition that what we cannot do on our own, we can do together with others.

3. The formation of witness-teams within local churches by people (a) who will meet regularly for preparation by prayer, study and discussion, and (b) who will take and make opportunities for witness locally, especially in the open air.

4. The organization by the leaders of the Order of Christian Witness of campaigns (a) of week-end duration with several teams taking part, as has already been done at Melton Mowbray, Neasden, East Grinstead, Acton Hill, Eastbourne, etc., and (b) one combined week-long campaign at the end of August 1947.

'The leaders of the Order would help teams in their preparations through a central library of information on appropriate courses of study, methods of campaign, organization of campaigns, etc. The Order of Christian Witness would be financed by voluntary and anonymous contributions from campaigners into team funds and from thence to the communal funds opened for each campaign. This method has been used in campaigns to date.'

On August 23rd, 1947, the Movement descended for its first long campaign on Huddersfield. This was a new beginning in more ways than one. The campaigners were invited by the Huddersfield Free Church Federal Council – and so escaped from Methodist leading-strings. It was organized in five areas with area commandants to capitalize the power of size while at the same time leaving space enough to manoeuvre. The area commandants were free to plan as best they could but they were joined by the other four in council every day and the whole mass of campaigners met also in a daily Assembly presided over by Dr. Soper. The 'family' principle was thus wedded to the large city-covering campaign.

Never before had the teams attempted to work in a great industrial conurbation – and indeed, the effort was a pioneer for much that has since been done in 'industrial evangelism'. It was soon discovered that casual talks with little groups or individuals outside the works was better tactics than talks in the canteen served up with the meals.

When approaching knots of young men in the streets, or calling in two's at houses, the teams discovered what Dr. Soper christened 'sanctified oomph'; girls could stop and interest people who would have marched by or brushed the team parson off the doorstep.

This five-area Huddersfield Campaign ended on a note of high success. Beginning with one consolidated Rally at the Town Hall, five area rallies were necessary to close it, and Keith Woollard master-minded these with great accuracy. Dr. Soper was billed to take part in each of them and elaborate car arrangements, together with stewards to see him through the labyrinthine passages of chapels to the pulpit or platform, contrived to get him spot on time in each meeting. All the earlier part of the day was used in slowly covering the area in narrowing forays until all the team was working on the site of the rally.

The meeting itself was arranged round the Sacrament of Holy Communion. With guides and stewards to help, it was made possible for 1,000 people to take the Elements together. The talk which went into the programme was a direct challenge to use the Communion Service as a token of decision. After the rallies came smaller counselling meetings, with people recording their names and addresses for following up. The long day ended with a team supper which welcomed the local leaders into a final act of fellowship.

The growth of the Order and its work produced seas of troubles which demanded continued experiment as the leaders analysed the work of this Campaign and the Cannock Chase Campaign of the following year. In the latter it was thought that a two-week period might improve the contacts with those influenced by the campaigning. So, year by year into the 1950s, attempts were made to cope with the problems of success and while the leaders would never claim to have solved them all, the effects of the Campaigns were to be seen everywhere they went. Worcester, South Shields, Oldham, Bletchley, some of the centres, demonstrate how the network stretched across the country.

Central organization became a problem to be solved and at the same time a solution tended to emerge from the work. Commandants of areas evolved as a central group to the Order, meeting in Council. So a programme emerged whereby campaigners

continued work through the year in their localities. This by natural development created a permanent membership of the Order.
A badge of a cross in hand was used and a Pledge of Membership was created which committed members to a permanent
discipline.

The Movement as a whole in this second stage of development
owed much to the influence of Harry O. Morton, then a young
layman. He was later to become a Methodist minister, member
of the Geneva Staff of the World Council of Churches, then
Secretary in charge of Central and East African affairs for the
Methodist Church Overseas Mission Department; and all this
was crowned by his designation in 1971 as President of the Methodist Conference of 1972.

The Membership Pledge as it finally settled into shape reads:

'Christianity demands communication. Modern Society
needs to be infused with the Christian Gospel.

I accept my responsibility to be a witness to Jesus Christ, to
the Christian life I know, the Christian faith I hold, and the
Christian world I seek.

Communication requires Community. Witness must be a
united activity of the whole Church. The effective unit of
witness is the Team.

I undertake to prepare and to make this witness in fellowship with others.

Comunity lives by Communion. Christians need to discover afresh in communion with God the means of grace,
without which this witness is impossible.

I turn for the strength and courage I need to the cross of
Christ, to Holy Communion, and to the incoming of the Holy
Spirit.

Therefore I pledge myself to the Order of Christian
Witness.'

It could be argued that there was nothing new here, but experience in many campaigns has demonstrated that, while the commitments in the Pledge are proper to all Christian people, in fact
the local churches are all too ready to leave witness out of their
reckoning and general membership of the Church is no guarantee
at all that the Christian will act as a Christian in mission.

The formation of groups of this kind to undertake seriously what is in theory a general duty has been a feature of Church life through two thousand years. More than this – it occurs in other Faiths than Christianity. There is a very real parallel between the threefold pledge of O.C.W. and the classical Buddhist pledge, 'I take refuge in the Buddha, the Law and the Order.' What is distinguishable as peculiar to the Order of Christian Witness is the content of its proclamation. It is difficult to find a parallel in the crusading groups of Christians to the social emphasis which Dr. Soper imprinted on his Order.

'Broadly speaking the witness of the Order, particularly in its earliest days, tended to centre around two themes: that Christ offered the way of social salvation, and that Christ had brought to the individual a pattern and power for his own life. The two lines of thought did not always link very obviously – and indeed, it is by no means easy to make the link between salvation of society and salvation of self. But it can, I think, be fairly said that from the beginning the Order of Christian Witness sought for a synthesis of the evangel of the social gospel and the evangel of personal salvation, and I believe that in so seeking it has been wholly right, and the fact that it may not altogether have achieved what it set out to do should not blind us to the importance of the task. The weakness of the social gospel pure and simple is that it is apt to be little more than a powerless moralism.

'The weakness of pietism, or the concentration upon individual salvation and subjective experience, is not only in its failure to do justice to the New Testament but also in its tendency to morbid introspection and excessive religiosity, with a corresponding loss of that naturalness which is characteristic of the real saints – not to mention its failure to get to grips with material evils that threaten the souls of men. Finally, in so far as the synthesis has been achieved, it seems to the writer that it has been achieved in the process of setting the witness of the Order (both in the sense of act of witness and its content) within the framework of sacramental worship and sacramental theology' (Errey *Experiment in Witness*).

Present day members of the Order have said that it is not and never was based on Donald Soper. The present Head of the Order has said, 'Had it been dependent on one man, even Dr. Soper, it would have died before now'. Nevertheless the quotation from Mr. Errey is as powerful an evidence as can be needed – on sheer textual examination as well as on observation – of Dr. Soper's basic personal life-creed, underlying all his works, as it underlies O.C.W. It is true he has not clutched this Order to him as his own – but it is the daughter of his own faith. Its uniqueness is that it uses the techniques which have been almost monopolized by the ultra-conservative wing of the Christian Movement right round the world, for the purpose of preaching a full 'Kingdom Gospel' which cares about material change and is so genuinely incarnational. It has done so by linking the urge which drove Donald Soper first into the open air as a counterblast to fundamentalist presentations of the Faith on Tower Hill, with the high Wesleyanism of his Sacramental Fellowship cult of the Holy Communion. This is an amalgam rising from purest inspiration – an act of the Holy Spirit.

Down the years the product has been remarkable and perhaps defies comparison. One young man fired by the Order took to the open air in Watford High Street entirely on his own initiative when other Christians would not touch the enterprise. Being a teacher and married to an artist he then conceived the idea of moving into some peculiarly needy multi-racial environment to live with its people. He found a school near 'Tiger Bay' in Cardiff, one of the oldest multi-racial centres in Britain, where Chinese and other Asians and Africans have been there long enough to be Welsh. In this place he turned his little home into an open art gallery of his wife's work and had hundreds of people through the home in coffee evenings for talk and friendship in the first year. He is now in the ministry of the Church of England. This was the direct work of the Order. This man when sick had been referred to a psychiatrist and then during subsequent treatment discovered that the psychiatrist himself had committed suicide. Under this shock he turned to Kingsway, Soper and the Order.

If anyone has come near to Donald Soper it is this host of young people of the late forties and early fifties who on campaign came physically near enough to share a communal bed and share the ribald songs of campaign half-days. They found him, to quote one of them, 'not dictator but leader, shy enough to hold off from us,

generous enough to share all our experiences'. Certainly outstanding men have resulted from the O.C.W. work, Kingsley
Turner, for example, now Chairman of the London North-West
Methodist District, is one who was organizer of the work at one
stage. Harry Morton, referred to earlier, carried the open-air techniques he learned into the Manchester Central Mission as a student minister.

There were others who did not develop into brilliance but into
that something just as valuable – loyalty and perseverance. 'Joe',
fired with zeal for the O.C.W., discovered he could not preach in
the open air, took counsel from the Doctor and as a result stayed on
as Quartermaster in charge of rations for years. A check round the
city of Leeds demonstrated that 78 persons could be traced who
had gone into social service professions of one sort or another as a
direct result of the O.C.W. work. It looks as though the Order
itself was its own mission-field.

As the years have passed, the Order has tried most of the techniques of evangelism and community penetration as they have
come and gone in the various churches. The house-group, the
youth squash, the two-by-two run down housing area streets
and – perhaps most gallant – their attempt to found a 'cell' of
O.C.W. in a house-flat in the Honor Oak new estate in South
London.

As evangelism fell out of popularity for some years this O.C.W.
dogged persistence has been of tremendous value to the Church
while new ways were sought by minorities, not unlike the O.C.W.
itself. So are the fires tended until they blaze again. In it all, the
submersion of Donald Soper's own self inside of the Movement,
rather than at its head, has been the enlivening factor. Things live
in many memories which were part of the experience of meeting
him on campaign.

His physical endurance, for example. For years he has struggled
with a leg trouble – phlebitis – and in addition a congenital in-
testinal problem (shared by Leslie Weatherhead, strange!). He
has always been sensitive about this difficulty being widely known
and there are those among campaigners who have had to
straighten him up in a morning when he could not rise from his
chapel vestry bed. 'Tell no one,' he would request them. It is a
memory which lasts longer than many sermons. From being on
every campaign he has slowly withdrawn to a visit to each cam-

paign on its high days and to work in the central council of the Order. 'I'm too old to lead them now,' he says, but Jim Bates and the other commandant types know that their Buddha is still within the shadows in their temple. They press on campaigning still and groping out after ecumenical experience with men and women of like mind in all the Churches.

Meanwhile the build-up of the work of a Central Mission went ahead in those post-war years and each section of it was an answer to some pressing problem which reared up and demanded a Christian answer. The recurrent tactical exercise, in accord with Dr. Soper's own viewpoint, was to act from the Church in such ways as to fit into the Welfare State as it grew under the political reformation going on in Britain. Not merely to fill gaps but to be part of the total system wherein the Church has a real and permanent part in the life of the nation at the points where it is hurt – this is the strategy beneath the 'social outreach'. Jesus the healer is as permanent a factor in history as Jesus the preacher.

It has been a conviction of Dr. Soper's that the Church should not be a social camp-follower in its outreach but should pioneer where the State has not yet arrived or simply cannot go. This formula – which is the one to which modern overseas missionary service is also trimmed – is of crucial importance in Christian advocacy. It has the advantage of mobility. When the State has caught up with some actions, the Church can move on to attempt another. Where the thing done is something beyond the capacity of a State service, it can be tried, improved, moulded and kept in line with changing circumstances at will – if the leadership is alert.

In all there have sprung up thirteen types of service in connection with the Kingsway Hall. Sterling Court, Argyll House, Kingsway Crèche, St. Luke's House, St. Mary's House, Grove House, Alfred Hartley House, Emerson Bainbridge House, Goodliffe House, Fellowship House, Katherine Price Hughes Hostel, Hopedene, West London Mission Clothing Store.

It is a principle in each type of work to have workers of professional standards as well as volunteer workers. Dr. Soper states, 'I've learned in the West London Mission that to acquire the kind of professional with a sense of vocation is the very essence of an effective social work. I'd be quite accurate if I say that our staffing is professional staffing. Some of them acquired their professional skills through being in the work, others have come with qualifications which are equal to any qualifications possessed by those outside the voluntary organizations.'

'That,' he went on, 'is precisely why there is now a happy marriage between statutory bodies and voluntary organizations. We have something to offer them; they have something to offer us. The result is creative and useful. The statutory bodies have now recognized their need to co-operate. In fact to do this work they still prefer in many cases to do it through us, because we can offer a particular quality of vocational skill. I think of it every Wednesday when we meet as a West London Mission Staff to co-ordinate what we are doing not only with a sense of love and a sense of vocation but with a sense of efficiency as well.' Here he surely has his finger on the difference between 'do-gooding' and true Christian service.

The Staff Meeting to which he refers is one regular feature of the whole enterprise and it ensures that he has the whole programme under his own eye. Even more importantly, perhaps, a worker in one type of service has an ear open and a heart with sympathy for those engaged in other, perhaps contrasting work. It is the persons doing the work which are of paramount importance to each other, not the chores of the work itself. Efficiency so often springs from the experience of being understood. The meeting every Wednesday – yes, Tower Hill Day – is not separated to the social work but takes the whole Mission into review, and the worship, preaching and pastoral work find an equal place alongside the social services. This avoids that awkward distinction which so easily creeps in which subjugates the religious programme to the social because the latter is more 'practical'.

The Katherine Price Hughes Hostel, named for the connection with the great Founder, Hugh Price Hughes, is dedicated to the care of girls on probation from the courts, and has had devoted leadership for more than twenty years by one lady, Miss Townson, who came into the work voluntarily as a reaction to the reputation and preaching of Dr. Soper in 1948. The whole object of the exercise here is to remove the feeling of isolated peculiarity which besets the life of a girl who, to begin with, has had difficulties at home and has had those difficulties increased by the public exposure involved in being brought to the courts. Confidence has been knocked out of the girls either before or after their encounter with the police and to restore it is a priority. Its absence can be expressed in many ways – brash vulgarity; contra-suggestibility; sudden bursts of submission to anyone to whom the girl is attracted, be that person good or bad; wild escapist longings to run away and disappear; extravagant adventures in self-salesmanship by dress and beauty-culture; violence against other girls or against themselves even as far as to self-wounding.

The Warden says, 'It's my business to offer them the kind of setting in which self confidence can grow and one in which we can help them to be natural and to be doing all the kinds of things they would be doing in their own homes if they could be there, and to mix freely with the outside world, and we hope by the end of the year, which is the maximum that they are allowed here, that they can take their place with everybody else quite naturally and with much more confidence than when they came'. These are words which screen all the anxiety and annoyance at the hands of truant girls, tantrum-flaring girls, sly and deceitful, tricky girls, which are part of every day, or nearly every day. It says nothing of such weird examples as the abysmally deep homesickness of a girl who never had a home at all. The girls are invited into the Hostel, not dragooned. They go to and fro to work from it, they make friends in it, they bring friends to it. It is theirs.

Down Lambeth way, there is the old Hungerford Club which presents its rather grim face to the modern world as St. Luke's House, a rehabilitation centre for male alcoholics. It is twin to St. Mary's House, which is in fact a wing of St. Luke's House, and to this come women who need the same service. People who want to stop drinking and whose lives have moved into uncontrollable difficulty come for cure or help towards their cure. The Houses can offer them sound background help, the companionship of people sharing their problem, and support and encouragement. They turn up from the reception centres, prisons, hospitals and just out of the blue. An Information Centre for Alcoholism offers any help that can be given, in job-hunting, family problems and guidance towards professional help in treatment.

People may dine at the Houses, where there is full board. They may meet and yarn with others without embarrassing silences, knowing each other in trouble. The men are mostly out at work all the working days, and at week-ends there is the friendly lounge for group meetings and discussions which are of such help in this sickness. Every man that goes is helped and better for going. Even when one drifts off again into his drinking and is simply lost, his clothes perhaps lying in the House as a silent memento that once he passed this way, it is always possible to know that he had those clear-eyed days of remission from his weakness while here. Others there are who never look back but go on along the disciplined path to conquest by strength and grace. Dr. Soper's 'puritanism', which often surprises those who come to know him and associate him with advanced thinking on so many subjects, finds practical expression in this modern approach to alcoholism. To him it is a disease which can only be avoided and not cured. 'I would close every pub in Britain,' he has said, and he means it.

Is London the most cosmopolitan city in Europe, perhaps the world? It sucks into itself people from less sophisticated places, village girls coming out of the quietness into the bustle and fascination of its limitless pleasure, overseas students who come unsophisticated or, perhaps, already city-conditioned and ready to exploit the great city for their amusement under the guise of studying.

Take the case of a girl coming, say, from Southern Ireland, trained for office work. Already initiated into town life in an Irish town or an English provincial town, she gravitates to church and makes friends with the contemporaries she finds there. She soon learns that this is an international setting and, indeed, her church life encourages her to be colour-blind.

Her circle of acquaintance includes, therefore, young fellows from that third world whose sexual experience has been gained in another cultural environment. They are away out beyond her experience of life but their interest in her is, to her, the love experience of a British person. She falls in love. The man is married at home but this does not mean he is kept back from the pursuit of the girl who has fallen for him. There is a tangle of cultural patterns; he thinks she is after occasional satisfaction; she thinks that life must be like this and that she has simply been sheltered from it in her earlier provincial life. They stumble into a 'common law' marriage and the girl finds herself pregnant. He chides her because she has not used any contraceptive precautions – she never dreamt of doing so but relied on his love to stand by her. The two drift apart: love has soured. The man is terrified of losing the financial support he receives from home if the affair becomes known there. He wishes to end what, perhaps, he always thought was a temporary association. Where does the girl turn next?

She may seek an abortion; but she is not that kind of person. It takes not a little sophistication to turn that way – and how make the turn? She fears to return home and in any case has to earn a living. She can see the pregnancy through and seek help to have the baby adopted but 'coloured' babies are not easily disposed of in this way. She has a few tormented weeks to find the answer before her problem becomes self-evident if unsolved.

Sometimes, and with the girl who is no child but in her late twenties or early thirties when this experience overtakes her, there emerges another factor – the man drops away from her heart – he means nothing any more – but the unborn child means everything. She yearns to keep it. The more Church-centred the life of the girl the more likely is this to happen to her. There is an enormous upsurge of responsibility. Few men can appreciate this drama; most women can. Nothing will now suffice but a place to be while baby arrives and a place to find refuge while the early days of the baby's life run on. It is in this situation that the two institutions – to use a most inappropriate word – of Grove House and Hopedene span the problem and create a solution.

At Grove House a family of some fourteen girls expecting their babies live together, going out to work until six weeks before the baby is due to arrive and their remedial effect upon each other is the greatest part of the 'treatment'. When a girl is too embarrassed to go on attending at her work it is largely the other girls who will stimulate her to persist. The Warden is in the background of the House life as a 'Mother' on whose bosom a girl may weep or against whose discipline she may rail – and both moods are valuable, as the Warden knows.

When the baby does arrive, at Hopedene the long process of finding how to be working woman and mother at the same time begins. Here with the baby in a nursery and with the co-operation of the other mothers and the staff a girl can go on with her work, perhaps at her original place of employment or in another post. It is a critical business. There are nights when the baby gives mother no rest but work is still there in the morning. There is the restoration of the pre-pregnancy psychological situation in the girl's own life. There is her future attitude to men. All these produce a host of problems which are best worked out in the atmosphere of a place where all are facing the same struggle. The stay can be two years. Not all succeed, some can repeat their original mistake, some grow weary. There are others who will find a new way of love and become the happy mothers of more children with the security of a home of their own.

Gone is the dread of being turned away from rooming houses because of the baby; gone is the lonely way of struggling along different from other girls; gone the mile or two every morning to lodge the child in a local nursery and the embarrassment of leaving office early to pick the child up as a day-nursery closes.

Dr. Soper has made in his own mind a distinction between what he calls 'rescue work' and 'philanthropic work'. 'Philanthropic work is work in aid, that is to say it is support work; whereas rescue work is in the first instance where people are incapable of helping themselves.' He instances the work that Kingsway has done in providing hostels for students as support work, since the student 'already has some competence and capability but needs to be helped to find a suitable hostel'. The objective is to assist someone who can stand on his feet to do so.

The philanthropic work which, at the time, lay nearest to his heart was the housing of elderly folk. In the average church of the forties this was not done so much as visitation with goods and pastoral care. The turn to church housing projects was still in the future. Dr. Soper saw a distinction in social service done by the Church between people who have got themselves into trouble and people who were in trouble because society is what it is. In the latter category no one could take precedence over the elderly caught in a world where hygiene and science make life longer in a world geared to the life of young people. 'It's not our fault we go living on, is it?' said one old woman.

An unusual feature in the West London Mission accommodation for the older citizen is providing some of it inside the busy heart of London and in earshot of its traffic. It is wrong that people should live in isolation and die unrecorded, but it can also be wrong to move some people out of the busy city and give them comfortable quarters away among the birds and the flowers. One of the residents in the Alfred Hartley House who had worked and lived in the West End only asked to be near the buses and the Tube. 'I don't like a very quiet place – I wouldn't want to live in the country. It's all right for a holiday, but not to live there.' There are, of course, people who are just the opposite, and for them there is a place outside the bustle on the edge of the great London complex.

It is this whole service industry, together with the crèche, the clubs, the Clothing Centre where people can buy clothes at reasonable prices and not feel they have accepted charity – or 'won' something to sell – which is the responsibility of the Wednesday Staff Meetings. They are the occasion for the shedding of headaches, the sharing of problems and the briefing of 'the Boss' between his visits to the various organizations. Some of the Staff have said that he is a 'father-figure' for them and their charges – it might be truer to add that he is also a 'husband' in the good old ships-chandler's sense of that word. The sources which he has tapped for money to begin and to operate the various houses are legion: the intricate work of arranging the grants which the Government or Local Authority provides in some of the work is an art in itself.

However much the growing life of the West London Mission riveted his attention in those post-war years of rebuilding, other things pressed in and the British Isles were no longer to have the monopoly of his time and energy.

8.

Far-Eastern Mission

One of the changes of the times was the strong pressure towards autonomy within the Commonwealth of the island of Ceylon – 'the brightest jewel in the English Crown'! Self-government within the Commonwealth came formally in 1948. In 1946 missionaries of the Island's staff, thinking forward to the day of independence, prevailed upon the Rev. G. E. Hickman Johnson, then Secretary in the Methodist Mission House for their area, to persuade Dr. Soper to go to Ceylon and conduct a mission to its Church and people.

Johnson was a friend of Donald Soper's and had shared his pacifist views throughout the war and maybe this tipped the scale for acceptance. Certainly something must have done. The Methodist Missionary Society was never Dr. Soper's favourite Department – which one is? He promised to go in 1947 in the months of September and October.

It was a journey into a land reeking with political argument and within the argument a range of Communist thinking and propaganda not to be found in many places. The three communist trends now identified with Marxism, Trotskyism and Maoism were all in battle one with another. On the other side, the socialist thinking of men who had been trained in this country battled with a high toryism of men brought up in English public schools and universities. Superimposed upon all was the relatively pure strain of Buddhism which is associated with Ceylon and its people.

Below the surface of all these competing thought-systems was the deep racial cleavage between Cingalese and Tamil, co-ordinating with the two religions – Buddhism, dating back to the third century B.C. and the Hinduism of the old Dravidian stock. In

1947, out of more than five million people, only half a million were Christians, sharing their minority status with some 300,000 Muslims. In both Cingalese and Tamil circles a caste system operated. Almost every issue which Donald Soper had ever raised on Tower Hill or radio at home was present in Ceylon in a vibrant, creative – or destructive – revolutionary situation.

He hit the situation like a tornado – only, perhaps, because it hit him. He was disappointed that the missionary staff knew so little of the theory and practice of Communism and had some blunt things to say to the Society about that fact. But during the campaign he co-operated loyally with the staff – a staff which, dating from the earlier days of British Empire, was used to ideas very different from his.

He began by sessions with the Cingalese ministers and the missionaries in a convention which lasted a week and produced the reaction in him already mentioned concerning communist theory and the modern missionary strategy. He then plunged into a public campaign which was to make history in the island.

The Chairman of the Ceylon District of the Methodist Church writing in his correspondence with the Home Church was lyrical. 'Donald Soper is doing magnificent work. Last night he took the first of two lectures on "Christianity and Communism" at which he had probably the largest gathering that has ever come together for a meeting of this kind. The hall where he had it was packed to capacity half an hour before the meeting began. He has exactly the message which our Church and particularly the young people on the fringe of the Church are looking for.'

The Colombo Campaign began a month's hard work. The second lecture on 'Christianity and Communism' drew such an audience that a second hall was wired in and even then the foyer had to be furnished with seats to make room for more people, drawn from every community within the commercial capital of Ceylon. The eagerness of the crowd was deeply touching. With the dawn of nationhood, section after section longed for a national unity which would make Lanka (Ceylon) a new nation for a new day. Soper became to the people the harbinger of that new day.

With an insight which did him credit, in talking to the morning groups of ministers and Church leaders he centred much of his instruction on the use of the Bible. In a pluralist religious situation the key does lie here for Christian people. It is so easy to fall back on the Word of God by treating the Book as a talisman instead of a human record of the mighty acts of God. The Bible has a revolutionary message for a revolutionary moment, but that is completely masked out if the Bible is dealt with in a verbal inspirationist manner. As the story of national Covenant the Book has no rival in the great Eastern religions, and many of the young ministers especially saw this in those morning sessions.

The lectures on Communism were a classical Soper operation. He simply turned the current argument used by Leftist thinkers on its head. They were prone to argue that any good thing which the Christian mission had brought to the country was a Communist derivative. He spent much effort on showing from the study of Communism that it had taken a large slice of its creed from the Christian tradition.

Mr. G. E. P. de S. Wickramaratne, a Cingalese, took careful notes of all the discussion of the campaign – and complained about the speed of the Soper delivery, though comforted by Donald's assurance that he was attempting something no Briton had ever attempted!

The following quotations are from Mr. Wickramaratne's records.

Question:

'Is the challange of the Christian Church dynamic enough to meet the challenge of Communism?'

Answer:

'It can be made to meet the challenge of Communism. I want to say that Christianity has all the good that Communism can show, plus something which Communism by its very nature cannot possibly give. We are not the only people who have to get together. I notice that you have here the Communist Party, the Bolshevik-Leninist Party, and the Lanka Sama Samaj Party. I think it is an instance of the way in which human nature tends to be fissiparous, that is, propagating by breaking up into bits. We have to get together. If the Christian Church gets together and says honestly what it believes, it is finally not my business whether we succeed or not. I believe that can be left in God's hands.'

Question:

'Is Communism as advocated by Karl Marx anti-religious?'

Answer:

'Yes, make no mistake about that. Read the records. Engels first used the phrase, "Religion is the opium of the people". Karl Marx repeated it and gave sanction and authority to it.

'Jesus did not say: "Say your prayers; go to church; read the Bible; and when you die, you will go to heaven". He said: "Seek first the Kingdom of God" and, when he was asked what it was like and where it was found, he said: "It is found here."

'If Karl Marx were alive today, he would have realized that without some sort of religion you cannot live. Karl Marx was anti-religious because he had unfortunate contacts with a few so-called religious leaders who were pretty anti-religious themselves.'

Question:

'Does Communism deny the existence of God?'

Answer:

'Yes: that is it denies the validity of God. Communism took over lock, stock and barrel a philosophical system which has long since ceased to enjoy the confidence of philosophers. I would say in all sincerity to any Communists who are here that there is not a single reputable philosopher in the world today who would support the philosophical Communism of Karl Marx.'

Question:

'Does Communism preach about God? If not how could it be a religion?'

Answer:

'First let me answer by defining religion. Religion is not a belief about God; it is an attitude to totality. Any philosopher will know that religion is a total attitude to a total environment. It is a way of life, not a way of thinking or acting.'

Question:

'You said the other day that Communism has borrowed Christian principles; what is wrong with that?'

Answer:

'Nothing at all. I am very glad that Communism has borrowed certain Christian principles, because Christian principles are the highest and noblest. If you do not believe in

God, what is the point that the world is a decent place and that the other man is your brother? If you do not believe in religion, how do you know that all these fine programmes will come off? We can have a new Jerusalem and a classless society because already there is a plan and purpose in the world. It is not something alien to nature but something planted in it.'

This battery of question and answer runs on through ninety-six crowded pages in the Ceylon Report of the campaign and it touches a vast number of issues which burn in the lives of people in a revolutionary situation. There is a fascination in the way in which, under the loom of two great religions other than Dr. Soper's own, all the social questions had a religious rider to them. It is possible to see in this series of answers that Communism, for example, has to reconcile its message with a religion or be rejected in the great Asian scene, just as Chairman Mao's Little Red Book has to take cognizance of the sayings of Mencius and the other Confucian thinkers. The reporters on this campaign remark on the speed and ease with which Dr. Soper picked up this thread in the weave of Cingalese life in 1947.

One of the most pregnant of his answers was that in which he defined Christian love – remembering that to the Hindu or Buddhist the claim of Christ is summed up in the word 'love'.

'Let the Left Wing – and I speak as a member of it – recognize the idea of "love" as an alternative to violence. Love is not a wishy-washy thing but a relevant activity to which man can apply himself.

'Let me give a definition of "love" as best I can. Love is first of all, according to psychologists, self-identification. Now, what does that mean? It means I love somebody when I and that person are no longer two but are united, in the sense that his choices are mine, and my choices are his. When you and I really think like the rickshaw coolie; when you and I think like the fellow in the slum; when you and I think like the fellow in the Moscow tenement or the man dying of malnutrition in Europe; then we have started on the right road of love.

'The idea of love is not to throw a coin to the man who is down and out and clear off as quickly as possible. That is a degradation of the word "love". That is why I do not say: "Give better wages to those who have insecure means of livelihood". You have to do that: but before that you have to do something more important; you have to give them the sense that you and they are together in the struggle, not that you, from the eminence of your benevolence, are throwing a few coins to them.

'The second definition of "love" is an attitude of utter tenderness. If you go to the cinema to see the average film, you will not see anything about love. If you read books produced these days you will find that many of them are just a travesty of love. Love is not merely a "kick" you get. It is a sense that, on every occasion and in every circumstance, you are under compulsion to seek the good of the other man. . . .

'The third thing is when you have identified yourself in thought with other people, when you respect them and are determined you will never do violence whatever happens. Then you have to live for them and work for them whether you "like" them or not. Is that something you do not understand? How many of you know how others live?'

We are fortunate in having the official report made by a professional literary specialist and publicist in Philip Penning. Otherwise it might be impossible to credit the impact of this whirlwind month. The questions fired came as much from non-Christians and Left party groups as from Christian people. One Saturday afternoon was given entirely to young folk on a vast open-air occasion. There is no more fashionable site in old Imperial Ceylon than the Green at Galle Face, a thrilling sea-shore viewpoint. The crowd for this highly sophisticated 'Tower Hill' of Ceylon was estimated by Mr. Penning at three thousand, the local Press said five thousand. Soper with his back to the Indian Ocean in the setting sun, the green sward and the palm fringe sweeping down to the road by the world famous 'honeymoon hotel' – any historically-minded Methodist might well have thought this is Gwennap Pit* modernised and now bigger than when Wesley addressed his excited Cornishmen. Here again the message was the utter need of Christ for revolution and reform of society in the new day.

Penning remarks, 'The young people of Ceylon were eager to hear and to pose their questions. The Forum was one of the high-

* The great natural amphitheatre in Cornwall where John Wesley preached. A commemorative service is still held there once a year.

lights of the whole campaign and did untold good in showing that the Christians were deeply interested in the political aspirations of the country and held high ideals about the standard politics should reach. Here was a strong, virile faith that was not afraid to look facts in the face and work for the common good along the best lines'.

Outside the planned activities Donald Soper worked in many extra events in response to invitations. The Young Men's Buddhist Association and the Ramakrishna Mission are examples of non-Christian groups of reformers who wanted him as their guest. A number of schools, Rotary, and the Christian Luncheon Club had a share. The University had a special student event to meet him and ask questions, and Colombo Radio Station took full advantage of his presence both for services and discussion.

The later Bible studies in the mornings were shifted to a new location and newcomers were welcomed to the tune of three to four hundred in a session. This was held for forty-five minutes before the day's work of the audience began. The public address type of meeting was transferred to the Town Hall and was crowded out into the streets.

The Colombo work over, Dr. Soper went on to Kandy and repeated the programme with similar responses. Meanwhile, Mrs. Soper, rarely on her husband's journeys, had been featuring on radio and in meetings of her own among women and for the 'Over Sixteen Club', with good responses.

The visit ended with a courtesy sermon by a Cingalese Minister! With characteristic Cingalese imagination a young minister just ordained during the visit preached the sermon. Dr. Soper had preached his Ordination Charge two days earlier. Rev. David K. Wilson, B.D., called his sermon 'Our Response' and among the actions resulting was the birth of the Order of Christian Witness in this other Island. The Kingsway Preachers had found their Asian brothers. 'A milestone in the history of the Church', concludes Philip Penning.

A milestone means more miles to travel and Soper flew out bound for Australia where he would deliver the Cato Lecture and do a whistle-stop tour of evangelism under the Southern Cross. F. Basil Jackson, then Chairman of the South Ceylon District, wrote in his Official Correspondence, 'We are accustomed in Ceylon to the visits of men like Dr. Stanley Jones and other much advertised but less reputable evangelists, but it is undoubtedly true to say that Dr. Soper's visit made an impression on Colombo such as no other Christian advocate has ever done.' This was the third breakthrough in the Soper story, from Hall to Hill, from Hill to national radio and Kingsway, from Kingsway to world evangelism.

There was one more breakthrough to come. Where is the Christian minister who is famous not only in his own religious world, even though that world be wider than his denomination? Noted Christian leaders are legion, but those who are acknowledged as leaders outside in the secular world for work they have accomplished in the secular world can be counted on one mutilated hand. There have, maybe, been four in three decades. This was still to come to Donald Soper. It came in the next act of his personal drama.

9.

The Battle of Preston

In 1952 Winston Churchill announced that Britain had her own atom bomb – the year was hardly born when he said so; it was February 26th. In the same year but a month later, in India's first national elections Pundit Nehru won 364 seats out of 489 in the National Assembly, and in the running sore of the Korean struggle China accused the United States forces of using germ warfare, which was strenuously denied. Dr. Malan introduced a Bill into the South African Parliament to make that Parliament a High Court and so avoid the criticism of race legislation by the Supreme Court. The ill-fated scheme for the Central African Federation of the two Rhodesias and Malawi was published. Mohammed Neguib seized power and formed a government in Egypt, only to rue it as his junior cashed in on his courage.

Japan made friends with Nationalist China, restoring diplomatic relations but at the same time Chou En-lai headed a Chinese delegation to Moscow – perhaps he was the more fortunate, though Taiwanese standards of living were soon to reach the high standard of Japan herself. The U.S.S.R. Communist Party held its first Congress since 1939; the Council of the Socialist International met in Milan, balanced, perhaps, by the London Commonwealth Economic Conference. But the Communist world came back with the World Conference in Vienna – city symbolic of imperialist conferences.

In the Western world Britain and her neighbours were struggling with a whole miscellany of Defence Plans for Europe and the expansion of N.A.T.O. aimed at the European Defence Community. The United States was in the throes of a Presidential Election in which a landslide swept Republican Dwight D.

Eisenhower into power. But the nation found the time to explode
its first hydrogen bomb at the miserable Enimetok Atoll in the
Pacific while Britain made her first atomic bomb tests in Monte
Bello, Australia.

A first attempt at a contraceptive pill, phosphorated hesperidin,
was made; London had the worst 'smog' of all time and was
thoroughly frightened by it, and the last London tram made its
parting journey. The public reading the national Press found itself
fascinated by the bestialities of Mau-Mau but missed the point of
what the rebellion was all about.

The Minutes of Conference of the Methodist Church for the
year 1952 read as follows on the opening page:

> 'The Conference of the Methodist Church assembled in the
> Public Hall, on Friday the 11th of July, 1952, and con-
> cluded its sittings on Wednesday, 23rd July.
>
> 2. The Rev. Colin Augustus Roberts was elected Presi-
> dent of the Conference; Sister Dorothy Hinksman Farrar,
> B.A., PH.D., was elected Vice President; and the Rev. Eric
> Wilfred Baker, M.A., PH.D., was elected Secretary.
>
> 3. The Rev. Donald Oliver Soper, M.A., PH.D., was de-
> signated as President, Dr. Leslie Ward Kay was designated as
> Vice President and the Rev. Eric Wilfred Baker, M.A., PH.D.,
> was designated as Secretary of the Conference of 1953.'

Soper's designation as President-elect was a famous victory – or
defeat – and followed storms and much tribulation which had run
through the years following his visit to the outside world of Ceylon
and Australia. There was a moment, at least, when he himself
thought that it would never happen. A man can be too much
exposed and no man was ever more exposed than he.

Colin A. Roberts, the President of the Conference, was a senior
minister, having served 43 years in the ministry, when he came to
Mr. Wesley's Chair. Donald Soper had 'travelled' twenty-eight
when he reached it. The Christian Commando Campaigns,
which had taken the Church to factories, street corners, clubs and
pubs on a wide map, were the work of Colin Roberts who headed
up the whole enterprise. He was known and loved through his
work in the Home Mission Department of the Church, and his
wiry, vigorous figure was known up and down the country. As
General Secretary of the Home Mission Department, circuit after

circuit was indebted to him for advice, grant-aid, planning and his constant demand for evangelical outreach and pressure upon the world outside the Church. He had an ecclesiastical image – his Church knew him, trusted him and loved him, and this was sufficient to ensure his elevation to the Presidency.

There were many likenesses between Colin Roberts and Donald Soper in those days – there still are – though it might be happier for Donald Soper if he too were afflicted with some deafness. Both were aggressive, demanding, autocratic, suffering fools less than gladly. Roberts, however, had the edge in tact, diplomacy and general ease in authority within the Church. He regarded himself, and still does, as a kind of father-protector to Soper, looking upon his ministry as an extension of Robert's own ministry. To be followed by Soper in the Chair, therefore, was to him to be a delight. 'If only he doesn't blot his copy at the wrong moment', said Colin Roberts in those days, rubbing his hands and shrugging his lean shoulders. 'You can't guarantee he won't say something!' Labouring the obvious, this. Truer to say he certainly would 'say something'.

And there was his exposure throughout the years which lay between the Ceylon journey and 1953. With 'Any Questions', with Brains Trust type of programmes, with Epilogues and casual questions, Donald Soper was all over the public screen. In addition to the radio, and then television, he was the newspaperman's 'pin up'. Feed him a question and get an answer; this was a guaranteed certainty. There was nothing coy, nothing elusive, just a straight answer and often one couched in a phrase which, though joy to the sub-editor, was misery to churchmen.

It is a solemn reflection that the controversy about Donald Soper's ministry and value to the Church produced within the Church again and again the very reactions which the man in the Tower Hill or Speakers' Corner crowd threw at him when he preached Christianity there. There is probably not one item which *Tower Hill 12.30* lists as criticism of the Church which the Church has not made of Dr. Soper!

Methodism in its beginnings might have been among the Kingswood miners and other under-privileged people of the eighteenth century, but in its modern guise, like all the Churches, it is middle class and wedded firmly to the capitalist system. John Wesley's 'Rule' for his people, 'Make all you can: give all you can', has been honoured among Methodist people with great enthusiasm. There is, therefore, an exposed nerve whenever capitalism is challenged as a system and that nerve has had rough treatment from Soper.

'So long as we live under a capitalist system we must expect trouble'. 'We live within a system which has its own decay written large upon it'. Such remarks as these, often thrown off with a swift, casual air of complete authority, have been an irritant of the first order. Added to this, in those years when the 'Cold War' broke across Europe, there was a fear of hot war until the balance of terror was established, which made any reference to the achievements of modern Russia extremely unpopular. As peace with Germany and Austria hung in the balance of debate year after year and Europe was littered with millions of refugees, any reference he made to pacifist lessons to be learned from the contemporary situations were guaranteed to disturb someone.

One Connexional (i.e., whole Church) Committee of which Dr. Soper was a member was the Methodist Ecumenical Council, which was the ancestor of the denominational 'Confessional Body' of the Church, the World Methodist Council, of today. Heavy pressures were applied within the Church to make this thing grow, but in 1948 the Methodist world population included 10.3 millions of American citizens, by far the greatest component on earth of Methodists – there are many more in heaven.

In 1946 the Conference arranged a deputation to go to Springfield U.S.A. for a Conference of world Methodists and in the list of delegates there is Dr. Soper's name. The Conference took place – and arranged a British return match in Oxford for 1951. Dr. Soper's name is in the list no longer, however, by 1948. Casualty? Non-co-operator? Which? In the desperation of Britain's poverty-stricken post-war condition, a warming towards the United States was natural – like some old lady, indeed, weeping on her grown daughter's bosom. But what could be more embarrassing than a minister who stoutly held that another young woman of another ancestry on the other side of the world had her own charms? To add fuel to the fire of resentment, Soper even said that the United States, daughter of Britain, lived by a system which had ruin built into it and could bring down her hoary ancestress with her.

Such a period of history throws up potentially controversial points in scores and a man exposed to the public and the Press can enjoy commenting on them all, while the man who never comments on anything but lives by well entrenched beliefs in an old system seethes with resentment more and more. Britain devalued the pound sterling; American aid to China ceased and the General Chiang Kai-shek fled to Taiwan; Klaus Fuchs was found guilty of passing atomic secrets to U.S.S.R. agents and Americans felt that Britain had sold the pass by bad security. Indeed, in the same month of 1950, U.S.S.R. did announce her possession of the atomic bomb.

The London dock strike stretched across a late spring fortnight; Pope Pius XII pronounced the dogma on the bodily assumption of the Virgin Mary. A 'Christian Socialist', pacifist, publicity-minded (perjoratively speaking) parson had only to make one remark on each of these subjects – and the *Daily Express*, not to mention the B.B.C., made sure that he did – to have a hive of enemies buzzing round his head; and such bees fly a long time without going back to their hive. He was now 'fellow-traveller', renegade, false prophet, wolf in sheep's clothing (red), or else he was the unblemished hero and crusader of tomorrow.

Exasperation knew no bounds; those who were his enemies suddenly found him making comments of which they thoroughly approved. For example, he who spoke death about capitalism suddenly remarked that Russian techniques were evil. Those who detested his 'modernism', being themselves stout fundamentalists, found in the morning paper that he was a confirmed teetotaller, hated Mickey Mouse films because they were sexy, and generally walked the puritan way as firmly as they. Even the open-air fans, who were lyrical about his social gospel, found on going to hear him preach that he talked 'straight religion' with never a hoot of revolution.

Loved or hated, he continued his journey through those years before his Presidency, in demand up and down the country, rung up by the Press perhaps half a dozen times in a week, gracing outstanding occasions in London or out of it. His image was stamped upon the Church and nation. In Order of Christian Witness Campaigns alone, 1949 saw work at Leighton Buzzard, Hereford, Risca Valley and Leicester; 1950 included Cheltenham and Newcastle upon Tyne; 1951 Cardiff and Barry, 1952 Reading. In both 1951 and 1952 there were campaigns over in Ger-

John Ray Photography

...rd Soper at Speaker's Corner,
...yde Park

With Mrs. (now Lady) Soper
and the Author

At Katherine Price Hughes House

Playing the tin-whistle at the annual National Children's Home Conference Rally

On "Meeting Point", BBC-1

many at Kassel. He was involved in all of these with what a recorder describes as his 'astringent charity' which means reward is given in terms of criticism of what has been done and advice as to what comes next.

If many parsons criticized him at that time and perhaps still do, his defence of them ought to be known, for many do not hear him but only read about him. Writing about 'Clerics and Critics' in his *Popular Fallacies about the Christian Faith* Dr. Soper says, 'Now all sorts of people do hold the most ludicrous views of what parsons are like. If these misconceptions were confined to a few peculiarly dense or prejudiced opponents of Christianity, they might be ignored, but, you know, they are not. I am continually being told that parsons are such a mournful crowd, a lot of 'spiritual Weary Willies' who create an atmosphere of gloom wherever they go. You know the old chestnut about the new Vicar who was to be met at the station by a reception committee. He travelled without his dog-collar, they failed to recognize him, and were compelled to ask several passengers if they were clergymen by any chance – to which one indignantly replied, "Good gracious no, it's my indigestion that makes me look like this."

'I remember the first time I had to conduct a service at Pentonville Prison. I had uncritically assumed that my congregation would all look like Bill Sykes, with the criminal type stamped indelibly on their faces, and from one or two lags I had met, and who did fulfil these conditions, I had fortified this idea. To my astonishment, when I came face to face with them, I discovered they looked very much the same as any respectable suburban congregation.

'No, to the non-churchgoing public, the parson is a stranger who is generally judged by preconceived ideas; and the critic who thinks we're a poor lot of human specimens needs to ask himself this important question, "What ought a parson to be like, in view of his vocation?" Because so few take the trouble to do this, their attitude must be at fault.

'In simple terms a Minister of the Gospel is a man, or woman, who has accepted the Christian faith for himself or herself, and feels called of God to express that faith, through the offices of organized Christianity, as a preacher and as a pastor, and has had that call ratified by the Church in some form of ordination.

'He is to be the intermediary through whom the Christian truth and Christian practice are made known in religious services and sacraments. He is to be the channel along which religion flows into common life, in the same way that Toscanini was the channel along which the truths and blessings of music were made available to all who cared to listen. In this sense he is a priest set apart, standing a hand's breadth off from the hurly-burly, so that he may concentrate upon his sacred calling. You would not expect a Toscanini to shake hands with everybody in the stalls just before he begins to conduct a concerto ... In the same way you have no right to expect a parson to behave in the pulpit as a "good mixer". Unless he can stand away a little from the entanglements of our little affairs he cannot see life steadily and see it whole. That does not mean he cannot be real and human when he stands before his people.

'We have been thinking about parsons. They are, I believe, called of God to do a hard job, especially now. Many of you stand outside the Church and tell us, day after day, how badly we are doing it. I am speaking for many of my brethren of the cloth when I say we heard you the first time. We don't disagree, *but* it's your encouragement and help which could make all the difference. We don't ask now for your approval, but we still believe so absolutely in the necessity that the Christian faith should prevail that we dare to claim your co-operation.'

The mood of the nation and its obsession with the 'Cold War' in the early fifties divided the nation and the people who spoke to the nation, as nothing had for years, and fearless people who dared to speak could not expect, nor did they get, general assent to any problem's analysis, let alone to any solution they might state.

The Methodist Conference meeting in Bradford in the summer of 1950 was a mirror of its year and reflected the tormented state of mind of the people more than the mind of its Master. How much the Conference was dominated by the times may be judged by the fact that while it fell into disarray in its debates, the President of the Conference under whom the debates took place was Dr. W. Edwin Sangster. If anyone could have ensured a peaceful Conference, surely it was he. But what do leaders do when a year contains such matter as that boys without any active service experience were being sent as National Servicemen to the grim jungle warfare of Malaya, after 'the briefest of training' to quote the Conference statement, and the hydrogen bomb was looming over the world already tormented by the existence of the puny atomic bomb?

Every year the enormous Agenda of the Conference is given to the Press by the Information Officer and it is combed through by them before Conference gets under way. That year it was not difficult to foresee at what sessions the reporters would gather to give an ear to and publicize the largest of the non-Anglican Church Assemblies of the year.

In the upshot the main battle was joined over the business of the Department of Christian Citizenship. Here a major resolution on the world anxiety about the dangers of a Third World War was presented and debated under the leadership of the Rev. E. Clifford Urwin, its General Secretary.

The Resolution as it ultimately emerged from the debate reads:

'The Conference shares profoundly in the deep and widespread concern which has been awakened by the advancing steps towards the manufacture of the hydrogen bomb, adding to the prevailing disquiet new peril and fear of war. The Conference believes that the invention of this new and terrible weapon of destruction throws into greater relief the shame and sinfulness of war. It is abhorrent to Christian men and accentuates their concern for the peace of the world.

'The Conference, while associating itself generally with the weighty expressions of concern which have emanated from the World and British Councils of Churches, records its own judgement that the present juncture in the world situation calls for a renewed attempt to break the dead-lock in international affairs which is dividing the world into two opposing camps, and to bring a new understanding between East and West, which is the basic issue. The Conference welcomes the efforts being made to this end.

'The Conference believes that the menace of war in the world today lays added burdens of responsibility on Christian people everywhere. It recognizes that the peril to peace rises not only from divergent policies but from opposing philosophies and social creeds, together with the recurrent threat of violent revolution. Christian people should face the situation fearlessly and maintain the steadfast will to peace and the effort for understanding and mutual trust, never doubting that in the last issue the Will of God must prevail. Above all, there should be unceasing prayer for the nations and their rulers, for social justice and the overcoming of class conflict and international and racial strife.

'The Conference believes that these grave issues should be made the object of special study by our people, if such understanding as alone can make possible effective Christian intervention in world affairs is to be achieved.'

There is another resolution of the Conference which gave effect to the last clause of this resolution – that a programme of education in these issues of war and peace should be part of the Church's preparation in the ensuing year. It so fell out that this education was given in no uncertain terms not only in 1950 but for some years ahead because of the notoriety Dr. Soper gained by his participation in the main debate.

His controversy with the sponsors of the proposition was really on the basic issue of whether the old catholic dogma of the 'just war' survived in the modern world. Clearly the emergence of the atom bomb which destroyed Hiroshima and Nagasaki had added needle point to pacifist arguments about the futility and horror of war. Pacifist leadership had to give guidance as to whether in their view there was any longer any war which could even border on justice. All the world's people cannot ever be parties to one particular international quarrel; but with the new type of weapon all the world's people could most certainly be obliterated by one nuclear duel between the two nuclear giants.

Having held for years that some Church, and preferably his own beloved Methodism, should take an unqualified pacifist position, Dr. Soper could not but intervene in this debate upon the immediate future under the hydrogen threat. He was sure that the Church which took such a stand would have the ear of mankind for anything else it might have to say. The modern story of the Society of Friends does not bear out this belief. Its numbers shrink. But it is true that nothing could stir the world quite so deeply as a Church of the size of world Methodism taking up a forty-million strong pacifist protest.

He said in the debate that he did see the difference between the use of the hydrogen bomb and the bayonet, but that the distinction lay not in ethics but in logistics and the strategy of war. In a crowded Conference he then administered his shock when he told the Conference that if he had to make a choice between a Third World War and a Russian occupation of Britain, he would for himself and his children choose the latter. Such an occupation could not last forever, nor be unmitigatedly evil, whereas the end of the war would be sheer annihilation.

There was a scurry of newsmen out looking for telephones and the nation knew the story in a trice. It was world news within twenty-four hours. The *Methodist Recorder* was shaken; the *Christian World* summed up Dr. Soper's many public utterances and deplored that the Conference should be ignored but for this one man! People who had been lying low, nursing resentments about his socialism and his attacks upon society based upon 'enlightened self-interest', at last had one really hefty handle of one really prickly broom with which to beat him. This was, perhaps, the least unfortunate effect of the statement. More to the point was the concern felt by ordinary church members who intensely admired his work in the open air and all the enterprise of the West London Mission. The flummoxed are always more important than the foul. The glee, for example, of the *Free Thinker,* a publication always ready to stick a lance in Soper, was not as important as some little paper like *Joyful News* dealing with its pious readership. The nearest to a commendation seems to have been in the *Church of England Newspaper* – something of a surprise.

The newspapers described the Conference as 'shocked'. How deep that shock was no one was to know for a couple of years, for a correlated issue underlying Methodism's reception of his statement was that Dr. Soper's name had by then already appeared in the totally unofficial and formally unrecorded list of names of ministers who were on the road to John Wesley's Chair.

The election of the President of the Methodist Conference is a process which has to be experienced to be appreciated. There is no Nomination Committee – many wish there were, there are no party alignments to produce suggestions of persons. All that exists is the free floor of the House of over six hundred representatives, half of them ministers and half of them lay people, who do as they feel led to do, free of all strings.

At the appropriate time, which is at the beginning of the Conference, the representatives are instructed to provide their nominations for the designation of the President of the following year. There could, therefore, be very large numbers of nominations. In fact the list is commonly of about a dozen names which, having been checked by the scrutineers, are printed and voted on for the first time. The first ballot – and the voting is always by ballot – rarely produces one minister with an overall majority of those present and voting, which is the required number. Sometimes the second vote also fails to do so; more often the third tells the result.

Those Methodists who are interested in such things – and being denied horse-racing as a sport they appear to be many – are apt to forecast the list of Presidents a few years ahead by counting the votes men receive in the discard of the early voting; a dozen would be significant, a hundred would consign a man to the task a year or two ahead. In 1950, the vote having been taken before his controversial debating speech, his name was bobbing about at the lower end of the list. Leaving Bradford for home after the storm he told a friend, 'At least I'm out of that list!' It was more a cry of relief than alarm. The 1950 Conference in fact designated as President for the following year Dr. Howard Watkin-Jones, a staid, steady and meticulous theologian who proceeded to have most successful designated and presidential years in which as scholar-evangelist he won many hundreds to faith.

As the year ran on through the autumn, Methodism's busiest season, Dr. Soper was never allowed to forget the speech he had made at Conference. It got into everything. Nothing he did, even the chores and routine fixtures, was reported without the added information that this was the person who had given up Britain to Russian occupation.

The Order of Christian Witness had a Campaign for Cheltenham that year including one of the most remarkable Youth Rallies of the summer, but it was overshadowed by the Press comment on the Conference speech and some denied the Doctor their patronage. Another Campaign in the late summer extracted a warm response from the Newcastle upon Tyne papers which were thrilled by more than 200 young people sleeping on church hall floors and Sunday school rooms who all came to support their Leader who at the Bradford Methodist Conference had said . . .

Back home in the West London Mission it was the same story. In the provinces mayors or senior citizens could cancel tea-parties or receptions, but the 'sinner' could survive knowing that people reach high local office only by dint of hard committee work and conventional tracks through the problems of the day. But when the senior treasurer of the West London Mission, Sir Robert Perks, resigned from the post in protest over the Superintendent's speech and belief, the blow was harder to bear, personally as well as administratively. There were, however, some comforters. At the Mayflower Celebration – a highlight of Congregational life – Dr. Belben, a leader of that Church, complimented Dr. Soper on his 'noble and independent ministry' which made him worthy of a place at a Mayflower occasion. Was the label 'For export only' attaching itself to him?

Two of the Mission's social institutions opened during the period, including the mother and baby work at Kingsway House which was matched by only one similar home in the London area and that run by the London County Council. The *British Weekly* which had been trenchant about the Conference speech managed to report the opening of this foundation unadulterated.

So the latter half of 1950 with its crescendo of criticism drew to its close with the Mission superintendent still in the maelstrom of conflict but with his young people trying out new open-air sites undaunted. In the sadness of those days – and they were sad and not puckishly gleeful days for Donald Soper – none supported him more than the Order's young folk. They could see his policies being illustrated in events as the Peace of Terror settled down over the world. The year of the Festival of Britain lay ahead – stirring memories of that wonderful past and of the 1924 British Empire Exhibition. Perhaps no comment on Dr. Soper's proposition had more point than this delayed action memory of the 1851 'Great Exhibition'. All the deep emotion which he roused surely stemmed back to the latent memory of those other and, for the affluent, more spacious days. Perhaps, too, as the years have gone by and left behind the Royal Festival Hall as a relic of that dream of 1951, Dr. Soper's faith that a world with Communists in it could be tolerable remains to us as a relic of the Conference's 'shock'.

The Communist pressure went on through all that he tried to do. There were formal debates with Communist thinkers on two occasions and there the pressure on him was from a different angle.

The *Free Thinker* and its debating nominees made a great point of beseeching the Doctor to come out from the isolation of the Christian Church, cease to bedevil the issue with religious side-issues or quarrels and himself join the great Leftist movement which was sweeping on to a new world of peace. Most of his church-going critics were, of course, absent on such occasions and so did not hear his passionate argument that the whole Leftist movement without Christ in it was doomed to miserable failure, as the last and decisive transformation which would make the new world possible lay not in man's hands but God's power in men. One paper recorded how in the sheer argument on Communist theory, quite apart from this massive religious criticism, he was unbeatable.

On a Sunday in May what the newspapers called one of the most notable occasions of the Festival year took place in 'The Cockpit' in Hyde Park when approximately 5,000 young folk turned out in a great rally for the Festival which Dr. Soper addressed upon the meaning of life in Britain today. Away up in the north his words had a ready hearing at the Durham Miners' great Camp Meeting, an occasion modelled on the miners' own craft rally, which the Methodist people there have held for years. Out in the open the crowds were enormous and the Left trend in Dr. Soper's reputation helped rather than hindered in that troubled county.

In the high summer of 1951 he went off on a trip which took him to the United States, Australia and Canada. He began by speaking at a Conference of Methodist Youth, meeting at Purdue University in the United States. He then went to Lakeside, Ontario, for another annual convention for the Fellowship of Reconciliation and then flew west for a mission in Vancouver. This mission was the fruit of the association of Keith Woollard of the Fire Fighting Service, assistant to the Doctor in London during the war.

One cannot measure the success of the mission by size but the largest church in town was filled on one occasion and another in a public hall had 2,800 people present – church people and outside people who wanted to know what this British speaker had that made him so world famous. The questions poured out of the audiences and they were the same questions that youth all round the world was asking. One of the big results of this campaign was the founding of a branch of the Order of Christian Witness in Canada.

In Australia the success of the tour can be gauged by the fact that in the Domain – the Hyde Park of Sydney – two thousand people gathered there on two occasions to listen to him and ask questions. On the banks of the Yarra in Melbourne fifteen hundred people gathered, two thousand in Brisbane outside the Town Hall, four thousand in a park in Adelaide and eight hundred on two successive Sundays on the Esplanade at Perth.

Apart from the Sunday meetings he spoke at a whole variety of places where people could ask questions – forges, iron works, factories. Social questions dominated all others and some of the earliest hecklers were men who had got into practice on Tower Hill itself. 'What have you to say about poverty in the East?' was a typical question with an Anzac twist to it in this particular setting. 'What are you Christians doing to prevent a world war?' There were very few genuine communists, though many who had not a clue (to quote the Doctor) about what Communism is took its name in vain when asking their questions or making their interjections. Most of these seemed to Dr. Soper to be disgruntled Left-wingers waiting for a really constructive Christian programme to help them out of their intellectual puzzlement.

The Australian tour had its difficulties because Dr. Soper had stirred up still further the already troubled Australian political waters immediately on his arrival. A Bill by the Government of Australia was being debated to control the entry of Communism into the country and on his arrival he threw his own views about such legislation into the pool. With a referendum in progress, and public opinion consequently being acutely sensitive, the Prime Minister, Sir Robert Gordon Menzies, publicly rebuked him. He bitterly observed that Dr. Soper had apparently acquired within a few hours of landing on the continent a knowledge of Australian affairs which he thought superior to that of native born Australians.

In the Spring he was back in Britain and engaged in an argument with the *Free Thinker* and its atheist or humanist supporters about the policy of the B.B.C. in presenting religious and philosophical ideas over the air. The critic, a Mr. F. A. Ridley, was grieved that the 'cautious modernism of Dr. Donald Soper' was as far as the orthodox pundits of Broadcasting House were prepared to go. Mr. Ridley claimed to have debated with Dr. Soper in the open air and to have drawn from him some remarkable statements which gave the Methodist image a strange slant.

In March Dr. Soper was across in Northern Ireland to preach at the 62nd Anniversary of the Belfast Central Mission in its great Grosvenor Hall. The trend of his thinking as 1952 moved on towards the summer can be seen in his choice of subject, 'The Christian and Peace-making', for this great occasion. Another strain, however, in his speaking and writing can be detected in the early 1951 and late 1952 period. He was concerned about the contemporary Methodist Church seeking the grace of God but neglecting the means by which that grace is received. He felt that the Church must regain the great catholic practices and find its place in the catholic tradition, while its place in the Protestant tradition continued to be stressed.

Proper to both these roles, he declared, was the sacramental nature of the Christian Church and its worship, the treasuring of the historic creeds, the maintenance of its liturgical glories, in short the great values upon which alone a true Church can be built. It is as though the great efforts of the world tour and the unrelenting 'fellowship of controversy' (to use his own description of the rough and tumble of the hustings) tired him, causing him to dig deep to the underlying rock on which his own faith rested. This is the Methodist Sacramental Fellowship side of his daily life, so little known to his open-air audiences but so vital to his own grip on faith and life. He saw this sacramental style of living as being the root of all unity in the world of divided Churches.

Dr. Soper was now, in spite of the 'clanger' of the 1950 Conference, a figure not to be ignored, whatever view people might hold of his value to the Church and the world. It was possible to be frightened of him and some traditionalists were. It was possible to follow him with a blind devotion, and young people especially did so. It was possible to dislike him and some did. But his 'charisma' was undeniable. This was a man quite impossible to write off. He was at the height of his strength, vigorous, physically attractive, brimming over with confidence and, as it were, carrying a vast open-air crowd with him as an invisible aura round his every action. The newspapers and B.B.C. were rapacious for his material and the religious Press carried his comments on his own life in an autobiographical background music to his daily activities.

'My ministry is me. I became a minister because I had to. I remain a minister because that sense of compulsion has grown with the years and my ministry has meant an integration of my life which I am persuaded would have been impossible if I had chosen any other sort of career. It is a great freedom from anxiety when we ask ourselves, "What am I likely to be two years from now? Will I discover one day that my call has died away? Dare I read communist literature or will it not undermine my faith?" The years have taken away all the sting and most of the meaning from these questions for me. I can sing now the old Boys' Brigade chorus, "Will your anchor hold" with sober confidence. "We have an anchor which keeps the soul, steadfast and sure while the billows roll." I can even sing the last two lines though I still shudder at the appalling marine prospect of fastening an anchor to a rock.' This is but one glimpse of the man as he presented his own inner life to the *British Weekly* at that time. So Donald Soper testified, as the 1952 Methodist Conference loomed over his summer.

The Conference that year was to meet in Preston, Lancashire, and it seldom meets in a town with a more distinguished history. It is a place with a large proportion of Roman Catholic citizens, a Caroline and Jacobite history, scene of great battles, with a Fair dating back to the Henrys, and here also was published the first temperance newspaper in Britain. The poet Francis Thompson was born in Preston. There is no wonder that the townsfolk call their home Proud Preston. The steeple of the most important Roman Catholic Church, St. Wilfrid's Church, was designed by Hansom, the inventor of the hansom cab! If it is remembered that the town was used to battles, that Roman Catholics are also 'nonconformists' and have usually a tender regard for the Methodists because of sharing troubles in the past, it is just possible to believe that Preston could bear what the Conference was to do with it between July 11th and 23rd, 1952. It literally became world-wide news.

The Conference met in good heart. 'At the Annual Visitation' read the Agenda, 'we reported over 27,000 new members received, 500 more than the previous year. After training and examination 738 new local preachers have been recognized and though we still need more, we rejoice in the continued loyalty of our lay preachers everywhere. Once again we have been proud to welcome twelve newly ordained Deaconesses and to ordain eighty-four ministers. We have had, too, an adequate number of promising candidates for the ministry.'

The Public Hall at Preston is rather solemn, externally forbidding but internally comfortable and of good acoustics. The Methodist Conference is of a size to make it just full enough and yet with space enough to have conversations break out among groups of friends assembling from the corners of the kingdom. Any lady serving behind the counter in the coffee room would tell that there was but one topic of conversation as the representatives came together. Conversations could begin at any point, 'How's your church?', 'Done well for Overseas funds?' 'Your wife found a decent manse yet?' But soon 'Are we going Bolshie this year?' or various party political alternatives to that question ruled the discussion. Somewhere behind the scenes Colin Roberts was planning how to handle that section of business of which all were thinking, guided by Dr. Eric W. Baker, himself the redoubtable contemporary of both the likely nominees for the designation to the Presidency of the 1953 Conference. It would be a Wesley House field day. The only palliative to this Cambridge pressure was that Colin Roberts in the Chair was trained at Didsbury, grandfather institution to Wesley House, and in his youth had actually been President's Assistant! He would be a proficient arbiter.

One of the comforts of the discipline of the Methodist Conference when it comes to electing a President is that there are no nomination speeches, in fact no speeches at all. Write the names, scrutinize the names, print the names, vote and that, mercifully, is that. When the time came, therefore, and the little 'short list' of names was prepared (including, prophetically, that of Dr. Leslie D. Weatherhead) the people nominated could meet, talk, joke and relieve each others nervousness without any embarrassment. It was a tough ballot which, dropping off the names with lesser numbers, at last brought into the lists two names one of which must get the majority. The votes earlier given to other names would now be switched to one or other of those two or cease to be cast. What a pair!

Sometimes when the vote is close an older man will take precedence in the Conference's mind over a younger, but these two men, the Rev. W. Russell Shearer, M.A., and Donald Soper were within two years of each other in seniority. Soper, then, was the open-air evangelist, surely what the Church needed at the time? Russell Shearer had begun his ministry in the Potteries by gathering large crowds on the chapel steps. Was he lively, eccentric, loveable and likely to gain the young men's votes? His period as a probationer minister had given headaches to his superiors and he was as handsome as a film star. Status in the Church, had he this? He was the Chairman of a District and there were only 46 of them in Britain: he was set apart for that work and so a rare forerunner of the new style of Chairmen all of whom were soon to be 'separated' to their work. Courtesy? The next Conference was to meet in his District. Was he of the Left or Right, pacifist or a 'just-war' man? Here the lines were less clear but there was really nothing to choose.

One other thing, Mrs. Shearer, of a distinguished Methodist family, was a dedicated worker for the overseas Church while Mrs. Soper was relatively unknown. Nothing matters to Methodism more than overseas missions and to get among the women supporters of missions in Methodism is really getting somewhere. Did this give Shearer the edge? Perhaps the tournament was most truly described as a joust between thoroughly structured Methodism and the world outside the Church pressing in on Methodism. For that reason let the world outside record the result of the two-man ballot.

Yorkshire Evening Post, July 12th, 1952. 'Donald Soper of Tower Hill fame and Kingsway Hall was today elected President of the Methodist Conference. Dr. Soper, an ardent pacifist, said he realized his election did not necessarily mean identification of the Methodist Church with his views. At the Methodist Conference at Bradford in 1950 Dr. Soper said he would rather see the world over-run by Communists than plunged into a third world war. Later he said, "I am not a Communist." '

The news broke right across the Press. *Edinburgh Dispatch, Evening Standard*, same news; *Star*, late night, same news; *Wolverhampton Express and Star*, 'Pacifist named Methodist President'; *Bristol Evening Post*, same news; *West Lancashire Evening Gazette*, 'Pacifist as Methodist President'. The *Lancashire Evening Gazette*, with sound northern earthiness, scored the bull's eye neatly. It recorded, 'He received 279 votes against 261 for the other candidate, the Rev. W. Russell Shearer of Birmingham'. Having published this quite phenomenal news, however, it slipped

into the same time-worn cliché as papers in less favoured parts of
the world – 'two years ago he electrified the Conference by declaring that he would rather see the world overrun by Communists
than see it plunged into a third world war'. At least 'electrified' was
a change.

*Daily Echo, Liverpool Express, Gloucester Echo, Cambridge
Daily News, Western Mail, Sheffield Star, Bradford Telegraph
and Argus*, the list of provincial papers seemed to be unending and
gave a demonstration that this Londoner had ceased to be merely
a Londoner, he had achieved a place in the nation. The great
London dailies, including *The Times*, as well as the *Scotsman* and
the *Birmingham Morning Post* were carrying the story by the
morning after and their praise of the Conference's choice reached
its crescendo in the *Manchester Guardian*.

Dr. Soper created one precedent after this phenomenal vote by
speaking to the Conference about it. Usually the President-
designate goes into a voluntary silence in the Conference's business
and only if his work demands it does he mount the tribune. Should
he have to do so, Conference will do no more than make a strange,
purring sound not unlike a lioness giving her cub a couple of
rasping licks of approval. He said he would strive to be an honourable as well as honoured holder of the office. This many took to
mean he would be discreet in his future utterances and they did
not forget.

That vote! It is hard to tell at this range whether it was unique
in Methodism's two hundred years – so few things are. Perhaps in
the early days of ministers-only Conferences it was paralleled. In
by 18 votes is narrow enough for any purpose but, strangely, for
years afterwards the national Press, reporting Dr. Soper's activities, or collecting views on controversial social or ecclesiastical
issues, has called him 'President of the Methodist Church'. It
cannot forget him. The historical situation dictated that Conference had to have him in this office. It is often said nowadays,
Let the world dictate the agenda for the Church. In this case with
an irresistable voice it did so. A Methodism which did not make
him President would have looked absurd. That vote nearly did.

The President of the Methodist Conference is in office for one
year only, but this statement is misleading. During his year as
President-designate he is almost as much in the public eye as in the
substantive year and in the year immediately after his Presidency,

as ex-President, he is still needed for many duties and is called upon for public appearances. For many years Past-Presidents occupied a place of honour in Conference for a period of five years, then lapsed into obscurity. Today the Conference retains its Past-Presidents on its platform until death or frailty removes them – a surprisingly slow process.

Donald Soper, therefore, went down from Conference a marked man aware that the newspapers, secular and religious, would record his actions or his pranks and would now tag them with the information, 'President-designate of the Methodist Conference' when they did not say 'the Methodist Church'. But had he not promised to be good?

The *Daily Worker* got in first by recording the next session in Hyde Park where Dr. Soper defended the Dean of Canterbury against the hue and cry then being made over the Dean's views on the peace and war issue. Many were determined to get the Dean out of Canterbury. 'Dr. Donald Soper, just elected President of the Methodist Conference said, "Leave the Dean alone. I have no sympathy with the idea of groping round for some mediaeval legislation to deal with him." Dr. Soper who is a well-known pacifist went on, however, to deride both the Dean of Canterbury and the Archbishop of York for what he called attacking mass-murder weapons rather than war itself. "They are both straining at the gnat and swallowing the camel." '

Soon there is the *Sheffield Telegraph* with its headline, 'No use for Ike'. Dr. Donald Soper addressing a meeting arranged by the Order of Christian Witness said, 'The Republican Party says it will endeavour to promote stresses and strains behind the Iron Curtain. I hope that statement fills you with a sense of the utter pagan futility and deadliness which goes unchallenged by the world today. We need more than ever today a Christian critique of the world in which we live.'

The Methodist Conference was hardly over; the two encounters were within July. By September the newspapers had one of those issues which they consider the public really enjoys. A choirmaster in a Methodist church made a win on the football pools and was asked to resign his office in the church. Because of his sorrow at this event or for some other reason, he took his own life. Immediately the hunt was up and the story aired on Tower Hill. Dr. Soper pleaded for clear thinking. The papers, he thought, had not the whole story. If a society has rules they should be obeyed or one should resign from it. The debate ran on for some weeks, now centring on Dr. Soper's replies rather than the original issue. The *Daily Express* obtained from him the final word. 'I condemn gambling whether by a Methodist millionaire or an obscure organist.'

At the House of Commons, in a meeting arranged by the Association for World Government, he told assembled Members of Parliament that he would welcome the opportunity to preach his pacifism to the Russians. 'I did have an invitation from the Patriarch,' he told them, 'to go to Russia. I had almost packed my bags when something went wrong.'

By December he was on the television programme 'Press Conference' and was subjected to a barrage of questions by a team of journalists; the crime wave, corporal punishment, gambling, the decadence of the Churches being among them. The *Methodist Recorder* gave as its opinion 'that it is clear that Dr. Soper is admirably suited to television and I hope this will be succeeded by many other occasions'.

So the pre-presidential year rushed round with an acceleration of even the normal Soper programme. The Preston Conference had taken up a suggestion from an earlier Conference to make 1953 a year of intensive evangelism in association with other Methodist Conferences across the world. Dr. Soper, now aware that a responsibility for leadership in this effort would fall upon him, turned to making preparations for the year's campaign. In the Order of Christian Witness he had his own special instrument for such work and began to get his teams ready. He drummed it into the Witnesses' heads that not one person in ten had any idea of what the Churches were like or what their contemporary message to the world was.

Hailed by his Church's newspaper as a 'television star', prepared to be an evangelizing star, he now prepared himself – the most difficult thing of all to do. It was the half-century mark in the Soper story.

10.

John Wesley's Chair

John Wesley's Chair has always been a hot seat; there is no easy way of discharging its associated duties. When occupied by the Founder of Methodism it supported the greatest autocrat in ecclesiastical Britain, his word law and his people willing followers. The autocracy has been modified by the years – there are lay people in Conference, unthinkable to Wesley – but nothing has changed in the 'mystique' of the office. The President makes the Conference operative. If he is absent, only his legal proxy can validate the session. His legal powers are enormous in between the Conferences, in stationing ministers, in the holding or disposing of property, in the discipline of the ministry and the members, and many other matters. The powers are his, however, only because he is the Conference itself between the annual assemblies. Conference is the head of the Methodist Church and the President is its president. He is known as President of the Methodist Church only by courtesy and to assist other Churches and organizations to which this Church looks a trifle quaint.

In World Methodism there is an extension of his spiritual function. There is but one Wesley's Chair; all other Conferences derive from this one British Conference and consequently there is something not unlike the Orthodox Patriarchate in the President's position in the wider world. No living President would deny that during his term of office he was perceptibly uplifted and enabled by the volume of prayer and affection which surrounds that Chair. The Presidency, mercifully, carries the man.

This is just as well, for tradition makes an enormous programme inescapable although the legal duties demand nothing from him save to ensure that the will of Conference is obeyed until the following Conference. In fact he is expected to go round the whole national Connexion which, in 1953, had 46 Districts in Britain, make a visit to the Armed Forces, preside over the sessions of the Methodist Church in Ireland, although that Connexion has its own President of the Methodist Church, Ireland, and also be present at the Welsh Assembly of the Methodist Church in Wales. The legal duties imply his presiding over the main Conference Committees during the year and he usually does do so in one session of each.

The President-designate, therefore, has an intricate itinerary to arrange. If he is attempting to keep his normal work going, the planning to fit that in somewhere has to be dealt with. Other duties will turn up, once the year begins, which also must be fitted in. Should the work kill him the ex-President must return to do it all again! It has happened.

A month before the 1953 Conference was due to meet in Birmingham the whole nation was cheered up by the great event of the Coronation of Queen Elizabeth II. There were special types of service and plays in the churches and the towns for weeks round the event. Winston Churchill had been back in power two years and the administration gave great encouragement to the celebration of the new 'Elizabethan Age'. Her Majesty the Queen expressed her wish that such associations should not be forced upon her reign and, viewed by enormous audiences on television, her own serious demeanour and manifest religious feeling left an impression upon the nation which had not worn away when Conference gathered in July. Some sense of the relevance of the Faith and some hope of better days were widely felt.

Leaving, therefore, the crowns, sceptres, orbs and green-room paraphernalia which had been used in most churches in their mock coronations and other junketings, the representatives arrived in the Central Hall, Birmingham, and from their Conference Agenda they knew that the Church over the country had just scraped a membership rise of 1,994, after receiving 28,404 new members and balancing off the erosions of death and lapsed members. The time was right for a Soper Conference. Few Presidents since have begun with better auguries. He came determined to be good.

The Central Hall, Corporation Street, Birmingham, is an enormous building, constructed on a design which must have been the joy of that great city in the days of the Chamberlains' power. Its main auditorium simply swallowed the Conference, but the tea-rooms and buffets were easily accessible, even if the rostrum, dignitaries and tribune seemed parts of another world. There was no cramping of visitors here; the President could have a mammoth audience.

It would be different from some; earlier in the spring of the year he had been knocked off the platform at Speakers' Corner by two aggressive and drunk opponents who complained that he was not talking religion. The magistrate, with that innocence magistrates sometimes display, told them he was certain that this could not be so and fined them £1 each for disorderly behaviour.

This incident had wide Press coverage, the *Evening Standard,* the *Scottish Daily Express* and *The Times* all commenting on it and linking it with the Presidency of the Conference. The *Western Mail*, with some admirable research into the labyrinth of Methodist ways, discovered that a month or so before Conference Mr. Arthur Henderson, M.P., who had been Air Minister and Under-Secretary for War, had become Circuit Steward of the West London Mission, where Dr. Donald Soper, the famous pacifist, now Methodism's President-designate, was superintendent. Mr. Henderson proclaimed that as both were Methodists there was no incongruity. To crown the process of sharpening up the public appetite for Conference, the Press picked up Dr. Soper's involvement in the controversy and demonstrations against the death sentence passed on the Rosenburgs for atomic spying. He addressed a Hyde Park Rally 'as President-designate of the Methodist Conference', the Press stated, 'whether I get into trouble or not'. So as Conference began his enemies and his friends could all hope for the best, their best, according to choice.

Safely through the second confirmatory vote which seated him, the Conference's first action was to make amends to Dr. W. Russell Shearer, M.A., for the tough passage he had at Preston. He was designated to follow his victor of the year previous with a satisfactory majority. It was a 'landslide', uniquely, it is said, one ballot only being necessary.

The *Christian World*, reporting through the pen of Dr. Maldwyn Edwards, said: 'It was a Conference resolved to look on the present "year of evangelism" as a beginning and not as an end, which assembled at the Central Hall, Birmingham on July 10th.

The tone was set by the speech of Dr. Donald Soper, the incoming President. He could neither have been true to himself nor his charge if he had not brought the contemporary scenes under the searchlight of Christian principles; but the general survey had a particular application. What must we do about it?

'He was not content to say we must evangelize; he declared that in his presidential year he intended to conduct his preaching services within the framework of the Service for Holy Communion. At night, whatever the time of year, he intended to take his congregation out into the open air to bear a public witness. Thus a speech salted with wit and informed by a deep social-evangelical fervour ended fittingly in the call to a great adventure.'

Dr. Maldwyn Edwards remarked that all the Donald Sopers were present in his Presidential address – 'the Field Preacher', the Christian Pacifist, the 'acute-keen-eyed student of affairs'. The argument of the whole was that the Church and world were separated by a ravine not yet bridged and the punch of the address was a mass of suggestions on how to bridge it.

The President said, 'What then lies behind and beneath the daily flux of thought and action which have as yet frustrated our advance? Let us with the spiritual equipment we already possess, and therefore with confidence as well as humility, try to peer into the future. It is our duty as well as our opportunity to do so.

'What is really happening in this tumultuous modern world? Religious leaders have been queueing up for some time now to announce that materialism has laid hold of Western civilization, and is every year becoming more powerful everywhere else. But to deplore this, to denounce and to appeal to men to forsake this materialism is not enough. Men believe in it and no wonder.

'It has bestowed great benefits, great freedoms, and if we are neither blind nor sour we ought to rejoice in particular at the prodigious good that applied science and technology are doing. If we oppose secularism it must be because we have penetrated its meaning by the light of the Gospel and, from a deep awareness of what lies at its roots and what must accompany its growth, we can descry its errors, and foretell its failures. . . .

'I now invite you to believe that these very facts, looked at more closely and particularly in the light of the future as we may foresee that future, constitute a challenge to the Christian because, far from making our faith questionable or irrelevant, they add tremendous weight to the claim we have made from the first day of Pentecost, "There is no salvation outside the Church."

'War which has been the chronic disease of human societies, is now acute, mortal and world-wide in its impact. Historically the Christian Church has failed to cure this disease. Confronted with this disease today, the Christian doctors as such are indistinguishable from the non-Christian. We are all impotent to agree with any remedy. Yet a remedy must be found or society will perish. Whether responsible statesmen are prepared to say this or not, let me as a temporarily responsible churchman say it.

'The armaments programme of the modern world must lead to two results – the progressive crippling of the world's resources and the unavoidable use of those armaments in a third world war. With the population of our world growing by twenty millions a year, the slogan "guns or butter" is out of date. It is the grimmer alternative, "guns or bread"; and we may well add a third result of this arms race, the poisoning of international understanding by the lies the armed communities must tell. No nation dare tell the truth about its armies, and navies and air forces.

'What, then, will break this vicious circle of fear and violence and lies? The Christians have hitherto failed but the champions of reason and science and humanism have also failed. I affirm that Christianity hasn't failed – it hasn't been tried since before Constantine. I believe that a Christian Church which was prepared to renounce all compromise with war and to take up its cross would succeed.

'I know that it would immediately put into the lives of outsiders a hope and a confidence in our gospel where now they have only more or less tolerant incredulity. Governments are hard-ridden by the fear that if they disarm they will expose themselves to attack and enslavement. I sympathize with them. Before they can be expected to take such a risk, someone has to demonstrate that in the last resort this is God's world, and what is morally right will turn out to be politically sound, and I say with boldness that nobody but the Christian and no community but the Christian Church can undertake this cross-bearing adventure of faith.'

Here is one of 'the Sopers' to whom Dr. Edwards referred. The great Soper dream of a mighty Church coming clean out in a pacifist, non-violence campaign. He must have known that it was the million-to-one-shot of all time that it should happen so, but his puritan soul would not let him be silent only because he could not hope for what he wanted.

He turned to his passion for the newly born Welfare State. 'I thank God for the Welfare State and treat with contempt the argument that because it is abused by the few it should be denied to the many. Yet I would say to those who say that human welfare can be promoted by secular powers – and that the gospel is therefore irrelevant – look more deeply into this matter; for there are grim reminders in every direction (and especially if we look ahead) that there is something terribly wrong with this claim.

'The facts are that welfare without God tends sooner or later, not towards family life but towards the Police State. Even in officially Christian England one lesson has been beaten into our experiences. Socialism is not a programme that can be carried out whether you or I are good or bad; its life-blood is the moral responsibility of the citizen. ... The true Welfare State, behind which I want the Christian Church to stand "four square and no nonsense", is utterly dependent on the gospel of Jesus Christ alike for its direction and its spirit; and may I add, after twenty-six years of field preaching, I know of no other claim that can be made in the name of Jesus that makes more immediate appeal to the honest outsider.'

The years which have rolled by since 1953 have served only to underwrite this diagnosis of the Welfare State's problem. The failure of national moral life, which has seen corruption grow in so many fields, has bitten into the Welfare system's application so deeply that some of its best friends are now astonished and silenced when it is attacked. Stoutly defending it down the years, Donald Soper has always reiterated this solemn fact – this is a religious question and some of the stripping down which the system has since undergone is part of the decline of religion. Religion is politics, after all.

The Conference experts, especially those who are 'conference elected' representatives with seats for three years in its deliberations, all wait hushed for the President's peroration. Will it bite? Will it point a way somewhere? Will it just round off a speech? The 1953 President knew this. He ended with them in mind.

He told them of his own way of handling the year of personal campaign which he intended, with his emphasis on the open-air –

which he knew many nominal Methodists simply detested or feared with a cold-sweat fear. He was going to be a trial!

'As for the evening meetings, you will not be astonished if I intend to venture out of doors and ask you to come with me into the open air. I know the weather may deter us now and then, but I refuse to believe (according to reports from some Districts) that the open air is only fit for use during about three weeks in the year, and that inevitably not in the weeks during which I shall be in those Districts. Without being fanciful, Christianity was surely born in the open air. It was certainly revived there by Wesley and Whitefield. Where today have we the opportunity of pressing the claims of which I have spoken, and many others, to the outsiders – where else shall we who are inside find a like exhilaration?

'How else for the time being can we invade the vast new housing estates and satellite towns – the new areas which set for us and for all Christian communities perhaps our greatest single task today? Come with me and we will hold our meetings, maybe on church steps or in market places, or best of all, next door to a Communist meeting. We will have fun in the name of the Lord.'

He was on firm ground in his own work, for the Oldham newspapers were carrying the story in July of the imminent invasion of their area by 250 Order of Christian Witness members who would conduct a week of campaign and this was only one effort of four planned in his Presidential Year, the others being Isle of Man, Exeter and Settle. The Oldham campaign went well and had a later follow-up in 1954 – it even made a surplus of money for use elsewhere.

Some momentous things occurred in Birmingham that Conference which were harbingers of greater changes still to come. One which was near to the heart of the President was a series of changes in the constitution of the Missionary Society's relationships with Ceylon, from which the old parent–child relationship was removed. Devolution, then a coming 'in' word, always has an acid test in the matter of financial control and the Birmingham Conference approved a Treasurer in Ceylon to care for money coming there from Britain. The 'block-grant' was still to come, whereby the local Church decided on what money was to be spent, but for the first time the spending was agreed with the British Church and managed by the Cingalese Church.

Strangely enough, the Missionary Committee asked Conference to appoint a Commission to review the whole work of mission in the light of the changing political and economic situation round the world. Conference did this and the subsequent Report, *The Missionary Obligation of the Church* was a key document. Yet there were no overseas representatives on the Commission! So swift is the movement of change that then this did not seem remarkable.

Perhaps one of the biggest things done by the Conference was the publication of a series of 'Judgements' for the guidance of the Methodist people.

'In a world where power groups struggle for mastery and the perils of irresponsible use of power are evident, Christians should stand for the principle that those who exercise power must serve the causes of justice and order, and that they are responsible to God for the way they use their power.

'In a world where men increasingly look to the State to ensure social justice and the just distribution of the fruits of industry, Christians must stand for the principle that there must be the will to contribute to, as well as receive from, the gathered wealth and service of the community.

'In a world where the State as the instrument of ordered government has taken increased power to itself, Christians should be vigilant to preserve and extend the right of free association, particularly in matters of religion, culture and industrial life.

'In a multi-racial world, composed of people of different colour and language, Christians should stand for the equal dignity and worth of all men in the sight of God, without discrimination of race and for the ultimate right of all peoples to freedom of development and self-government.

'In a world where some races are highly developed and others are under-developed and the standard of life is unequal, highly developed nations should accept the responsibility of helping less favoured peoples to a higher standard of life.

'In a world of armed nations, where the menace of war is ever present, Christians should be vigilant for peace, pressing for policies which assuage discontent and division and which, by promoting freedom and international justice, lessen the peril of war.'

There followed a series of five petitions to Her Majesty's Government bearing on the issues then alive within the categories of the statement.

It has to be remembered that the Cold War situation was then in such disorder that there had been imposed a renewed conscription for five years. The posting of young people under adult age as conscripts to Korea was a matter of deep concern. There was a prescience about the list of six Christian judgements listed above which now makes the Conference's mind rank as of high intelligence, and it can well be imagined how much the list of practical attitudes to problems then troubling the world could be used as a practical casuistry by the members of the Order of Christian Witness on campaign at that very time.

Every Conference passes some Resolution which takes on an ironic twist in following years and perhaps that, with Donald Soper in the Chair, it condemned commercial television in no uncertain tones is the irony of 1953.

There were indications of the knowledge gained in the Ceylon visit in his repudiation of the old Christian belief that the world had only the choice between Christianity and chaos. His declaration startled many who had not been plunged into the world maelstrom of conflicting ideas. Our Faith today, he argued, is only an option. 'This modern world offers mankind a variety of bazaars where he can market the spiritual and intellectual goods he possesses or buy the goods he desires. A better knowledge of the other world religions must make provincially minded Christians humble, though it will fail to shake faith. In particular I have noticed this in those who have compared the non-violence of the Hindu Ghandi with the power politics of so-called Christian statesmen or the tolerance and charity of the Buddhists when compared with the Christian sects'.

This free-for-all interpretation of the missionary situation has now become the framework of Christian Mission as is evidenced by the 'Institutes for the Study of Religion' dotted about the world under the auspices of the Division of World Mission and Evangelism of the World Council of Churches. Ceylon led the way in this type of encounter, together with the great work of Reichelt in

China. To this day there are Christians who do not accept it: it was early days for Conference missionary 'fans' of the old school to swallow such doctrine.

His nearly contemptuous pillorizing of the motive forces behind Western economic and industrial systems also stirred opposition in some members.

'The most erosive element in Communism is not "dialectical materialism", whatever that may mean in Moscow this week ... but the manifest evidence it offers that the public and private "goods" at which Christianity strains itself in production can be produced by political and economic machinery. The old capitalism had at least this practical merit – it ran best on the crude oil of selfishness, mutual distrust and fear, what are politely called "the checks and balances of private interest", and there was no lack of such fuel. The Welfare State is a much more delicate machine and will only run on the refined fuel of unselfishness and personal honour. There is not enough of this spirit to go round and so we have to fall back on the old fuel and when this crude oil is fed into the machine it clogs and the machine breaks down.'

There were delegates who did not know that their accustomed world was driven by 'enlightened self-interest' – they simply lived in it without examination. Curse the Communists, of course, but us and our world? The shock value of a Soper lies as much in the awakening he causes to a yawning gap in one's world view as in any new idea he may thrust down reluctant throats. The Faith we live by, having existed under all types of social system, can be assumed to belong to the type dominant in our own times and simply lie upon it like a jewel displayed on a velvet cushion. Then 'the Troubler' jabs men into seeing that this Christianity belongs to no social system or age but is itself a system, a timeless system, with a built-in explosive power. I got a bomb and I never knew I had it!

Conference Sunday is ever one of the great days in the Methodist year. Every representative capable of preaching is planned to preach somewhere in the District which is host to Conference and the people look forward to seeing and hearing some of the well-known preachers. Of the galaxy of talent spread through the churches the President, of course, is the central personality and for him there is the Conference Service. This is always conducted on the liturgical framework of John Wesley's own revision of the

Anglican Order of Morning Prayer – a pattern now being questioned by revolutionary pundits – and the Office is read by the Secretary of the Conference, the President preaching.

The Birmingham papers seized upon the fact that the Birmingham Conference and Dr. Soper created a precedent. 'Moseley Road Methodist Church was packed for two hours for the Official Service of the Methodist Conference which began in Birmingham yesterday. For the first time the service was televised. The Church is one of the newest in Birmingham. The sermon was preached by this year's President of the Conference, Dr. Donald Soper'. It is not clear if the 'two hours', the 'packed', the television or the preacher is the main point of the report.

It was a field-day Conference for the Press; they were not even denied the customary paragraph or two on the ever-popular theme of sex in society. 'Sex Revolution', says one headline. Dr. Soper is quoted as declaring: 'A wholesale revolution has taken place in the attitude, particularly of the youth of the Western World, to Christian sex morality. It is said that the use of contraceptives has made a bigger difference to our world already than anything since the domestication of fire. Can any of us doubt who are really in touch with people and not just with schedules that the removal of the fear of dire results from promiscuity has at last undermined for multitudes the sanctity or even the value of chastity. Chastity in their eyes is not a spiritual virtue but a severely practical price you pay for ignorance'. There is either a concealed 'Soperism' or a Freudian slip in the phrase 'domestication of fire', for the first impact of contraception among the common people was felt in the domestication of careless love-making which previously had affected the male world only outside the home. Marriage without anxiety is probably a greater social solvent than all the libertarian factors in modern habits of contraception.

The televising of the Conference Service was a 'first time'. Perhaps a more startling example of 'first time' occurred in the evening when instead of the usual prestigious service in some suburban church, 'Dr. Donald Soper', to quote the *Birmingham Post*, 'packed the Bull Ring', over a thousand people being there to help in beginning his open-air presidency. This was right up the Soper street, the Bull Ring being a forum as well known as the Speakers' Corner in London and a site of open-air preaching by the young student ministers of Handsworth, the Birmingham Methodist

Ministerial Training College. Extra police had to be called out for Sunday duty on that Conference Sunday – surely a momentous 'first time' – and as far as modern history records, a last time too.

All that followed was not so easy as this dynamic Sunday might suggest. Dr. Soper was indeed being a President after his own prescription, and in the open air and on the television screen all Methodism was behind him. It was not so easy to guarantee that the Church was with him when later in the Conference he waded into one of the summer controversies which always adorn the Press in Britain in the 'silly season'. The juicy item of the summer in that year was the friendship between Her Royal Highness the Princess Margaret and Group Captain Peter Townsend. Should a member of the Royal House marry a man with a divorce in his life?

It was actually suggested that there should be a national plebiscite to determine the will of the people on the matter! At this point the President made his official comment. 'I want to protest,' he said, 'in the name of this Conference as vigorously as I can against the disgusting intrusion into the affairs of a Royal Personage and I regard this newspaper as having behaved very badly indeed in opening the floodgates to all kinds of prejudice and probably perverted opinion. I therefore make this protest as strongly as I can and I believe the Conference will support me.' It did, and in view of what was to happen not very long afterwards it probably supported the opinion rather than its leader in doing so.

Conference is nothing if not an enormous mixture of grave and gay, mighty problems and tiny acts of grace. In one day the Conference had before it all the horrors of the Mau-Mau movement in Kenya – upon which, because of the big stake the Methodist Church had in that country, the Conference was better informed than the mass of the nation's people. The China-trained and therefore politically wide-awake Chairman of the District, the Rev. E. A. Bastin, speaking of our losses and the murders among the Meru people, could offer the Conference no hope of an easement but prophesied that the worst of the tragedy was still to come. He was right, as the Meru Martyrs Memorial Church now witnesses.

With this grim business on the agenda during the day, suddenly there was the magic switch and the President fulfils his promise to continue his regular support of the Conference Rally of the National Children's Home in spite of his new duties. There were 2,300 people massed in the Rally and they and the children giving the concert items were delighted when he gave an extended presidential-special on his tin whistle. 'The Girl I Left Behind Me' and 'O Solo Mio' brought such a burst of applause that he had to give an encore, on the piano, 'Annie Laurie'!

The busy days wound their way through to the end and while some of the news media complained that the President had all the publicity and the acts of Conference fared badly by comparison, it was the religious papers rather than the secular and national which made the complaint. One of the Conference acts which did get through was the preparation for the Second Assembly of the World Council of Churches, to be held in 1954 in Evanston, U.S.A., to which Dr. Soper was elected to go among the Methodist team.

The *British Weekly* deserves the praise for picking out in its issue at the end of the sessions what was, perhaps, the phenomenon of the whole Conference. 'There have been occasions when Dr. Soper has obviously been hampered by the essential impartiality of his exotic isolation. Some discussions of international and political questions have made it seem as if Alec Bedser were in the middle in umpire's coat and not at the wicket! The temptation to take the ball must have been enormous but it was manfully conquered.'

Conference dispersed, leaving the Secretary and his team to the weary midsummer labour of preparing the Minutes of Conference. Many ministers set about the task of packing ready for one more move in the constant itinerary which is their lot, and the President went down to the country. He did not choose the respite taken by some who had preceded – and followed – him of disappearing while the disappearing was good, but turned up within days quite his old self.

That year the Labour Party held its Party Conference at Margate and, as has so often been the case, he attended to preach the Conference sermon there before the sessions began. In August he was down in Cornwall and chose, in surely a very strange place for the purpose, to express an adverse view of Dr. A. C. Kinsey's study of sexual behaviour which he suspected was read for 'kicks' rather than scientific interest.

He next turned up at Oldham where over a thousand people gathered to hear him debate the prospects for peace with Tom Rowlandson, Communist Parliamentary candidate, arguing whether Communism or Christianity held out the best hopes of attaining and preserving peace. There were people standing in the aisles.

As the Government set up the Royal Commission on Capital Punishment in the autumn of 1953 he issued a Presidential Statement to the Press on the task of the Commission. He was concerned at the terms of reference of the Commission and wanted to raise the basic question of whether the death penalty should not be completely done away with. (With the introduction of the Silverman Bill in November 1964, he was better placed to take a part in this momentous debate.) In the same period he took the initiative in demanding that a Royal Commission should be set up to enquire into the whole question of homosexuality, which enquiry he described as being long overdue and neglected for the wrong reasons. He asked for a private Commission to take the question out of the world of publicity and sensation. He had no luck, witness the *Daily Herald*, 'Dr. Soper calls for probe into vice'; and 'Sins of Sodom; Enquiry urged', *Daily Recorder*, November 1953. His turn came later in that 'other place'.

The *Manchester Daily Despatch* then found him outside Gladstone Dock, Liverpool where he was one of two rival speakers addressing a crowd of 200 dockers on a piece of spare land. 'There was a stocky man in corduroy trousers and check shirt; his line was numerology with a guaranteed cure for catarrh as a side line. The other was a much taller man in a black cassock talking Christianity, or, as he put it, "common sense" to the dockers. He was Donald Soper, this year's President of the Methodist Conference, and he out-talked his rival as he appealed for greater importance to be placed on decent living as a means of preventing a third world war.' The Methodist year had flown round to November by this time. 'He never talked down to the dockers,' the report said. 'Instead he lifted them up to his level and the crowd stood in silence, giving up their lunch hour to listen to him.'

The Soper presidency was going true to form up to this time and he was being listened to and reported with unusual regularity. Then it came, what his friends had feared might come, what his enemies had known was bound to come. It happened in Manchester, that royal city with the outstanding story of loyalty to monarchs good and bad.

On November 16th, 1953, on a site near Deansgate, he told eight hundred good-humoured listeners. 'I wish the Queen didn't go to horse races. She would be much wiser if she kept away from the sport of kings. It is very obviously a household of racketeers; you know it and I know it.' As though this were not enough, he went on, perched on a green box, to praise the Duke of Edinburgh's lead in the demand for playing fields but ended his commendation, 'but what a lead if he told us what he thought about God.'

From all corners of the kingdom the heavy guns were trained on him for this one. You can't tell a Queen to be wiser, or question a Duke's faith. The *Scottish Daily Mail* slipped in a piece of good reporting by mentioning that the President's remarks, also reported fairly, were made in answer to a question. It troubled to fill out some of the detail missed by snap reporters, reporting him as saying, 'I had no intention of talking about the Queen or horse-racing but at an open-air meeting one cannot refuse to answer questions. I started out by saying how much we all were indebted to her and to all the Royal Family. I also said how impressed I was by the speech the Queen made on her twenty-first birthday, dedicating herself to God and her country. I am against gambling and as a Left Winger I think it is an anti-social habit. I believe wealth should be distributed according to need not to chance. I prefer that the Queen should stay away from a vested interest like horse-racing. We in this country cannot afford to gamble on horses. That is why I personally wish that the Queen would not go racing.' This was a good interview which gave him a fair chance to put the record straight. But in the eyes of many it was not so much put straight but tangled into an even greater indiscretion. The *Daily Telegraph, Daily Express* and the *Daily Mail* all had the story and were typical of the whole range of the Press. 'Stop nagging the Queen', cried the *Daily Sketch*.

Then what surely must be another first event occurred when the paper which is the household reading of the Methodist Church rebuked the President of Conference. The *Methodist Recorder* said what it felt it could in defence of one beset by a Manchester crowd. It also agreed with the Doctor that gambling was not to be encouraged, though expressed this in strange terms for Methodism

– 'We hold no particular brief for gambling, it is a necessary evil'. It then went on to its criticism.

'But the particular circumstances of the question did not warrant Dr. Soper bringing Her Majesty into the argument. For one thing neither the Queen nor the Duke of Edinburgh, nor any other member of the Royal Family, can reply. They are thoroughly democratic, they embody in the best sense of the term the spirit of the age, but at the same time propriety demands that they should be held to be outside of all sectional controversies, whatever the nature of these may be. And then, too, the Queen and Duke are hard, eager workers each doing an indispensable job. As such they are entitled to a little relaxation on the few occasions when it is possible.' No one told the *Methodist Recorder*, 'Stop nagging the President.'

He seemed beyond reform. On the Mount, Edinburgh, he told the crowd that he wanted the Duke to give a lead to young people, but at Berwick-on-Tweed, a town that had a history of frontier disputes over centuries and where he was to have a civic reception, the mayor cancelled the engagement because, he said, he was 'a loyal subject of Her Majesty the Queen'. As an old soldier of twenty-three years' military service, he refused to meet the President.

This was not the only cancellation which sprang from the affair. On the other hand, it was at this juncture that the *Radio Times* publicizing a broadcast, gave the work of the West London Mission a warm write-up. Elsewhere Dr. Soper was attacked by a clergyman who alleged the President had the habit of swimming on Sundays. This brother of the cloth asserted that Dr. Soper was known on occasion to wear his bathing trunks under his canonicals.

With all these newsworthy items popping up with regularity in the Press it is by no means easy to realize that the normal Presidential visitation programme wore the character which in fact it did – not everything gets reported. Down in East Anglia, out across the West Country, an eye was kept open for his visits and all the reporters prayed that on their patch he would drop a 'clanger', have a jab at the 'American occupation of Britain', sketch in the more notable achievements of the Soviet Republics or otherwise brighten their lives. Not all were disappointed, but some things they did not notice.

The Methodist Recorder

...rd Soper leading
...Demonstration

...Anti-Coursing Campaign
...with Mr. E. Heffer M.P.
...d (right) Mr. Raymond
Rowley, Chairman)

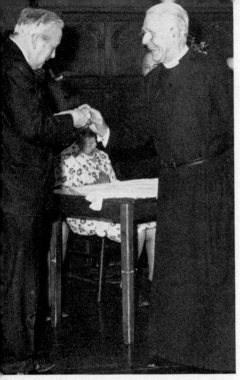

◀ With the Rt. Hon. Harold Wilson M.P.

The Methodist Recorder

With his sponsors at the House of Lor
(left, Lord Inman; right, Lord Hende
▼

Universal Pictorial Press and Agency Limited

His visit to the Portsmouth Central Mission perhaps serves as an example of what was happening to the churches. With Mrs. Soper he descended on the Eastney Central Hall in that naval town and to a Hall full of Christian people he preached in the afternoon and presided over an enormous celebration of Holy Communion, nearly a thousand people communicating in one great festival of eucharistic joy which was born along on wings of song as the people moved up to the Communion rail to be served by the President or the Superintendent Minister who assisted him.

Utterly tired, he spent an hour or so on the settee in the manse so weary it was a pity to disturb him. But then, in poor weather, down to the sea front at Southsea he went, to where already a group of those who regularly answered questions there had begun a meeting. He got up on the platform at Speakers' Corner, Portsmouth, and engaged in a furious multi-party argument with tough ex-naval men and other folk in a crowd of two hundred or more people. That complete, he was back at an evening Rally, with the Hall once more crowded, to preach a sermon. The evening gone, he was asked about his expenses. 'Fill the tank with petrol and that will do,' was his response, and off he went into the night, headed for London and whatever came next in the itinerary. This was the impression which was gained by countless Methodist people up and down the country.

What happened was that, on top of the inspirational work in the churches, the outside world made the agenda because of the open-air witness and this was the root of the news coverage. The country knew more about Methodism by July 1954 than it had ever known, and probably thought more about the Church's Master than it had done for many a year. Through the closing days of the Presidential year how Soper must have prayed for his successor, Russell Shearer's good health and safe passage.

11.

All Stations to Kingsway

The overseas missionary activities of the Methodist Church in Britain centre on the Centenary Hall , Marylebone, London – the much-loved Mission House – and through the hectic days of controversy about the President's deeds or misdeeds there was more than a little interest in the minds of the Missionary Officers.

As early as April 1954 negotiations were taking place to have Dr. Soper visit the Caribbean Area and the work in Central America which is now comprised in the enormous Methodist Conference of the Caribbean and the Americas. The Methodist Church there is almost as old as that in Britain itself, being founded in 1760 by a convert of John Wesley. It is deeply dug into the life of the area because before emancipation in 1834 the Church moved with and followed up the migrations of the slave population and the incoming of indentured labour so closely as to become part of the inter-racial whole which is the Caribbean.

In 1954 negotiations for the West Indian Federation, comprising many parts of the Caribbean Area, were well advanced. The Federation came into force in 1958 but the tension of the situation was known to the leaders of the Church as early as 1954 and they could have forecast the end of the experiment which lasted but four years and ended in 1962.

Those who have spent a lifetime in the area cannot be guaranteed to have a finger on each island's pulse. Within twenty minutes flying time of Miami are the Bahamas, which are self-consciously not of the West Indies at all but themselves. Here in 1954 rule was by the white section of the population which proudly looked back to a history of loyalist settlers in the Southern parts of England's old American Empire and who left it rather than be part of a republic.

Sophisticated, neatly segregated, old Britain on the doorstep of upstart U.S.A., but not averse to upstart capital entering the islands. Soper was to preach there.

Mercifully, Cuba was part of the responsibility of the American Methodist Church, but nearby was Haiti, fragment of French culture, and political dynamite. Tucked cosily in away from Atlantic storms lay the great and successful island of Jamaica, big brother to the other churches of the area but not demonstrably loved by the little brothers. On the other side of the Caribbean Sea lay Honduras, Costa Rica and Panama, with its penetration of the indigenous Americo-Indian culture.

Westward of Haiti lie the Virgin Islands, with both British and American rule, and beyond the Virgin Islands, like a string of pearls facing out into the Atlantic, were the Leewards and the Windwards, with Antigua, now the tiny home of the Methodist Conference's administration, and Barbados, with cricket enough to cheer a Soper. Nearly touching the South American Coast was Trinidad, perhaps just a little jealous of the power of Jamaica.

From the Grand Bahama there are sixteen hundred miles as the crow flies down to Port of Spain, Trinidad, and most of the miles are water. The ex-President was to preach here. Another four hundred miles south-west to Georgetown, British Guiana (now Guyana) made the round two thousand crow-miles and every mile of land which the crow passed over was guaranteed to have a struggle for liberation, change, development, or a struggle against change and development for the retention of the good old English bond.

The hottest spot of the whole vast area was British Guiana, where the incoming of Indian labour over the years had produced a second population all too often standing over against the African. Here all the techniques of East Indian politics were part of the scene and party politics thrived. There were British troops there to keep the peace, and now and again the British Government had to take action and intervene in local government. Anyone could think of a dozen Soperisms which might be prompted by such a situation.

In early July the Chairman of the District wrote. 'I have just seen an announcement in the Press which suggests that ... a member of the deposed People's Progressive Party will try to "adopt" Dr. Soper when he comes as something in the nature of a "fellow-traveller". We will have to guard against any move of this kind. I am sure that Dr. Soper appreciates the very delicate situation here: British Guiana is not England'. By July 30th, however, Dr. Soper having flown in from Caracas and done his tour in Guiana, the Chairman recorded in his official correspondence, 'We had a great time with Dr. Soper. Our only regret is that his visit was so short'.

Behaving very well, Dr. Soper left Guiana for Antigua, where official guests are welcomed to the great old house in which Princess Margaret and Lord Snowdon were to spend their honeymoon, and which lacked no royal portrait except that of King George VI. Within a flip of an aircraft lie St. Kitts, steeped in Methodism and sugar, Nevis and Anguilla, to which he paid a brief visit. Travelling on through Trinidad up to Nassau in the Bahamas, he preached at Trinity, which is the historic white people's church, and at Ebenezer and Wesley Churches in the one Sunday. They survived, as did he, though the congregations spanned members of the white Government and leaders of the black community, including stalwart fishermen and the lighthouse keeper. And so to Jamaica and the historic church dedicated to the founder of American Methodism, Dr. Coke. He was then to go on to the Second Assembly of the World Council of Churches and follow this with a lecture tour in the United States. In the upshot affairs at home were pressing too heavily at Kingsway and the lecture tour had to be abandoned.

It was a tour which began with trepidations. 'We hope that he will be good, but there is no safe prediction about his utterances on certain issues; some of us wonder what he will be likely to say.' But it turned out to be one for which Chairman after Chairman wrote sincerest thanks and the Area gladly helped with travelling expenditure. There is a grapevine stretching through that Western Ocean. It could well be that the reception and the reactions of Dr. Soper were alike affected by the 'accidental' fact that one of the very brightest of Caribbean probationer ministers, back in England on training, heard the ex-President preach an Ordination Charge which completely won him. There is nothing that Donald Soper does better than this and few that can equal him. So the message left Bowes Park Methodist Church, North London and was round the Caribbean before ever he arrived.

'Evanston', the second meeting of the World Council of

Churches, still awaits the verdict of historians of the future. Some who went to it dropped out of the ecumenical movement in later years – perhaps the atmosphere of nearby Chicago had something to do with it. Survivors of it at New Delhi, where the Third Assembly met, were legendary people who took a deep breath and began again in the atmosphere of new India. Its chief contribution was in the field of Inter-Church Aid; its chief difficulty in mixing the different Christian bodies which came together at the earlier meeting in Amsterdam.

The summary of the encounter has a heroic quality, 'We have come together and we intend to stay together'. That pledge has certainly been kept through years of change hard enough to separate many other unities. It is pretty certain that the factual negotiations to turn the Jamaican Theological College into a united self-governing body in association with the University of the West Indies, or the attempts to run a new mission under the wing of a Canadian bauxite company in the heart of British Guiana, were more to the Soper liking.

The Methodist new year was on the threshold by the time the ex-president became again the Superintendent of the West London Mission. He was more than fortunate in his colleague within the Mission, the Rev. B. Arthur Shaw, stationed at Hinde Street Church, just behind Selfridge's store off Oxford Street. He was bursting with energy, resourceful and making a success of student work within the University. His ability to take care of things is to be judged by his subsequent career as Chairman of a District. Of Wesley Deaconesses there were three in that difficult time – Sister Lottie Hudd, Sister Megan Capon and Sister May Smith – whose loyalty was best demonstrated in their tireless service.

It was just as well things were well under control for in November Dr. Soper was appointed to lead a delegation on a visit to Moscow and Leningrad. He had an earlier invitation from the Russian Orthodox Church but then said he wanted to find things out for himself. In the November journey Canon C. E. Raven, a kindred spirit within the Church of England, was one of the team of religious leaders on the expedition.

In a Press Conference on his return he neither pleased the party which wanted him to be utterly critical nor those who wished him to praise all he had seen. At that time the churches were full on every occasion but this was partly because they were so few. The people's certainty that their own way was completely right and their resistance to outside information struck him. The selectivity of what the public was allowed to know was noticeable and consequently no critic of the Soviet régime could be found. He was quite sure that sullen resistance to the régime was a 'comic' Western myth.

Writing sixteen years later, after a second visit to the U.S.S.R., his comment is much more percipient. In the famous *Tribune* articles he wrote, 'In 1954 the dominant impression was of a country determined to express a new forward way of life by the simple process of seeing to it that everything was different – and obviously this difference had to be demonstrated either in emphasis or in style, in the field of architecture. The palatial splendiferous 'Metro' in the midst of squalid tenements represented the new emphasis. The 'chocolate box' apartment blocks and the Moscow University represented the revolutionary (or at least the manifestly extraordinary) style of the new régime.

'The process was indeed beginning to run down by 1954 but the building programme was intended to be of a new earth. Nothing was going to be as it was. More important still, nothing was going to be like the capitalist world which still for the time being continued to exist outside the boundaries of the Soviet Union and its satellites.

'From the uniform, almost pietist demeanour of the crowds in Gorki Street to the quite tremendous sense of community responsibility everywhere; from the total prohibition of religious propaganda to the all-pervasive Communist placards and slogans, the Soviet Union was indeed a new earth if not a new heaven, and it seemed to me then that this gap would tend to widen even further. Even those who abominated the terror and the violence, and the regimentation and the destruction of so many human liberties were caught up in a sort of wonder.

'Were we seeing the emergence of a society radically different and we hoped finally better than all that had preceded it? Well, I don't think so now. It may well be that the Soviet Union is becoming a more humane society, as it is unquestionably becoming a stronger and more prosperous one. It is certainly not the sort of new and unprecedented society of which there was so much evidence in 1954.'

The complaint of the rest of this important article is that the

Soviet Union is becoming just like everywhere else, a situation reflected architecturally by what the writer calls 'concrete Esperanto' and there is no evidence of new categories of men. The 1970 summary asks the question, 'The old Adam in the new Jerusalem?'

'Life in the cities seems to me to pose the questions: Is the Soviet Union moving, albeit slowly, towards the kind of human existence which marks a fundamental change from all previous societies? For, after all, this is their classic claim. Or is this vast experiment turning out in the long run not to be fundamental after all – but on the contrary obedient, like all other historic societies, to processes which overrule even such totalitarian and ideological principles as have been claimed in the names of Marx and Lenin?

'I will hazard a guess. Communism is at heart a mixture of two elements. The one is the ultimate dynamic of community which can be stronger even than self-interest. I believe that this element is indestructible even in a changing Soviet Union. The other is the element of finality in communist thinking such as the consummation of the dialectic process, and here time and change are tending to lay bare the fallacy.'

More than eleven overseas journeys followed in the years up to 1964 and all of them were the results of invitations to lead or speak in campaigning or for lecture tours. Japan, Canada, the United States of America, East Germany, Switzerland, Spain, Nigeria and Palestine feature in the list. One aircraft is much like another and the meals are indistinguishable, but the visit to Poland some months after his Russian visit was certainly different enough to remember.

The Methodist Church in Poland is of peculiar origin and, with the other European countries of non-Latin Language, has close relationships with the United Methodist Church of America rather than the British Conference. In the years following the First World War the relief programme of the (then) Methodist Episcopal Church, South (within the United States of America) entered Poland with an enormous shipment of relief supplies, so great that it required the chartering of a special ship. Soup kitchens were established in the great cities. In Warsaw alone three thousand people were fed daily. The impact of this programme caused Poles living in the U.S.A. to seek the establishment of a Methodist

Church within their homeland. The Church in Gdansk (Danzig) was founded in 1922.

To this Church Dr. Soper was invited, following on his visit to the Soviet Union. But a Church with these origins could not escape all the difficulties such an origin implies under the tremendous changes in government following the Second World War. Carrying letters of welcome from the Head of the Methodist Church in Poland, Dr. Soper arrived by air in the black of the night. As the aircraft stopped on the darkened airfield he was greeted by an unfamiliar official who disowned the letters he was carrying and informed him that the writer was not Head of the Church, he himself was that Head. Gently persuaded by an armed guard of some strength, the pacifist ex-President was escorted from the airport by this second Polish Methodist leader. He was an unwilling participant in a Methodist putsch.

'In journeys oft', to quote the Apostle Paul, was clearly part of the life of Soper from his presidential year onward and remains so. But the other side of St. Paul's experience was even more truly his – 'that which comes upon me daily, the care of the churches'. Every flip round the world had Kingsway as its last stop. Only those who have done business with him and discovered the time for the appointment to be 9 a.m. at his Kingsway office, and who, keeping the appointment, found that he was doing the Epilogue on the air the previous midnight, can credit his capacity to get in world touring and the care of the Mission.

The principle of delegation in the institutional life of the Mission had meant a great deal for the fulfilment of his national commitments – and his colleagues have had to bear some heavy loads. They have been known to grunt quite loudly, but the experience has in the long run produced a series of men who, having hived off into responsibilities of their own, have done extremely well in their own spheres – including the knack of devolving their work.

The development of the work at the Hinde Street Church is an example of this relationship. Beginning with the Rev. Ernest R. Richardson, who came home from the Trichinopoly District of South India after eight years there and then did six more with the Missionary Society before his appointment to what was then a weak church indeed, the colleagueship in the West London Mission created a new prospect. In hospital visitation, student

care and a ministry of the ever-open door the Hinde Street
Church began an upward lift in usefulness which went on after
Richardson's five year pastorate.

Richardson, described by Dr. Leslie Weatherhead as one of
London's saints, moved out and the Rev. B. Arthur Shaw succeeded him. He had no missionary experience but had served in
Her Majesty's Forces as a Commissioned Chaplain – which is
nearly as useful – and he came to Hinde Street from the north. It
is not always that one's man's work acts as base to another man's
effort. When it does, there is a tremendous uplift. This was the
case in this appointment.

Hinde Street was filling up with keen young people. He stuck to
the task for six years and once again the miracle happened, a true
successor as distinct from 'another man' came to the West London
Mission and to Hinde Street, the Rev. Arnold H. Cooper, B.A. His
advent made the third lift in the history of this fortunate church.
London University student breakfasts there now reached 200–300
people eating bacon and listening to guest speakers. Hospital,
prison and other duties were made to fit into the programme
somehow.

The student programme stretched out into the colleges round
London and points at which Holy Communion was celebrated
dotted the metropolitan map. The little flat on Thayer Street in
which the minister lived became a refuge for people in many sorts
of distress – girls adrift, ex-prisoners finding their way to a new life
or just hitching between sentences, overseas students both
Methodist and non-Methodist. Long ago it had been a 'horse and
carriage church'. Now it was a resort of overseas High Com-
missioners and their like. Lay leadership built up until there were
influential people in the various offices of the church of such
calibre that it would have been impossible to guess that the church
served the miscellany of people which it did. A conundrum might
have been constructed: When is a fashionable church a down-and-
out's refuge station? The answer – When it is Hinde Street
Methodist Church.

By 1959 the cause was so strong that it was divided from the
West London Mission and became a Methodist Circuit in itself
within the London North West District. But the same type of
protective mothering of a project which had to prove itself re-
curred in 1960 when the Notting Hill Team Ministry had its

beginning and the Rev. David M. Mason, B.A., S.T.M., moved to the staff of the West London Mission.

In the middle fifties the Rev. Geoffrey Ainger, B.D., was fired with the vision of trying new methods, in particular among the immigrant population in Britain, and had set his heart upon learning the technique of this work by a spell in the internationally famous Harlem Project in New York. This was by no means easy to arrange in those days but, with some encouragement in the right quarters, permission was finally given for this young minister – then with only nine years experience in the ministry – to have his wish. He experienced the 'shop front Church' and all the other excitements of Harlem for two years and came back with a deep certainty that he had found his *métier*.

This was only a fragment, however, of the problem. How was the idea to be realized? He dreamed of two or three men sharing one compact single appointment and this was, to say the least, highly irregular. Three men! Were there not many places who would covet one man? He prodded round, sought advice from the Mission House and anyone else who happened to be interested in multi-racial solutions. The area was sought and found in Notting Hill, where there was a Methodist church with a very poor response from the people around it, but with a community problem big enough to test any method. But the three men?

Long discussion, close collaboration between the Missionary Society and the West London Mission, and pressures on the Conference itself to permit the use of such a Team, finally brought the beginning as David Mason, Norwyn Denny – an old hand of the Jamaica District – came to the West London Team and were joined as soon as he was free by Geoffrey Ainger himself, Kingsway and the Missionary Society making some money available.

This outreach of the West London Mission, which could not have begun without its support, has proved itself in more fields than one in the years since. In liturgies, in music, in housing experiment, in house-group techniques, and in the gathering together of new people in worship, it has been one of the most pleasing activities in London. The Soper control of it has been consistently of the same general, benign, remote-control pattern as in so much that has been done by him. The day has come when the finance of the work and its management have earned an independent life and today the London Mission, Notting Hill Circuit, stands autonomous in the Methodist List of Stations.

In the years immediately following Dr. Soper's presidency, changes in social conditions in England and in particular in the life of the Churches began to press in on his consciousness. They raised problems for a man who in years of dramatic preaching and open-air evangelism had grown accustomed to hearing crowds posing questions as though the Christian Faith really mattered to them. He would pinpoint the beginning in the decline of mass congregations to the year 1956 and this date, for most churches and ministries, would perhaps be late. It was only such pulpits as Kingsway Hall, City Temple and Westminster Central Hall which could put it so late.

Dr. Edwin Sangster's great ministry at Westminster Central Hall ended in 1959 when he was taken out to lead the Home Missions Department of the Church. He was followed by a magnificent minister, the Rev. Derrick A. Greeves, M.A., but the day of great crowds there was over. Dr. Weatherhead left for retirement in 1960 and was followed by a most carefully chosen Canadian minister who combined all the traditions of the City Temple's life, but here, too, the mass support faltered. Soper alone of the great trinity was left soldiering on. His crowd, at least at worship time, also melted. It was a national phenomenon. Other central halls and great preaching places of other denominations shared the change.

The Church leaders puzzled about this – the great enigma. Why this fall off in congregations, at this time, in this way, and what was to be done about it?

Diagnoses have been legion. The easiest and particularly among older Christians the most common, is the simple cry, 'How are the mighty fallen!' The strain of orators has run out, they think. The people search for a prophet and find none. The 1950's Dr. Graham campaigns were undoubtedly a response of this type of diagnosis. Bring in the really great man and the tide would turn. The tide did not turn, there was simply a short-duration strong wind which piled the waters up at Harringay for the space of one tide.

Economic pressure has been used as explanation. It is now costly to journey to the city centre, and this is undoubtedly true, and relatively true in all the nation's cities in proportion to provincial standards and wages. It is also true that it is costly to get to a football stadium, yet they fill up, while the local clubs to which people need not travel far lack supporters.

National decadence has been adduced as an argument. The people have gone to the dogs and they don't want to know. Hosts of factors in our contemporary civilization which are not necessarily evidences of decadence are brought together to support this assessment. With an enormously expanded output of social service at home, and more than 3,000 volunteers overseas from among the nation's youth, doing service in developing nations; with old folks' clubs which visit the sick as thoroughly as ever did any vicar, and with the prodigious incomes of Oxfam, Christian Aid, Help for the Aged and the others, it is a trifle impertinent to dub the British nation decadent.

Others cry despondently, or angrily, that the Church has failed and lay the blame at the institution's door. They have not observed the success of suburban churches with intricate social and fellowship programmes and the rash of 200–300 seater churches which all the denominations have planted in the suburbs and the new-town areas, nor have they noticed the enormous charity output of the Churches, where, for example, the Methodist Church exports a million and a quarter sterling annually for church-support overseas; or the number of children in the care of the Anglican and Methodist Churches in their Church of England Children's Society and the National Children's Home. The years since 1956 have seen a magnificently engaged Church in Britain. There is little room for doubt that lesser numbers of committed churchmen have achieved a greater output of witness and service both in personnel and money than their Edwardian ancestors – and that in spite of the decline in the number of clergy and ministers. But people are not listening.

The Kingsway point of view, shared by many churches in the world, is that the times we have entered are not times for weeping, wailing and the gnashing of teeth. They are times for re-assessment. There is a new type of Western man and a new type of Western society to which to witness and minister. They are times of a multiplicity of gospels; they are times of extreme communication facilities, so that the business man is inundated with words twenty-four hours a day and is not too anxious to go somewhere to hear more. They are times of technical omni-competence ranging up to the potential of synthetic man himself. They are times when astronauts and cosmonauts have deluded very ordinary, baffled men and women into thinking that they, too, are pioneers of a new age. 'We fly to the moon – that debunks heaven.' Does it?

For his Order of Christian Witness members in 1960 Donald Soper wrote: 'What I do feel ought to be said after all these years (years of campaigning) is that it is the silliest of fallacies to think that those who are embedded in a secular civilization and quite outside the Church can easily be influenced towards Christian thinking, let alone brought to the feet of the Master. The acids of modern society have bitten so deeply into the traditionally Christian way of life that the task of witnessing to the saving grace of Jesus requires a thoroughness and a patience which those who ask "too much and ask it too soon" are unable to provide.

'We dare not any longer assume that the response of the lapsed churchgoers, or the half-Christianized children of religious parents, is in fact a response from the community as a whole. Generally speaking a genuine outsider is not susceptible to the invitation to come into an ecclesiastical building even if there is a semicircular bait attached to that invitation. It is only those who are already acquainted, however superficially, with the apparatus of the Church who can be brought inside through an O.C.W. campaign.'

A little earlier he had told the members of the Order that, 'Today as never before, the witness to Christianity must be set within the framework of (so-called) scientific criticisms, comparative religion, secular communism, and world violence' (*O.C.W. 1957 Year Book*).

A pattern has emerged of the lively suburban church with a very complicated fellowship programme, in which worship is one feature of the congregational life, but only one, and where on Sunday the attendance is wholly church people. This is in true alignment with the first of these quotations from Dr. Soper. On the other hand, the concept of witness has widened to include lay-witness in factory, college, hostel, shop and business house through the daily life of the Christian, and in particular within a context of joint social service with other non-Christian friends. This points to the mode in which the faith is now being propagated in Europe.

Many keen young Christians would think it quite absurd to expect their non-Christian colleagues and friends to line up in thousands specifically to be indoctrinated on the premises of the indoctrinator. But they would not hesitate to suggest a friend turned up at Tower Hill or Speakers' Corner and might even recommend that he listen to a session over the air in which Dr. Soper was a participant.

Approximately from the mid-fifties, therefore, the type of programme in operation in Kingsway Hall or in Westminster Central Hall has supplanted the mass congregation and the change is not the mark of failure. It is the mark of pioneering in a new generation. There are the canteen, restaurant, the numerous interest groups, the equally numerous committees, a programme of befriending, experimental worship-forms for Christian people and training in the inner meaning of the Faith. The Church has become what, years ago, George McLeod called 'Christian strongpoints': and they are strong points for Christians.

The evangel is to be presented in individual or group activity off the premises on the principle that it is best to fish in waters where fish breed. Consequently, if the great congregations thinned out from the mid-fifties, the witness of the open-air forum continued – it will last as long as men do discuss any subject in this way. The institutional programme of social aid has increased rather than decreased. It is the modern idiom for all who are idealists. Concomitantly Donald Soper has remained avid for secular openings wherever his personality has created them. 'Give me air' for him has meant, 'put me on the air': 'Give me significance' has meant 'plunge me into situations which make differences in communal living'. Very often, 'O for a trumpet voice' has been changed by him to 'Give me a chance to whisper in the proper ear'.

One of his ministerial critics has said, 'A Methodist minister's success is judged by the simple question, "Does he leave his church stronger than he found it?" Donald Soper inherited a full Hall and now has an empty one.' This criticism, if honestly made, is basically a misunderstanding of contemporary revolutionary history. He did not empty the Hall and one of the pulpit giants of the past, revived, would not fill it. The $64,000 question is, When the decline in mass congregations set in was the great preacher felled by it? Was he also an ephemeral phenomenon?

The change is not unlike the changes in military tactics between the First World War and the Second. There is a passage from the massed ranks of sheer numbers to a new independence of attack in which the platoon corporal becomes a thinking, free-moving person acting in association with his handful of completely known comrades. It is the difference between the Haig manipulated masses of whole regiments and the 'snatch squad' of today.

'Put me to what Thou wilt, rank me with whom Thou wilt.' So runs the historic Methodist Covenant prayer. It is a Christianizing formula fit for transmitting the gospel in our times. In 1958 there occurred an unusual example of 'ranking'. Following on the years of collaboration in the Mission's institutions with the government of London and the Borough in which the premises lay, as well as with national ministries who controlled grant-aid, not to mention with the Labour Party, so long controlling London, Donald Soper was made an Alderman of London County Council and then the Greater London Council.

In 1965 the Greater London Council controlled the life of 7,986,100 people. Its predecessor, the London County Council set up under the Act of 1888, to which he was first elected, controlled some four million lives. This latter Council with 124 County Councillors could appoint 20 Aldermen. When in 1963 The London Government Act became law there were the same number of Aldermen. Traffic, much housing, drainage, sewage, fire services, the ambulance service, parks, building regulations, licensing, both of entertainment and cabs, driving licences – these are just some of its duties. It is the principal body for the planning of London's growth. Twenty men at the heart of a 'commune' of nearly eight million might be said to be a key group. He threw himself into this work and his attendances and work in the main Committees of the Council won genuine praise from other Councillors. He left the Council only for another forum.

Overseas commitments, work on the radio and television, work in the London County Council and in the Press – all these were essential parts of the years between 1954 and 1965. But in fact, as from the beginning, the work at Kingsway was the broad base of the whole pyramid of service. The decline in hearing which we have noted had not in those years reduced the Sunday preaching to the degree to cause alarm. There were still large congregations at the Hall if not the milling crowds of earlier days.

Published sermons taken from tapes and edited into manuscripts are indeed dominantly from this period. *Keeping Festival*, a series on the Christian Festivals from Rogation-tide to Trinity Sunday, was published in 1954. *All His Grace*, a Lenten book, but reflecting sermons, belongs to 1957, and *It is Hard to Work for God*, a series of five sermons based upon Faber's hymn, also saw the light in that year. In 1963 *Aflame with Faith*, a series of fifteen sermons was published by the Epworth Press.

That sequence of published sermons, preserved by tape-recording but not originally intended for publication, when compared with the earlier 1938 volume published by Hodder and Stoughton, *Popular Fallacies about the Christian Faith*[1], allows a judgement to be made about the progression of thought wrought by the years and by changes in the community life.

The earlier work appears to assume that the people outside the Church want to have a religion explained to them and can be challenged to accept it. The tone, language and thinking all blend to urge men to take up their natural inheritance of the Faith. Much of the labour is an attempt to re-state the Faith cleared of its parodies, its misapprehensions, its myths.

In the later work the preacher has changed his opinion about his audience. Now he is speaking to folk who have the root of faith in them and with great care and much tenderness he gives them pastoral counsel, with skilful use of the world facts which surround their attempt to live out a Christian life. The Chinese Church was in the habit of building its chapels in two sections, one into which the crowd could wander, coming and going at will; and another, often lovelier, where the Christian folk worshipped and the pastors taught them. 'The "Outer" and "Inner" chapels.' There is much in the earlier sermons which, allowing for the English inbred folk-faith of a 'Christian country', belongs to the 'Outer Chapel'.

To quote from the 1938 volume, 'Fallacies about religion are popular in the first place as a result of the decay in the habits of public worship, and the accompanying decline in the study of Christian Theology. Theology is certainly not a popular intellectual exercise nowadays, and crowds of intelligent people are content to cull their views about spiritual matters from fifth-rate sources. It is surely dangerous to think that Hollywood or Fleet Street will give more than the sketchiest information as to the vital

[1] Re-issued as a Wyvern Book by the Epworth Press in 1957

truths of the Gospel, and yet they are all too often the only authorities quoted in discussion.

'What a well known political propagandist has to say about the
inspiration of the Bible may be interesting, but I should no more
think of accepting his verdict . . . than I would accept his diagnosis
of a sore throat as the correct one . . . in a word fallacies abound
because so few enquirers about religion consult its textbooks or sit
at the feet of its undoubted authorities.' (Wyvern edition,
pp. 9–10.)

This is good stuff if the audience consists of 'outsiders' who have
a deep-level deposit of vestigial Christianity and are prepared to
come into church or hall to hear an 'undoubted authority'. When
the 'outsider' will not do this, there is no longer need to say this, in
church.

The contrast caused by the passing years is reflected in the
following quotation from *Aflame with Faith* in a sermon on
'Men for a New Age: What does he think?'

'This is God's world through and through, and if there are other
planets, well, God is the Father and the Master, and the Lord is
there too. And God is the Lord of eternity, as well as of time, and
whatever men may do to us in this life, nothing can separate us
from His love.

'Jesus may speak with other tongues. Jesus may come clothed in
other habiliments. The truth may be presented in forms of which
we know nothing. But if this is a universe – one universe – it has a
central characteristic of life, and we should not fear wherever
truth may raise its head. It is the false we should fear.'

The product of this type of preaching is strong believers going
out, armed, into a world which, though alien to their ideas, is
loved by them for the sake of their Master. For the moment
churches exist to produce strong believers. Propagandising belongs
elsewhere. Why harangue the converted or empty pews? There are
other times and places, and Soper had the entry to both.

12.

Mirror to the Times

Dr. Soper's year of Presidency fell within the period of British
history dominated by Conservative Government, beginning in
1951 and continuing through the Administrations of Winston
Churchill, Anthony Eden, Harold Macmillan and Sir Alec
Douglas-Home – what Labour politicians were to dub, in 1964,
'the thirteen years of Tory misrule'. Had this not been so, the story
of his life might have been quite different. Now acknowledged
across the whole nation by friend and foe alike as one of the
commentators on the times to whom attention had to be paid,
backed now by the aura of leadership in his Church, he became a
mirror to the times through which the nation was to pass.

From 1954 onward little escaped his comment – on most things
people sought for it. Conservative historians have nominated the
second Churchill Administration from 1951–55 as the most successful peacetime ministry that the country had experienced since
the end of the First World War. The main ingredients of the
national life were ones familiar enough. There was an acute balance of payments situation; there was a Tory desire to reverse
large areas of nationalized planning instituted by their opponents;
there was the austerity budgeting; there was an electioneering
type of promise of houses galore; there was the change on world
markets which did in fact improve the British economic picture
enormously to such a degree that rationing was finally gone by
1955. Wartime purchasing devices were abandoned, while two
great thrusts at nationalized industries changed the steel and
transport situations. There was a generous slice of good luck in the
terms of trade overseas which would have benefited any government in power but it did mean more employment.

Abroad, the whole world's fate pivoted on the relationships between the new-born Soviet Union, the United States of America and the Western world for which the Aministration believed Britain to be the spokesman. America had assumed a posture of protection to all and sundry who were alleged to be in danger of communist pressure. In this field the rise of Chinese Communism within the Eastern world, challenging Russian Communism, added a new factor and a frightening one. British reactions to the Chinese situation did not run evenly with American and our interests in the Middle East also threw up differences of viewpoint. There was a basic Conservative hope – and belief – that the relations within the Commonwealth were a viable foundation for political world action. This the Americans did not believe and sometimes seemed to attack. They were very busy with Korea's war while Britain was making headway economically in India.

There was an American attempt to fill the vacuum left by the old British Empire – regarded, prematurely, by the Americans as dead – by a system of American guarantees which might have been tolerable to a Labour Administration but was not so to a Conservative Government. The outstanding first case was the offer to New Zealand where an arrangement was made which cut out the British Government. In Indo-China similar activities involving the struggling French nation sowed the seeds of the long horror story of the Vietnam sixties.

At home in Britain a rearmament programme joined the benign trade balance situation overseas to give Britain a good time. The Armed Forces rose from 800,000 to 1,500,000 with all that meant for industry. The Labour Party was passing through a period of inner tensions largely prompted by the knowledge that the people were enjoying the 'fleshpots' now theirs and consequently a planned economy programme was hardly good electioneering material. But where find another? Some said it lay in reconciliation to the long prospect of a 'mixed economy' and therefore the need was for a muted Socialism. Others of the Left demanded the complete adherence to the basic socialist dogma. Attlee, Bevin, Gaitskill, with Harold Wilson coming up, and George Brown in the mêlée, were immersed in such issues.

Eden came to power on Churchill's retirement in 1955 and those in the inner circles could smell the approach of a new Sterling crisis but were not too keen to tell the nation about it. There was an election Budget and the outcome was an election result with an overall Conservative majority now risen to sixty. The total poll fell to 76.8 per cent – from 82.6 per cent in 1951 and masses of Labour supporters appear to have lost themselves, voting neither way. The nation was comfortable, the victorious Party went in with 421,000 votes less than it had previously obtained but stronger than before!

The new administration moved on to the drama of Suez and the intervention there, by the circuitous route of a sharpening of inflation affecting trade and industry. Overseas the position of Sterling just could not be defended in spite of stringent measures at home. It was a situation which Gaitskill found he could assail with great effect. Budgets could deal with hire purchase and the other running sores in British life, but the drain on overseas finance continued.

Within the 'steady state' induced by the nuclear stalemate in terms of Russo-American rivalry, both these great nations turned, to many people's surprise, to the gentle pressures of economic aid used as a political inducement. Aid could be offered, adjusted, withdrawn, to satellites, or friendly nations, according to their performance. This became a principal weapon in the Cold War and, on the whole, perhaps the Russian leaders showed greater agility in using it. The Cold War spread to include the Afro-Asian nations and by the end of 1956 Russia was offering general aid in the Middle East. An attack on 'British Imperialism' in these quarters of the world paid better dividends than an assault on the U.S.A.

Out of these tensions arose the Suez crisis as Nasser rose to power and both America and the Soviet Union refused to leave the Middle Eastern Area as a British field for 'exploitation' – even Washington could breathe sentences on 'colonialism' now best forgotten. So in a world filled with armed action, in Korea, Hungary and Indo-China, British/French armed action in Suez was declared outrageous. Perhaps it was, but more for the reasons Dr. Soper marched to express than for those the diplomats quoted. Gaitskill tried to rush his fences in an appeal to the nation to unseat Anthony Eden, but this radio sortie did not achieve what ill health did and, to the embarrassment of the Party, Eden had to hand over to Macmillan.

So Britain arrived at the 'never had it so good' era when the general standard of living reached heights unknown in living memory.

The Macmillan Administration continued until 1963 when Douglas-Home took over for a brief period.

A skilled and cool politician, Macmillan did give the nation a continuance of the 'fair weather' government enjoyed under the Conservative party at the start of their thirteen years of rule. He kept the process of government as quiet and discreet as he could, the leave-it-to-me type of administration being natural to him. Two or three things stood out, 'the wind of change' speech connected with his African tour; the revision of the gambling laws which helped poor little parish churches to raise money – and opened some other doors for making money also; the creation of Life Peerages in 1958.

By 1963 we had the 'affluent society' but it was not very nice and there was a great deal of boredom around. Labour leaders were looking round for the 'working class' which appeared to have become 'middle-class, Mark II' and within the Unions to behave as arbitrarily as any group of gentry meeting in a Mayfair Club. If there was 'full employment', based upon careful job restriction, there was on the international scene the Russian missile to the left of the world's people and the American to the right. In fact the world was in prison, and the people hostages to power. The rations were good – in some places – and the others were far away.

In the autumn of 1955 Donald Soper journeyed off to New Zealand at the invitation of the New Zealand Methodist Church's Public Questions Committee and spent a very busy period in the great cities of that nation in the time when the swing in New Zealand policies from Britain to America was in discussion. He left this country in a storm. The *Sunday Dispatch* in July picked up a report that Dr. Soper was unwell and strongly criticized his programme for resting. He who had condemned the Duke of Edinburgh's polo programme on Sundays was to go into Cornwall, and indulge in surf-riding, with his bathing trunks under his Sunday clothes, and then was to go on a trip to New Zealand.

In the six months previous to this departure, Dr. Soper had run a series of articles in the *Tribune* stating his case for socialism being the political outworking of Christianity. Shortly before his departure, Lord Hailsham attacked this series of articles and confessed himself shocked. This he did in the *Spectator* and attempted a theological argument in response. A little later this feud still continued. Writing in the *Sunday Graphic* Lord Hailsham said, 'The rule of the crowd is reaching levels of insecurity; in the land of freedom, turning men out of their jobs, sending men to coventry are contemptible features of group action all out of proportion to the offences committed. What amazes me is that those church leaders who for ever are preaching socialism and inveighing against the capitalists and the despised Tories never come out boldly and say, "This is sin". No squeak is heard from churchmen, not even from Dr. Soper'.

Donald Soper was back in Britain by October of 1955 but his health was by no means restored and the autumn's work and controversies quite exhausted him. He was reported in the news as suffering from constant insomnia, though he found energy to take part in the discussion which had flaired up on the question of Disestablishment of the Church of England. He wrote in *Tribune* that the appointment of Church leaders should be on the basis of men selected by the Church itself. 'It is theologically impudent,' he said, 'that the Crown should ever appoint the spiritual leaders of the Church and it is preposterous that, with the virtual extinction of those royal powers, Church appointments should have fallen into the hands of the Prime Minister.'

In December one of the great current issues, the testing of the British atomic bomb, made news and he wrote to the newspapers protesting against the test, with the result that a widespread controversy sprawled through the headlines for some time. This was but the prelude to the enormous protests which were to follow on the establishment of the Campaign for Nuclear Disarmament (C.N.D.) which occurred in 1956 and with which Dr. Soper was closely associated throughout the most influential period of that Campaign's activities.

Minor issues buzzed round like flies, as is the case so often in the life of a famous or notorious person. His views on circuses, to which in January 1956 he decided no longer to take his children for their New Year treat; the guesses whether his family actually played tennis on Sundays or not; his comments on the death of Dr. Garbett, and their impact on Anglican–Free Church relationships, are examples of this endless pressure to which he never failed to respond.

So it came about that in January 1956 he was prevented by

illness from taking normal preaching appointments in the provinces and had to look forward to catching up with them in the spring. This did not prevent him from joining that year's President of the Conference in complimenting Princess Margaret on her decision to go on alone, unmarried to Captain Townsend. 'This is the action of a brave and good woman and will do much to raise esteem for the Royal Family among many people.'

In that springtime the team was set up by the Methodist Church to negotiate with the Anglican Church in Britain for terms of union between the two denominations and many folk noticed that Dr. Soper was not included in the team although he was, so it was said, 'a High Church Methodist' and would have been on that score a suitable negotiator.

It was in the early summer of that year that the Cross disappeared from the front of the Kingsway Central Hall and the Picasso Dove took its place, not without adverse comment. This Dr. Soper rebutted by saying that the Cross for many had become a meaningless symbol, whereas the Dove would be flying off from a nailprinted hand and so demand attention.

In the summer Harold Macmillan introduced the 'lotteries budget' and the Premium Bond was born, condemned by the Methodist Conference and described bitterly by Donald Soper. 'It is indefensible for any government to take gambling into its system; quite apart from my Christian opposition to all forms of gambling, I regard it as evidence of the bankruptcy of government policy.' The Archbishop of Canterbury in the House of Lords opposed this Bill and the Conference marshalled Methodist people to support him. The newspaper reactions were very vigorous but only extracted from the Government a series of statements of the type which suggested that 'it is only a little sin' and therefore defensible. They added some remarks about how ungrateful were the Churches which could under this system run little gambles to their own great and endless comfort.

Mighty forces in the contemporary world came to a sharp head at Portsmouth that year in the visit to that naval town of the Russian Naval Force which was entertained generously by the Lord Mayor and City. But in the midst of the jubilation Commander Crabbe disappeared. Where, how, why? Was he, enthusiastic aqua-lung fan that he was, acting alone in nosing round the ships in port? Was he an agent doing something under orders? There were a thousand guesses, none ever really confirmed as the truth. In his *Tribune* article Dr. Soper plunged into this whirlpool of speculation. 'Violence is the devil. It corrupts everything it touches.' His argument was unchanged. Allow for armaments being part of natural, civilized life, he asserted, and things like this crop up because they are integral to the system approved in an arms-industry society.

Back in health again by the August, and fit enough to lead his daughter to the altar to marry 'the boy from next door', he was plunged into the hectic storm over the Suez Crisis. There was a Labour Group deploring the act of aggression in the attack and pointing out that it was condemned under the United Nations Charter. There was widespread debate in which Dr. Soper declared himself to be appalled at the 'blatant idiocy' of the Government's attitude and equally disappointed at the woolliness of the Labour Party's opposition to the attack. Nor did he spare the Archbishop who had called for a day of special prayer that the will of God should be done. He asked the Archbishop of York to declare what the will of God was, rather than speak vaguely of something it might not be diplomatic to speak of plainly, before praying. A meeting in the Caxton Hall booed Anthony Eden and there were 500 marchers.

The *Spectator* in particular was enraged by the opposition to the Government's action. In August that periodical said: 'We have the fact of the continued existence in this country of a group of people who are deeply and intensely suspicious of any positive action of Britain overseas. They include pacifists, communists, liberals as well as socialists. A sample member of this group, and a sample in a state of chemical purity, is Donald Soper. He said in London this week he was appalled at the "blatant idiocy" of the Government's action.'

Whatever the state of Donald Soper's chemical purity, the resistance mounted rather than faded. On a Sunday in September there was a rally of 5,000 people in Trafalgar Square to hear six Labour Members of Parliament. Kingsway's congregation contributed 500, who marched after church from Holborn to the Square, led by Donald Soper and a banner shouting 'Stop gunboat diplomacy'. Another march, a thousand strong, followed later in the autumn.

Nor was all peace within the confines of the Methodist Church which had shared that summer in the meeting of the World Methodist Council at Junaluska, U.S.A. The Message to the World of this Conference appeared in the autumn, long, dignified and portentous. ' "What a performance!" as the immortal Sid Field would have said,' declared Dr. Soper in the *Methodist Recorder*. 'What a spiritual minnow this ecclesiastical meeting brought forth. It seems to me quite shocking that we should be saddled once more with such a mixture of platitude and escapism masquerading as a Message. It all has the tepid familiarity of a Tuesday rissole.' Dr. Benson Perkins, British 'father' of this Confessional Body, did not like this one bit and descended in fury on Soper in the *Methodist Recorder*'s columns. Good clean fun! Perhaps it was, but it was also the joining of battle between ecumenicity and denominational power within the Church which is not quite so funny.

At this time the *British Weekly* ran a series of Kingsway sermons under the title of 'The Pulpit of Kingsway'. The Mission bought the Langham Hotel in Worthing for a people's holiday home and on the occasion of one of Dr. Soper's televison appearances it was arranged that he should conduct the service in the Independent Television studio while a screen in his own pulpit should give his own congregation their share in the televised service. Then, in the height of summer, he dashed out to Japan at the call of the Japan Christian Council to head a national campaign in Tokyo.

In 1958 he was a member of the Campaign for Nuclear Disarmament committee and in March the famous trek to Aldermaston nuclear centre took place with Dr. Soper leading the march on its second stage with banner flying – in the rain. In June and July of 1958 he was marching again, though now Alderman of London County Council, and took part in the formal laying of a pacifist wreath on the Cenotaph in Whitehall. He shared in a mass lobbying of Parliament by the Movement. When on one occasion the party was not allowed to enter the 'security' precincts of Aldermaston, they sat, foodless and wet, outside the gates and he expressed his gratitude to the guard for allowing this.

At this time the nation's attention was drawn to the possibility of artificial insemination of childless women both by donor and by physically handicapped husbands. The papers were full of the discussion and the Methodist Conference voted against the principle of artificial insemination (donor), with Dr. Soper speaking and voting against the resolution. A similar topic arose in the publication of the Wolfenden Report on homosexuality and prostitution, released in the autumn of 1957 but catching public interest in 1958.

The *Sunday Pictorial* picked up a story of Dr. Soper talking with a girl who had recently arrived on London streets and entered the ranks of prostitutes with the intention of making £4,000 and then retiring from the business. He told this 20-year-old that, after thirty years in the London world and talking with many of the women, he had never known a single person to keep a promise to leave the profession. 'I tell you that if you save that amount you will be in no condition to enjoy it.'

One of the television programmes of this period took the cameras to the open air in a programme called 'Soap Box Sunday'. Later, in a closed studio effort of similar type, he complained that the audience's questions were too remote and contrived when compared with his open air freedom. In the summer he was involved with a leading Jamaican citizen in an enormous Trafalgar Square Rally on international friendship.

In 1959, Pope John XXIII, having succeeded Pope Pius XII, called the Vatican Council and raised a thousand hopes of ecumenical change by his ready and charming reception of his 'separated brethren'. It seemed to Dr. Soper that the magnificent hopes raised by Pope John's humanity would match the great service which Pope Pius had given in the cause of world peace. His mind was more on the problem of peace than ecclesiastical affairs and the subject came up everywhere in his miscellaneous work; in 'Sunday Break', the television youth programme, which set him real problems; in the Methodist Conference sessions; in the March 1959 Aldermaston march, said to be the greatest protest of this century, when 4,300 people took part. There was nothing which appeared peaceful, however, when on May Day Frank Cousins and a Labour platform had their crowd in opposition to Dr. Soper's regular one!

In the midst of all this political and social turmoil, the *Woman's Mirror* took up the question of women being admitted to the ministry of the Church and asked Dr. Soper to contribute to the discussion. The result was a foretaste of what subsequent Conferences of the Methodist Church have had to accept as the result of enquiry and debate.

Dr. Soper said, 'We ordain women as Deaconesses and they have the same status as men. That God can work only through the ministry of men is a preposterous idea. If women are similarly qualified they should have the same status in the Church as men. I think women should not want to do exactly the same work as men. On the whole I imagine they would be better at pastoral work'. There was, perhaps, a fallacy here which left the door open to the argument that a woman would never be a superintendent minister in Methodism, still less a bishop in the Established Church. Had not his case a vulnerable heel? It has turned out that the Methodist Conference had sound shoes to cover that heel. Surely, with a Queen on the throne, it had to happen!

In August 1959, two men who hold crowds faced one another with exciting results when in Ballymena, Northern Ireland, Dr. Soper, speaking in the open air, fell foul of Ian Paisley. Things warmed up, a woman in the crowd was hit by a Bible someone aimed at Soper, the meeting was one long barrage of heckling and leaflets were handed out to the crowd accusing Dr. Soper of blasphemy. The indignant 'main line' churchmen of Ireland forthwith issued summonses against Mr. Paisley and two of his 'ministers'. The whole of August was taken up in the *Belfast Telegraph* with letters and comments on this foray.

The autumn brought an election which Harold Macmillan won with a tidy majority of 100 seats. Dr. Soper's politics were much discussed during this election period and his claims that Christianity and socialism went together were greatly resented by Conservative Parliamentary candidates. They complained in particular about his assumption that a 'free for all' type of political philosophy must mean that those who held such views could not love the common people. The notable illustrated magazine of the times was *Picture Post*, now gone, and in this welter of political discussion it featured an article in which Middleton Murray and Dr. Soper discussed their life views and in detail their views of pacifism. Early in the new year a wave of anti-Semitism sprang up in Britain and especially in London. This kept Soper busy in the open air and in the Press.

Not before time, the West London Mission authorities turned their attention to Kingsway Hall and gave the premises a new look with a new foyer and, within the Hall, new seating. Dr. Soper seemed to have celebrated this event with a 'go' at the Beatles, then in their ascendancy. To him they stood for a false trail which people could easily follow into wrong values and social disruption.

The miscellaneous character of the several interests which make up the record of Dr. Soper's public commentary during these years towards the end of the Conservative administration are a true reflection of the age through which the nation was passing. A similar stream of minor events become major ones has come down to us and is part of our own national discussions today. They are as the froth on the top of a glass of beer.

By the dawn of the sixties a quiet social revolution had worked itself through the nation to make a situation which brought the number of white-collar workers in the country nearly into balance with its industrial workers. Macmillan was broadly right in saying the people had never had it so good. The problem lay not in getting a better personal deal but in the abiding fact that a goal achieved only serves to open up new demands. A further problem then appears if there are not any big goals evident on the horizon. Where do we go from here? If there appears to be nowhere to go, the people tread water with a great splashing but no real joy. It was said that in 1960 the working family in Britain enjoyed a standard of living so luxurious as to be unprecedented in modern history. It served to create demands for more, through hire purchase, wage demands and the race to get well ahead of the local Jones's.

Macmillan as skipper of the nation's vessel was the all-time expert at the simple chart-room exercise of 'keep her as she goes'. The deft adjustment of mixed economy measures took the place of a policy on the Conservative side, but it also eroded in the minds of Labour supporters the idealist dreams of the benefits to be gained by Socialism. It was an extraordinary situation in which each Party weakened the other and the instrument used to do so was 'the good time'.

In the upshot the big bad wolf of the Western world's economic pattern began to bite. Inflation gripped and began to reduce the value of the good time. Those feeling the pinch now were not the Union members, still less the men at the top labelled 'Captains of Industry'. They both had means to hand for countering the first onslaughts of inflation. The new poor were clerks, non-union white-collar people, civil servants and the bungalow dwellers of the perimeter of London. The trend was evident when Orpington fell to the Liberal Party, a 1959 Conservative majority of 14,760 being turned into a Liberal majority of 7,855. The well-heeled were bored; the suburbanites were cross. Modern man is baffled when it is the affluent times which are out of joint. No Western nation has yet produced an answer to this problem.

It is natural that the 'stick-a-patch-on' type of government of which the nation was wearying was no government to please Donald Soper, though he knew that the exploitations of planned society were true to a large degree. As marked an opportunist as ever breathed, Soper did not believe in opportunism in government, he believed in planning.

In 1958, writing in *Tribune* he had said: 'I did not join the Labour Movement to sing "the Red Flag" and join a campaign to turn a pundit's capitalism into a people's capitalism. I joined because I was theologically and experimentally convinced that there were only two possible forms of society that are even conceivable in a modern world, one a Marxian Socialism the other a Christian, or if you prefer it, a democratic socialism'. His problem lay here as the nation turned towards an election. It had been a critic's free-for-all during the decade past for anyone with Left tendencies. But now, as the day dawned for something different, the tendency to continue to play the same tricks was manifest in the Labour Party itself and, should that Party win the election, the new problem arose of criticizing one's own Party – which is occasion for new techniques. Not that he was unfamiliar with this; he had vigorously attacked his own Party in the London County Council over the matter of Civil Defence.

There was little doubt that his kind of socialism would not win the election and Labour leaders most likely to come through to the top of the administration, should the Party form one, knew this as clearly as he. Total planning; total disarmament; total dedication to a new order – these were just 'not on' with the nation's mood as it was. In 1964 there was a moment when the election nearly came in the early summer. It was postponed, and he spoke of Party consolidation for the autumn struggle.

His political remarks grew tougher. Asked why he could not accept the Conservative position he said that Conservatism ran on the crude oil of selfishness. It was the life of the jungle. It was worse than that, because animals only killed when they were hungry. This did not mean, he explained, that Conservatives did not go to heaven, but it would be a circuitous route and it would take rather longer to get there. Unfortunately, should the Labour Party win, it would have to venture into the jungle and do its best.

In June 1964 he got away from the British problem by visiting the Holy Land. But there really is no holiday for those whose eyes have been trained to see people and their problems and the Holy Land served only to show him the deep mess into which that country had sunk. He came back to take his part in a debate which that summer rocked the Methodist Conference as one of its ministers sadly left the Church over his beliefs and the news media picked up the story.

October came and on the 15th the great political event took place. In the election the Labour Party polled 44.1 per cent of the votes cast, Conservatives 43.4 per cent, Liberals 9.0 per cent. The seats in the House turned out to be Labour 317, Conservatives 303, with Liberals taking nine. The turnover in opinion was a swing to Labour of 3.2 per cent, not a famous victory. It was as though a fat man had flopped into a Turkish bath and probably the reasons were the same as his. The minute majority had not a hope of producing the revolution which alone would suit Dr. Soper, but his Party was in. It needed all the support it could get and the narrowness of a majority is a very useful instrument for closing gaps in ranks.

Harold Wilson, Prime Minister after all, proved swiftly that the tiny hold he had on power did not cripple him and the Members put in a very hard winter maintaining the voting power. Concessions to the Liberal 9 were essential, but it transpired that the job could be done. There was, however, 'the other place', drenched in Tory presence. Some improvements could be made there without tinkering with the voting membership of the Lower House.

Through all those years of increasing publicity for Dr. Soper, the Press ever and again switched its attention from him to his own 'outreach' through his young folk. His persistent aggression, albeit pacifist aggression, is matched as the years rolled by in the campaigning of the Order of Christian Witness. Year by year their touring took in at least two places in the year, often more, and usually he was with them for the campaign or for part of it.

The usual pattern of reporting is of things he has said coupled with astonished description of the way his Order's members lived. Back in 1957, in Cornwall or in the Rhondda, they were in tiny chapels. Then they turned up in a busy 'growth-area' like Bletchley. In Yarmouth they found new problems, having the year before taken a stab at Manchester. 1960 shows three campaigns – in the Doncaster coalfield, Liverpool and Birmingham. Their casual life, sleeping on chapel floors, their deep belief in the Kingdom of God, interpreted in concrete social terms suited to the times – all were an authentic part of the whole movement of Soper's ministry and the Church's contribution to the national debate.

It would be very difficult to find a comparable group of people moving through the country speaking with one voice and one message over so many years. Their socio-evangelism made them relevant to the issues of the day and this went on throughout the sixties. Their leader's message, that good government is a matter of morals and not expediency, and that the morals are needed among the governed equally with the governing, was their message and his rising reputation among the people owed something at least to their faithful following. There are those who would boast they created Soper; the degree to which the youngsters put him on the map is, perhaps, more easily documented.

Just a decade after laying down the Presidency of his Church, in January 1964, that office caught up with him again and gave to him a permanent place in the history of Central Africa. The Annual Report of the Methodist Missionary Society for 1964 reads: 'Less than three months after Zambia's political independence, the 27 ministers, 18 lay missionaries and 2,404 members of the (Methodist) District's 11 circuits became part of the new United Church of Zambia. This union with the United Church of Central Africa in Rhodesia (itself a merger of Congregational and Presbyterian churches) and the Church of Barotseland (founded by the Paris Missionary Society) is the natural outcome of a long period of growing fellowship and co-operation between the three Churches.'

The deep reason for the union is the subject of the next paragraph. 'The speed with which the union negotiations were carried through bears witness to a conviction that, in a new country, where the existence of many tribal groups scattered over a vast area makes it difficult to achieve national unity, Christians must, as far as possible, speak with one voice if they are to be heard at all.'

It was essential that some noted leader of the Western Churches from which the Zambian Churches derived should be present and preside over the solemn acts of unity and with one voice the presence of Dr. Soper was requested. Not without difficulty and sacrificing some other engagements, he made a flying visit to preside over the inauguration. Responsible officers of the four missionary Churches were present to do the chores of the business. His was the privilege of giving the older Churches' blessing to the new beginning.

The occasion was a national event, Dr. Kenneth Kaunda being a member of one of the uniting bodies. A lunch at his home afforded an opportunity for long discussions of Zambia's future. The great inaugural service took place at the All-Africa Church Conference Centre at Mindolo – a place of lovely tree-studded lawns. At the service Dr. Kaunda himself spoke of the nation's future and the Church's ministry of unifying people of many tribes and traditions.

There was a football-ground Sunday rally held with great gusto and Thanksgiving services followed in the great centres such as Lusaka. Here again Dr. Kaunda was present and warned the minister in charge of the meeting that he had a Cabinet Meeting to attend which would make him leave early. Sitting in the front seat with his family and friends, the President was quietly guarded by a Zambian army major sitting on a side seat. As the time for the Cabinet meeting drew near this officer went and whispered in Dr. Kaunda's ear. Dr. Soper was in full spate at this time, having been introduced by an old British colonial service official who had once administered the territory. Dr. Kaunda waved his aide away and settled down to hear the end. The Cabinet could wait.

In the lecture programme attended by large numbers of European people in Lusaka, many of whom were not at all fellow-travellers of his, Donald Soper made a speech on the Christian contribution to nation building which pulled not a punch. It was quite fascinating to see opposition melt into sheer interest.

It was a strenuous business, phenomenal distances to travel across the sparsely populated country, endless queues of friendly people in the towns. He was not sleeping well and in pain with his old leg trouble. When, however, some of the staff members felt that one who had given his life to civilization in a place like London really could not return home without seeing Christianity at work among a prehistoric people just emerging from the Stone Age, he cramped his weary leg into a car and took the hundreds of miles return journey down into the Zambesi Valley, well below sea level and stifling hot, to the Kanchindu Circuit where this new work was being done. He returned grey with fatigue and spent a sleepless night, but said that his grasp on life would be deeper ever after because of what he had seen. The Mission House officer who persuaded him to make this Zambian journey was one of his own boys, Harry Morton. Generation speaks to generation.

13.

Peer of the Realm

Reform of the House of Lords has been an item of agenda in British politics for many years, and still is. The Conservative Administration's Life Peerages Act of 1958 was one, generally accepted, step in the direction of modernizing this Second Chamber. It was not surprising that the Labour Administration coming into power in 1964 should turn its attention to the opening this Act presented to it for strengthening their weak forces in the House of Lords, nor is there any great evidence that the Conservative Peers of the time made any demur about this move. They are a very level-headed body of legislators.

So it came about that in 1965 there were created twenty new Life Peers some of whom, with their forerunners of the earlier List, were humourously known as 'Wilson's Marauders'. Among their number, in May 1965, was created The Reverend the Baron Soper of Kingsway and a new, consummating phase in the life of Donald Soper began. He is careful to point out that he ranks among the Lords Temporal, not among the Lords Spiritual – which body has still to be modernized to include a conspectus of the religious denominations and interests of the whole nation. He frequently says, 'I am a lay Lord'. Nevertheless, his contributions to debate have a distinctly theological, moral and ecclesiastical ring to them, as though he were indeed the modernizing element in the spiritual field to which the nation still looks forward.

His creation as a Baron – such being the status of Life Peers – was a cause of great surprise, and some humour, in the Methodist Church's inner circles. It was also a matter of some criticism among people who followed his work in other sectors of the nation's life. The preliminaries to elevation are the subject of the deepest secrecy. It is almost impossible to take advice from anyone, should a nominee wish to do so, and the decision has therefore to be taken largely as a personal responsibility.

There is a story that a whisper was going the rounds of the Pressman world before the List was issued and that one enterprising journalist with great experience rang him up to ask whether if he were nominated to be President of a North Lancashire Cricket Club he would be pleased or uninterested, to which Dr. Soper replied that in such circumstances he would try to do the job as best he could. But then, these stories do get round and furnish the material for the contemporary apocrypha.

He has been repeatedly asked why, as a socialist and critic of the administration of the nation, he accepted the Peerage. His reply is usually the same, when the question is honestly asked, the latest reply being given in December 1970 on the B.B.C. radio programme 'It's Your Line' in which some well-known figure answers the telephone calls from questioners over the air.

The House of Lords is basically a Christian Forum – its place in the structure of British Government is within the context of our religion, even if some members of the House are not Christians. (This in itself is another matter of debate within the British constitutional field.) The non-established Church within the Realm needs representation. It is a very efficient organism, and in the reply given on this particular occasion he instanced how, on the subject of alcoholism, he had cleared up in minutes, with a statement in the debate in the Lords, what might have taken six years through any other channel.

The subject of his peerage remains one which can cause all kinds of comment and will do, so long as he is in the public eye and his own Church's councils. Barons in the long story of Britain have a chequered history. They muzzled kings, as in Magna Carta; they also muzzled many of the common peasantry of England. They fought for liberty, but it was mostly for their own liberty with the people's liberty as an appendage. There is not a large list of socialist among them!

In Church life, was the Church to remember the 'Lord' and forget the 'Rev.' or ignore the 'Lord' and stick to the 'Rev.'? Either device seemed to have theological overtones. In the long run the Church was asked to leave it as 'The Rev. the Lord Soper' and so it is – which is a long way from the Sangster nickname for the young man of Kingsway, 'Donald Duck'.

It is a splendid place, the House of Lords Chamber. It is intimate, the members being eyeball to eyeball in the debates, yet its glory of red and gold, its dominating Throne, combine to give weight to anything said there. Its members sit in an entirely different atmosphere from that of the Commons. As A. P. Herbert noted in his poem 'Big Ben', this is the place where people speak because they have something to say and not because hordes of electors are thumbing through Hansard to see if their elected Member has been present and vocal in the Chamber. To be there and to speak there by sheer environmental pressure could lift the barrow-boy into the aristocracy in the true sense of that term. It did not need to lift Lord Soper; he was born to fit into just such a council. The Lower House, people might say, would have brought out the worst in him; the Lords brought out the best.

To demonstrate this it is only necessary to go into a public library and browse through Hansard's record of the transactions in the House of Lords. This is a thing which many who covet the power to speak and influence people should do in any case, Soper or no Soper. It is quite impossible to find a higher standard of debate or a higher standard of research-perfected information deployed to illuminate an issue than occurs regularly in the Lords. There is no 'catch-as-catch-can' speechifying here. If a peer wants to speak he will find opportunity to do so, put down his name, and it is done. Points of view may be outrageous, boring, infuriating, but within their category they will be well done.

There is no section of Lord Soper's life which is less known than his participation in the life of the Lords. Within his Church his peerage is accepted as part of the ecclesiastical drapery of Methodism. On Tower Hill and at Speakers' Corner many try to forget it and in any case are interested more in the other sides of his nature. That his contribution to the House is considerable and in its way unique is a fact which is obscured.

He sits with the Labour phalanx of peers and votes with them, now in opposition, but his is not a day-by-day 'Not content' vote. He chooses the issues for which he attends and on which he speaks and they are usually matters of moral judgement or of social reform about which he would be speaking in other places. Occasionally he takes part in a debate which affects the religious life of the country, which in terms of the Lords means the life of the Church of England. Now and again he will suddenly do a little 'marauding' when something crops up which savours of the old pre-history of the British Constitution and the Chamber's place in it.

There is a fascinating change in sheer style in his early speeches in the Chamber, with its own conventions of speech dating back through many centuries and far removed from the Tower Hill Soper vernacular or the roving-mike technique of his Kingsway pulpit. Clearly, he learned this before he ventured to rise in the House and it is marked in the early efforts – it tends to rub off as he has grown to be part of the place. The smooth, courteous and time-honoured phrases, cosseting the Noble Lords, ring strangely and a member of the Order of Christian Witness might be forgiven if he were to wonder 'Is this our Donald?'

He wasted no time. His daily work and the responsibilities of the West London Mission were often the sources from which he drew lessons and examples to shed light on debates in the House. In July 1965, when the House was discussing Community Care, he instanced work being done in Notting Hill to make the point that care is a whole-life issue which cannot be broken down into ameliorative actions applied in isolation from the total social setting. 'Community Care,' he said, 'is not a bad description of the characteristic qualities of the kingdom of Heaven. Quite the most Christian thing that has happened in my lifetime is the Welfare State.'

In October 1965, by now well settled in, when the House debated the Sexual Offences Bill, he put down his name to speak. None could deny that this new Baron had the right to put the views of the non-Anglican Christian community and those of his Church. This is what he did. He told the Noble Lords that so far nothing had been heard of the non-conformist conscience and he wondered whether their Lordships assumed that this famous thing had gone into liquidation. He offered the views of the Free Churches, giving as example the debate of 1958 within the Methodist Conference, evidence that the Churches were thinking of this matter earlier than the House. He paired the opinion of the Methodist Church with that of the Congregational Church, where both agreed that homosexual problems were proper matters not for penal sanctions but for special caring.

'Your Lordships will forgive me if some things suggest to me that noble lords walk with nonchalant ease in the realms of moral theology as if this particular area of human enquiry were part of the light that lightens every man coming into the world. In my judgement it is not so.

'Having among my friends many homosexuals, I know that they are in error and un-natural. I cannot comprehend their motives nor enter into the psychological reactions that are theirs. But I am convinced that within the light of what seems to them to be the world in which they have found themselves . . . it would be totally wrong to think it a heathen world and they evil.'

It is of the genius of the Lords that each member brings with him a life experience which contributes to the communal wisdom of the Chamber and there are plenty of examples of analysis in Lord Soper's work possible only to deep Christian pastoral experience. In the same debate, for instance, when the discussion veered round to alcoholism, he is recorded as saying, 'Alcoholism is a disease. This is a clinically distinct episode in the kind of society in which we live. It is not untrue to say that it is proper to the modern society in the same way as drunkenness was to societies which have gone before it.' This comment, raising the whole problem of the effects of affluence, is effective because it is an historically informed comment by one whose judgement on wide issues is based on Christian practice and theory. It was made palatable to their Lordships by the side remark, 'I am certainly not going to give a lecture on total abstinence, or the devil in solution.'

In a further debate on alcoholism, which he initiated, the question of adequate facilities for helping those with this trouble was raised by his four questions to the Administration. What were the figures for the incidence of alcoholism in this country? What were comparative figures for Europe and the U.S.A.? What facilities in fact exist for treatment? What are the plans for their extension? In the course of the discussion he argued from work in the West London Mission's own Alcoholic Information Centre. The debate filled a whole Tuesday session of the House.

He spoke more than once as the Rhodesian Independence affair wound its weary way through the House, always pressing the pacifist point of view and commending the refusal of the Government to use force, because it was a killing cure. 'If the only bottle by the bedside of the patient contains strychnine or arsenic, it is better to leave the patient alone than to fill him with strychnine or arsenic.'

He deployed information gained for him by people on the ground in the Rhodesian world and backed by this his gorge rose at the complacent talk of 'kith and kin' who were perhaps to be denied their pensions. He referred to the 'kith and kin' concept as 'impertinent' and reminding the House of the six hundred people who were 'inelegantly called "restrictees"' said that some also regarded these as kinsfolk.

Some of his encounters with the Bishops, Lords Spiritual, were happier than others. One of the happier was in the discussion on the 'Prayer Book: Versions of the Bible' Measure. His first delivery came straight down the wicket; 'This is not my business, nor yours either,' he told the House, making plain his resentment of the constitutional position of the Church on its liturgy. He went on, however, 'I as a Methodist must look at the Prayer Book very much as the pious look at the harp; though not much involved with it at the moment they hope to be much more involved with it later on.'

Things were not so friendly when in 1966 the long debates on the Abortion Bill began and he found himself opposed to the Bishop of Exeter.

'I have no particular pleasure in opposing my noble and ecclesiastical friend. But I would gently break a lance with the reverend prelate when he uses a phrase like "the unborn child's right to live." If you wrote down that and studied it with some care, I think you would find it semantic nonsense. No unborn child has any right to live at all. Furthermore it seems to me there has been a fallacious and almost ridiculous attitude to compare the value of a foetus within the womb and a fully-grown person. We who talk so much about the sanctity of the foetal life are, I think, under the strong condemnation of being prodigal in our attitudes – the way in which we are prepared to see adults live and squandered in warfare over the years, I do not think we stand on very sound ground when we make such an extravagant case for the eternal rights of what medically, it seems to me, cannot be regarded in a preformative sense but must be genetical.

'You will allow me to reinforce what I say from practical experience which some of you may not have had the opportunity of sharing. I am at this moment responsible for fourteen pregnant girls in a house. I am quite sure, from a careful analysis of their condition and what approximately their conditions are likely to be, that it would have been a very good thing if this Measure had been on the Statute Book. I believe that at least four of these girls will be permanently impaired, spiritually and psychologically, by the trauma of child-bearing particularly at an early age. I am also responsible for a hostel in which we receive and care for delinquent girls. I am perfectly certain that in your Lordships' House you will not doubt or treat as trivial or frivolous this comment; that anybody who has had any protracted experience with the psychological conditions of girls who pass through the experience of childbirth under squalid and dirty conditions, knows that they themselves in some way contributed to these squalid conditions.'

He was engaged in the work on this important and controversial Bill clause by clause as it came through the House and always insisted upon the wider humanities of the whole life of grown people being paramount. From time to time the debate became bogged down in the argument about the whole concept of abortion being an affront to Christian principles and the Bill therefore an added affront to this principle of the sacredness of life.

He was at pains to state that, in his view, the doctrine on which this principle was stated was in itself in confusion within the Churches and that, once any abortion had been permitted anywhere, the question left the realms of principle and became one of adjustment of practice. He felt it to be evident that within the world of Christian theology no new doctrine of birth had been worked through since man's knowledge of genetics, and the sheer fact of being born, had attained its modern shape.

He saw that the old doctrine of the male spark of life being entrusted to the mother, as though she were a mere receptacle for an already living something, was a cause from which much cruelty could stem. For him the unborn child was an unborn person-in-the-making; the mother a person in being. Some of his words are in answer to the prophecy that, the door being opened, abuses of the law would follow – as has been the case. To this Lord Soper then answered that it is impossible to hold back from doing what is just merely because that justice will be exploited by some.

No one acquainted with Lord Soper would expect him to be

silent when the Defence Estimates came before their Lordships, but few would guess into what close conflict with the military heirarchy the debate would bring him on one occasion.

He complained about some of the statements made by some who supported the Estimates. 'I have jotted down many of the statements which have been made more or less dogmatically by some of those supporting the Estimates. One was by the noble and gallant Viscount Lord Montgomery of Alamein. He was reported to have said, "We have fought all our wars on other people's territories." If there are any Cavaliers and Roundheads who are still in their graves, I am sure they will rebut that charge. I know that very many splendid people in the church where I work will feel strongly that the last war was definitely fought on their territory and that the "blitz" caused the destruction of their own homes.

'When it is said as an accusation against the Government that they intend more butter and very few guns, what in the name of God is wrong with that? That would seem to me a very admirable intention for any government which invites the people of any country to support it.

'What is the average man likely to think when we seem so concerned about the preservation until 1975 of an aircraft and a further provision that the aircraft carrier will still be viable in the year 2000? Is he not likely to say that anybody who engages in this kind of debate would better serve in devoting his time to trying to bring about the time when there will be no need for any aircraft carriers in 1975, let alone 2000? And might he not think that if we are in possession of these weapons for very much longer, according to my noble friend, Lord Snow, the probability of their accidental use with catastrophic results is almost as great as their intentional use?

'The debate is concerned with the possibility that we shall have to deal with Russian submarines. I do not think that one could convince anybody outside this House that if we had to deal with Russian submarines there would be any eventuality from this excursion into madness but the total destruction not only of our life in these islands but very largely of the life that goes on in this world as we know it today.

'I make no secret of it and I make no apology particularly in a country which is supposed to be Christian, for the fact that I am a pacifist. I shall not argue the pacifist case but I shall be untrue to myself if I did not witness to it or testify to it and I propose to do just that, I have no right to expect from the Episcopal Bench a chorus of "Alleluias" as I make this point, but I might perhaps wish for an occasional "Amen" which has not been forthcoming. I would have been happy to remind myself and I would have been happy to remind my episcopal brethren, that the immortal Dr. Temple said that the pacifist position is a reasonable one and an inference from the Gospel that is justifiable. I believe it to be true. I believe the whole apparatus of violence to be morally wrong and I am further convinced that it is totally wrong.

'May I invite your Lordships to do a simple exercise? What is the difference between putting a baby on the fire and putting the fire on the baby? Surely the answer is the anonymity of 25,000 feet? If the airman were compelled to see the effect of his napalm bomb on a child, I do not believe he would find cause to put the child on the fire or put the fire on the child. Ecclesiastically and morally I believe that in many cases, and in particular in the case of modern war and modern defence, the cure is morally worse than the disease.'

This impassioned speech in defence of pacifism, delivered in the nation's highest council, was interrupted by a noble lord with precisely the question which had dogged Lord Soper during the famous period after his Conference speech and to the interrupter he gave the same answer; that he could not use violence to repel an invader under any circumstances.

He ended his statement by saying that he believed that in a Christian country it was relevant in the councils of the nation that the pacifist position should be put. He reiterated his constant declaration. 'I believe that what is morally wrong, and I believe that war under any conditions is morally wrong, can never be politically right.' In practical terms he urged that the statement by Lord Gladwyn was the adequate answer. Diplomacy is the proper instrument of policy and not violence.

'Furthermore, I present to your Lordships what is to me an incontrovertible case, that the true answer to these people who now opt for Communism is that, if you and I were in similar economic conditions to those in which they find themselves East of Suez or South of Suez, we too would opt for Communism. Therefore instead of putting our resources into violent expenditure on weapons, which will become out of date before they are obsolete, how much better would be a plan to feed, cloth and nourish those whose only reason for turning to violence and totalitarianism and Communism is that in many respects they have no option.'

Throughout the autumn of 1966 the nation was in the turmoil of the debate about the Rhodesian negotiations. The Churches, and especially those with interests in the Churches of Central Africa, were deeply involved and under great pressure from those who were more concerned for the British section of the public in Rhodesia. All kinds of methods were brought into service to make the African case within Rhodesia known to the public and, after the meeting of the British Council of Churches at Aberdeen in which the Council supported the reinforcement of Her Majesty's Forces in Rhodesia, the Churches could be said to be a main protagonist in the debate.

There was a great deal of diplomatic activity among the Churches, in the construction of joint statements, in meetings with members of the Government and through letters to the Press. The weight bore down upon the Anglican, Methodist and Presbyterian Churches in particular because of their connections with the territory.

December 8th, 1966, became the date when the question of sanctions to be imposed upon Rhodesia was to be debated in the Houses of Parliament. Careful briefings for this debate were made by the Conference of British Missionary Societies and presented to speakers who hoped to take part in the debate.

An old custom of Methodist members of both Houses, as it happened, was revived that very day by holding a dinner in the House at which the President of the Methodist Conference was guest of honour within a group of as many Methodist members of both Houses as could be present. A less favourable night could hardly have been chosen as so many members of the Commons wished to take part in the debate on sanctions. The Speaker of the House, Dr. Horace King, himself a Methodist, was weighed down by the number of people who hoped to participate in the debate but squeezed out the time to be present in a dining-room within the Lords. Lord Soper was differently placed, he could not be relieved of his duties.

So it came about that a large number of churchmen met in joint session beneath the Chamber of the Lords and the President gave them practical examples of how life was being lived in Rhodesia by Methodist ministers and members at that very time.

Meanwhile, up in the Lords, the Archbishop of Canterbury spoke to their Lordships and Lord Soper made a speech of twenty-six minutes based upon similar material to that used by the Archbishop. In the Commons there were those who wondered whether it was not Mr. Speaker who in fact felt the burden more than those who did speak where he could not.

Lord Soper's speech began with reference to some which had gone before which to him were 'cynical' and 'utilitarian'. He drew the attention of the House to a letter in the Press that morning signed by the leaders of the Protestant Churches. He expressed the belief that the Roman Churches could also have signed the letter. He felt that the Church had a right to be heard. He associated himself with the statement. He referred then to the action of the Rhodesian authorities in making it obligatory for all kinds of welfare organizations to be government registered before they could operate. He saw in this an evidence of the 'police state'. Relief of the distressed was regimented by having to seek consent to aid them. The objective of such legislation was evidently suppressive.

He drew attention to legislation passed in Rhodesia in 1965 which was identical with laws passed in South Africa. He mentioned specifically the clause whereby those who were subject to restriction or special conditions were prohibited from issuing any form of communication. They were left without any method of presenting their case.

'I believe that Smith is the man that is blowing the coals of the fire and not the Government. I also believe U.D.I. is the instrument he is creating for his work and not the work to which we in this country ought to be dedicated. Therefore, with heavy heart the next step seems to be the right one, we should now proceed to selective sanctions. We should do everything in our power to persuade those to whom we are committed in love as well as in justice that we are seeking to do what is right, unafraid of the consequences once we are persuaded that it is right.'

It is quite surprising how much legislation within Parliament is of a moral nature and has consequences or aspects of approach which are directly within the Church's world of interest. So the watch-dog function which Lord Soper has fulfilled, and continues to fulfil, in this field is of enormous benefit to the Church's cause.

There is a peculiar comradeship within the House of Lords. Its tea-room and other places of meeting are places where people really get to know one another, or can do should they wish to know and be known. Unlike the Members of Parliament, the Lords and Ladies know they are going to be together a long time. It is as well to find out just what lies behind each face, its prejudices, its obsessions, its cynicisms, its loves.

Lady Stocks, as well known and as well beloved by the public as Donald Soper, tells of how it was only when he became a colleague on the Labour benches in the Lords that she really began to know and appreciate his qualities.

She found that he was quite ready and eager to espouse an unpopular cause or to dig his trowel under some carefully hidden thing that needed to be exposed. She admired 'the courage to say it', so long admired by the Methodist Conference. She recalls an occasion in the discussion of penal reform when she proposed following the Danish precedent, the employment of voluntary castration as an alternative to imprisonment for persistent and compulsive (but otherwise harmless) sex offenders and Lord Soper supported her in this proposal. She has seen him 'gently and tactfully' help his colleagues when in distress. 'I have grown to admire and even to love him,' says Lady Stocks, and there is no commendation higher than that.

It is permissible to wonder just what hopes Mr. Harold Wilson had in mind when it was first proposed that Donald Soper become a Life Peer. Nothing is more certain than that his productivity index has risen far higher than could have been guessed in 1965. It is equally certain that the Free Church world has reason to be grateful to the administration which elevated him to the Lords and the Methodist Church to be 'content' with its one-man Bench.

Others are content too. In the Week of Prayer for Christian Unity 1971, Methodists from eight parishes were among the congregation in Sandringham Parish Church when Lord Soper preached in the presence of the Queen and members of the Royal family, the first Methodist to preach in Sandringham Church. Forty Anglicans and Methodists made their communion. The rector summed up the sermon. 'Just a simple gospel of love as the one road to unity and the only answer to starvation.'

14.

Far to Go

John Wesley, sometime Fellow of Lincoln College, Oxford, was born in 1703 and lived until 1791 to be ultimately honoured by the nation. He thought himself on the threshold of departing a dozen times before that March day in 1791, but contrived to preach his last sermon in the February of that year, having written his own valediction in the Arminian Magazine in 1790!

In 1966 on March 24th, the *Cambridge University Reporter* carried the announcement of the election of two Honorary Fellows of St. Catharine's College, Cambridge. In alphabetical order they were, Lord Franks, Provost of Worcester College, Oxford, formerly Ambassador to the United States of America; the second, 'The Right Honourable Reverend DONALD OLIVER, Baron SOPER of Kingsway, formerly Pensioner of the College.' To be elected Honorary Fellow of one's College is the rarest of Cambridge honours.

Grey-headed, with that troublesome leg now more troublesome than ever, the aftermath of a serious pneumonia to cope with, and in moments of tiredness himself proclaiming that he now works 70 per cent of his earlier output, Donald Soper is still left with far to go. He cannot let Wesley his great forerunner, beat him by two decades, give or take a year, and there is little sign that he intends to do so. Surely modern gerontology can improve upon the eighteenth century record in the case of this other '03 man. He hardly stops to ponder on these things, there is too much to do now.

When a life contains within it certain fixed convictions to witness to which is the ruling passion of the person who holds them, the unchanging in that life dominates the temporary and the temporary, of necessity, includes the process of ageing. This is the secret of longevity in many cases among notable people. Dr. Scott Lidgett, that great forerunner of Soper, might be cited as an example; or Bernard Shaw, or Bertrand Russell. There is the 'spiritual' element to living and geriatrics is the field in which to see it working actively.

It is sometimes said of Lord Soper that he is still saying the same things as young Donald Soper, the probationer minister of the Old Kent Road. He even states them in the same phrases. This is true; it is also true that the same heart muscle is tugging away within him when he growls today on Tower Hill as kept him going when singing to the strikers in Cambridge. It is for the verities which have not changed that he goes on working some years after the time when the average Methodist minister superannuates.

The Methodist minister does not 'retire'; he becomes supernumerary to the men on the active list, but available for such service as he can perform. A supernumerary in the old Methodist terminology was described as 'worn-out'. Latterly the Methodist stomach became too delicate for such crudities. But it is only when the vehicle will not express the verities any longer that the Wesley-pattern minister preaches his last sermon in the February and dies in the March – worn out.

Among those permanent features in the Soper ministry some are easily identifiable. There is the conviction that it is possible to have the Kingdom of Christ expressed through the medium of this world we live in and this social pattern he identifies with socialism of the Christian or democratic type. This has persisted right through, all the way from St. Catharine's. Perhaps the conviction had a starry-eyed quality in it years ago which is now missing; perhaps there was an omnibus or pantechnicon shape to the Kingdom – everything is in here – which is not now there. But the Kingdom still is.

There is the complete commitment to the laws of the universe as being moral and because they are moral being physical, biological, scientific. This genuine insight which was one of the treasures of the twenties in theological studies has not failed him any more than it has failed others. It is valid. One of the Soperisms which make people say 'he says the same things', is the phrase, 'That which is morally wrong cannot be politically right' – or 'economically' or 'socially' right – across the entire human field. The moral law underlies the natural law and, indeed, is that law.

Efficiency is but the obverse side of righteousness. It is on this conviction that he condemns war and violence. However hard man tries he will not get good out of these things.

A third fixed point concerns motivation in the human life. It could almost be said that his Christology is simply that Christ is the Lord of human motives, the love-drive in Jesus being the key to human action. From this stems the derived conviction which he so often states about 'enlightened self-interest'. This recently-revived political motive he has railed at and condemned through forty years, only to find it glorified in recent years. His dislike of what it implies is almost a physical nausea: it masks cruelty and contempt towards other people with such gentle, civilized smoothness as to appear utterly respectable. It is Satan in a dinner jacket and bow tie. He cannot see, and never will, what is the light which enlightens this philosophy. He knows only one light which enlightens and it is the light of the love of Jesus.

There is a realistic conviction that sin has penetrated deep into all corners of human society and individual personality. Much of his political thinking is affected by this conviction: it is this entrenched sin which blocks the road to the classless commonwealth which is the ordered expression of the Kingdom. The Capitalist, the Socialist, the Communist and the Mugwump sitting on his perpetual fence, all contribute decay and corruption to life's scene.

After his recent journey to Russia the second half of his *Tribune* report was under the headline, 'The Old Adam in the New Jerusalem' and the whole argument of the report was that, 'There is no permanence in their New Jerusalem, for the "new" man who will cherish and maintain it is yet to be born.' He noticed more drunks on the streets of Leningrad in three nights than he had seen in London in three months: but he knew that this Russian weakness for the bottle is part of the old Russian. Same old man, different setting; same old sin spoils different setting – the proposition winds like a snake. No wonder the devil turned up in Eden as a serpent. 'Sin is the most powerful thing in the world next to God.' So he said in the twenties and so he believes today.

There are many of these basic items of mental furniture in the Soper mind and each of them is tagged with a phrase which the world knows by heart which he repeats as shorthand for the philosophy by which he lives.

One other deserves mention largely because it is of enormous import for the contemporary scene. Detached from its conventional Christian connotation, faith is of the utmost significance in man's journey. In the name of God or, if God is out, in the name of humanity or, if humanity does not matter, in the name of personal sanity, believe in the thing by which you live. This is a constant Soper cry. Let a man argue his case with faith if he is capitalist, socialist, unionist or individual free-lance. There is an antiseptic quality in a faith to act by which destroys decay. Better a believing Communist than a waffling Christian. It is as though God said: Give me a believing man and I can get on with my work. All faiths tend to Faith.

All for the Kingdom; the universe is going my way; the love of Jesus is the core of existence; sin is master of camouflage but he is a poor Christian who cannot sniff out the old smell; Faith is the victory – here is his five-pointed framework to a life's work.

The rest is the apostle James writing of the faith of Abraham. 'Surely you can see that faith was at work in his actions, and that by these actions the integrity of his faith was fully proved'. There is something peculiarly fitting to Donald Soper in James' argument, one example employed in it being a wandering soul who sought a city and the other a harlot who saved herself by natural generosity.

Whether in the forties or the seventies, the truths are abiding, but the environment changes with relentless persistence and demands new expressions of the abiding. It is in this sense that the present decade is a challenge to Lord Soper, to his Mission and to his political colleagues. It is the mercies of the 'constant' God which are new every morning, and there is no time to be old if a man is to keep pace with God's changelessness set in the heart of change. If God would grow old, there might be time for his ministers to retire.

Writing in the *Tribune* in February 1971 Dr. Soper speaks of the ministry of 40 years and the Speakers' Corner platform today. The actual setting has changed into a noisy square formation where speaker seems to be shouting at speaker. This is simply a technical trouble which has to be overcome. Today other changes are more significant. Once it was rare to see a coloured face; today there are perhaps 40 per cent coloured people in the crowd and coloured speakers on a February Sunday were five out of six operating. 'Let us make no mistake about it, these coloured speakers are excited, eloquent and endowed with more lung power than many of their white competitors. Speakers' Corner today is a race forum and not infrequently a race cauldron.'

Even more significant, the speakers today are a group of quite anonymous persons in contrast with the marked individualism and piquant personality of the regulars of decades now gone. The disappearance of rare characters is matched by the patchy attendance of the leading political parties – occasionally a Conservative, now and then a Liberal, will put in an odd appearance but never a Labour speaker. Once this was their regular assignment. The Communists and Socialist splinter groups persist with little fervour.

'The argument has declined,' writes Lord Soper. 'In the religious sphere, secularism expressed in what the critics of religion believed to be scientific terms is no longer the menace that once it was to the Christian advocate, either of the Right or of the Left. In the political realm the economic propositions that drove me as a youngster to read Marx and learn about communism seem to have faded away.

'This does not mean that religion is validated or that Marx is repudiated at Speakers' Corner. What it indicates is a move away from propositions and a preference for protests. Declamation has taken the place of debate and, most regretful of all, there is a marked tendency at the moment to shout down the opponent rather than controvert him.'

Observing the stream of Sunday marches which begin at or end at Speakers' Corner, Lord Soper compares them in his mind with the sombre but deadly earnest Hunger Marches of the really unemployed of years now gone and notes how today's more numerous marches, which are rarely self-explanatory, decrease in effectiveness as they grow in number. He comes to his verdict.

'Speakers' Corner is a sign of the times and those times have radically changed over the years. The old certainties of Christian, communist, socialist, fundamentalist, as well as the British Israelite or Seventh Day Adventist, have largely wilted and given place to a sort of petulant indecision. Nowhere is this more obvious than in the field of socialism.'

The article ends with a plea to the Labour Party to give people a theme and a programme at least to argue about, at best to argue for. In this decade the Christian cause has its representative still prepared to state a case where the others have faded: the Labour Party point of view still has the Christian Socialist Movement with the same person at its head to state the idealist case which must underlie any good that Party may at last achieve. He still quotes Jehovah: 'I will do a new thing.'

In the House of Lords also time has marched on. It is a different world now from that when he came into the company as one of the dominant Government attempting in spite of the enormous pressures of ancient history and in the medium of a *laissez faire* society, to create a planned society. Then the argument was as much with such members of his Party as wished to make a compromise between what existed and what the movement had dreamed. The task was to see that the 'mixed economy' was not the mixture as before. Today he is in the ranks of the Opposition and the task is heroic in its proportions, as much defensive as creative. Once upon a time, when he pressed his own people to some more socialist way, the Tory Lords could taunt him with voting for the Government on this issue or that. Here at least the modern idiom has simplified life – which is a pleasant change.

In the world of broadcasting he long ago made the transition from the, perhaps easier, medium of radio to that of television, but that successful transplant was only a stage on a journey. He predates the period in which it is common enough to refer to the British society as 'post-Christian'. He has lived through the time when television newspaper critics complained that the broadcasting authorities appeared to think that they had only to put two or three clerics together to have a successful programme. Today it almost looks as though the authorities heeded that criticism and the parson is regarded as a television character to match the 'corner-man' in a minstrel show. Not that the producers are totally to blame; there are parsons eminently fitted for the job of feeding the comedian.

Today his television and radio work merits the phrase which he commonly uses, 'Speaking as a Christian Socialist', or 'As a would-be theologian', so much has the atmosphere of tolerance of other views of living than the Christian view prevailed. Fortunately, in this Christian advocate the Corporation and the Independent Authority alike realize they have a man who enjoys being the parson who rides like one of the handful that came back from Kabul. A world well travelled has taught him that Christianity is nowhere more at home than where the ideological battle rages and all comers are eligible for the tourney.

More difficult is the insertion of the Christian point of view into programmes which are dominated by the 'pop' of the day. If one newspaper reported, with as much joy as anger or sadness, that in a youth group Lord Soper got in a few useful digs at modern music and a commendation of the purposefulness of life but Christianity or 'religion' had only a look-in, it is as well to examine the skill which contrived the look-in. However that may be, he is still 'on the box' in a medium which so resolutely drops participants who have said their say.

The open-air propagandist situation and the 'secular society' situation are alike symptoms of the current age and both point to the sobering conclusion that what Donald Soper has said about social organization through forty years is only too demonstrably obvious in the seventies. American National Service men throwing their medals contemptuously into a pile in their nation's capital are unknowingly acting out the Soper thesis as though their action were one of those dramatized sermons which that other prophet, Ezekiel, found so useful. The British Government trying its best to corral the Unions could also be a dramatic preachment of this old but new theme.

'We become aware that war doesn't work any more, and the evidence from Vietnam to Sinai adds weight day by day to this reflection. We are, at the same time, aware that the non-violent attempts to solve the problems of Vietnam or Israel do not seem to work either. We become increasingly aware that the industrial system doesn't work and the traditional checks and balances of the capitalist system are being reduced to nonsense with each successive strike.' So said Lord Soper in *Tribune* in March 1971.

He goes on: 'Not only in these islands, but almost everywhere else, the cherished ideas that were associated with stability are overtaken by events which could apparently be neither foreseen nor averted. . . . There is, I believe, perceptible evidence that, because such attitudes are assumed in the prevailing atmosphere of thought, a situation not unlike Wicker's assertion that "life doesn't work any more" could develop.' (Tom Wicker of the New York *Review of Books* created this phrase.)

Lord Soper points out that contemporaneously with the decline in religious faith, which kept whole centuries alive, secular faith in science and a predictable earthly, technological heaven has also died. He finds himself therefore in this new atmosphere and has to adjust his proclamation that life is a billion times worth living when God and the gods are not dead. His recipe for a faithless situation is the doctrine of works. Do the deed because the deed is there to be done, 'salvation by works'. The experience of many young people who out of the faithless cynicism of our age have gone on Voluntary Service Overseas from the most mixed of motives, only to discover faith and themselves, and return to work on the tasks permanently, suggests that there is much wisdom in this answer. He who does the will shall know the doctrine. Jesus himself offered this guarantee.

That wartime baby, the Order of Christian Witness, has been no more immune from the changes wrought by the contemporary scene. Recent reports of campaigns have frankly admitted that the people completely outside the Church have not come in great crowds to hear the open-air preachers. An allergy to open-air witness has sometimes been discovered within the Churches themselves and sheer open evangelism has fallen into disrepute among many denominations. The leadership of the Order has in consequence had its own crisis problem. Lord Soper has of deliberate intent handed over the leadership to others, though remaining as the central adviser and encourager of all that has been attempted and wise man within the discussions of policy. Conceived as an open-air witness Order, it would not have been surprising if the whole organization had gone into liquidation, but this is far from the truth. Instead it has adjusted itself to the society in which it now has to work.

The 1970 Report, for example, describes Campaigns at Fulham, London, and Newcastle-under-Lyme in Staffordshire. There has been a channelling of the programme into house-to-house visitation and small group meetings in the homes of Church members or people on the fringe of the Church, though open-air witness continues to be part of the plans.

Such a change fits in with alterations noticeable in large-scale advertising, where the mass talk is left to the television medium while the campaigning is done on the doorstep, or with highly individualized correspondence. 'You have been chosen for one of our lucky numbers.'

Lord Soper still manages to get in a visit to the Order at work and has had again and again to emphasize the importance of factual witnessing being in itself more than worthwhile. Ecumenism has introduced new factors and the Order has drawn closer in its organized life to others concerned with renewal and mission in the Church through an experiment called *ONE*, as well as finding campaign opportunities in the service of both the Anglican and Methodist Churches.

Denis and Muriel Gardiner, joint secretaries of the O.C.W., in a recent report write: 'One thing is sure and that is that our concern is for the society in which we live and the individuals which are part of it, rather than with the Church. The Church is the agent of God's mission in society, and it is as part of the Church that we do our work. But when we think of the Church we can no longer think in terms of Methodism or any other denomination. We need to affirm the oneness of Christ's Church against the human divisiveness which would split it into fragmented parts.'

In this new method of getting personally alongside of people, in the street or the home, the club or the school hall, it is still possible to bring into one serving Family forty young people ready to live together and witness, as in the Erdlington and Conisborough Campaign – itself a joint Methodist/Anglican effort. Here the open-air work was backed by a guitar group and there was a welcome revival of audiences. House groups begun on campaign were kept going when the campaigners had left. 'It is possible for very ordinary folk to do things for Christ when they do it together.'

Doing it together is the very lifeblood of the long-term project of Community House in Notting Hill which is designed for ten people, with no 'encumbrances', to live together while they work in London on their own jobs. Sharing in communal finance and the chores of housekeeping each, according to his or her gifts, serves some local community project – clubs, youth work, political parties, local action groups. The ten form a nucleus round which other volunteers can gather from among students in the colleges of London.

The last decade has seen a prodigious concentration of thought upon the nature, future, shape and relevance of the Church. No denomination has been outside the discussion and the number of books and reports is beyond counting. Each section of the Church has produced a galaxy of young men and women who have become well known because of their criticism of the Church. Some of the men have been within the ranks of the ministry, have written their criticism and then later left the ministry, seeking new ways of service.

Others have had the patience to stay within the ministry of the Church to work out new ways of expressing the worship, life and community programme. Yet even among them there have not been many who have turned their attention to the techniques of a new evangelism. Much of the debate has begun with analysis of the way in which the 'secular age' has rejected the Church but has then turned away from defining any mission to the secular age and ended up in talk on how to re-arrange the Church's interior life.

Indeed, the Church has never been so interesting as it has been on the dissecting table of the years following Vatican Council II. But so many who have taken part in the exercise appear not to have realized that they themselves were parts of the cadaver on the table, and that the observation gallery in the dissecting theatre has long since been empty.

Nevertheless it would be ridiculous to say that as an establishment among the establishments of the Western world – and beyond – the Church as a world-wide whole has been irrelevant. On national and international scales the Church never had greater efficiency than it has today. The upper echelons of power are remarkably good at their job.

Great British missionary Churches have over a decade successfully turned mighty ecclesiastical empires into real and working commonwealths of co-operating self-governing Churches. The East Asia Christian Conference can show its heels to the South-East Asia Treaty Organization. Faced with the same problems it has done a better job. The All-Africa Church Conference has less danger of splitting down the middle than the Organization of African Unity. Even Europe can show a degree of ecclesiastical co-operation hard to parallel.

These, however, are areas of human activity where thought, planning and tough labour are still in fashion. Where the world situation has demanded ordered thinking, the Church, through some of its best minds, has not failed to produce a contemporary product as good as any other organization. The Division of Interchurch Aid, Refugee and World Service of the World Council, for example, will bear comparison with any international effort of our times.

All this chimes in with the Soper thesis about Tower Hill and Speakers' Corner – Give us an arena of argument and we will argue and win. Give us a new nation situation demanding development, containing young nationalist zealots, and we will provide such a programme and such resources as to startle the nations. Give us a situation where the white man has long dominated the programme but new, eager people are now bred into being and we will show you a Christian Revolution.

In these overseas fields, all the agony of thought which has purged the Church through the last decade has toughened her for intellectual, reformatory, serious activity. But on the home ground she is like the 'blue stocking' at the 'pot' party. Who wants intellect, planning, reformation? The Church is not alone in this philosophical isolation, indeed, at the time of a General Election in Britain the audiences gathered to hear politicians arguing their case from Right or Left are not so numerically strong as the regular weeknight meetings of the churches and far behind the average of morning congregations. All too often the Press report of a political speech, subsequently relayed to the nation, does not mention that it was delivered to fifty or sixty persons in a chalk-dusty classroom of an Infant School. It is not for nothing that the campaign directors introduce a 'shopping basket' election. Their diagnosis is not far adrift: in the flavour of the votes cast you can't tell the difference between a thoughtful vote and a trading stamp vote.

Writing in that brilliant little magazine of the West London Mission, *Kingsway*, before the last election Lord Soper told his people of the signs of the times which affected the election to come.

'The first is the manifest impact that the economic condition in which the man-in-the-street finds himself has upon his political interests, let alone his political thinking. The concentration of attention upon personal convenience and economic well-being is a brute fact that every political psephologist treats with the utmost attention. This is moreover a brute fact which poses a profound issue for the Christian. I expect that the outcome of the next election will ultimately depend on the way in which millions of voters relate what political principles they have to what personal economic prospects they anticipate. In the light of the faith we profess this is simply not good enough.

'Hence I believe that our job is to argue, to press for, and illustrate the primacy of service to the community rather than the benefits to be derived from it. In no sour criticism of present trends in the political spectrum, I am none the less persuaded of the urgent need for the recovery of, and deepening of moral earnestness.'

It is off the beat of Lord Soper's immediate argument in that particular 'Diary Note' in *Kingsway* but it is a legitimate projection of the same argument to ask whether this contentment with the immediately comforting 'thing' is not an element in the low-keyed life of the Churches. The old 1000-seater chapel can be quite cosy for the 120 members if they simply forget the pew glut. The legacy left by the deceased over-eighty spinster is enough to do the repairs on the boiler, so all is well. We have no young people, but then they all have to go away to find work and the Senior Citizens' Club is growing. The youngsters will return, on pension. We don't get many to service, but look at Kingsway, look at Westminster, look at City Temple; *they* are not what they were.

Lord Soper has been looking at Kingsway for a long time and all through the period of Britain's religious recession. He has looked at it in the context of the whole ecclesiastical occupation of Britain. Not surprisingly he has been in trouble because he has looked.

On a late night and satirical programme on B.B.C. television in 1968 he unburdened his heart about the state of, and future of the Church.

'I have to confess that I don't believe the Church has a permanent place as it now stands and operates in the life of the community today.

'I don't believe that the Church has the monopoly of stated truths in stated words about everything in particular and everything in general.

'I do not think, in fact, that we can any longer believe that the Church is the kind of institution which can require people to behave in certain patterns liturgically and in particular sabbatarian patterns.

'I do not believe that the Church is indispensable as we have known it down the centuries and to go on pretending that it is, is a piece of self-deceit. It is not essential because, quite frankly, a great many people get on pretty well without it, and even more important is that there are so many intellectual propositions attached to it, and so many practices have accrued to it, which manifestly have no relevance in the kind of world in which we live today.

'I do believe that Christianity is true, and therefore this effervescing Word must be expressed in new wine put into new bottles. The Church can no longer contain the fizzy, explosive stuff that the true wine of the bottle ought to be.' (Report in *Methodist Recorder*, January 18th, 1968.)

There was, of course, a storm of church-centred criticism of this statement but, as the *Methodist Recorder* drew out from Lord Soper, the argument really revolved round the view of the Church by those within it who have struggled to re-interpret its life in terms of a new theological look, and what the man who passes the rather grubby church on the corner of the street thinks the Church to be.

People do not know that the churchman thinks 'the fellowship of all believers' is the Divine Society. He is not aware that the parsons and the minority which follows the parsons regard themselves as the Body of Christ. Here is the Great Estrangement, the people not knowing the Church; the Church not knowing the people. Life goes on in a world where there are tens of thousands of younger people and children who are totally unaware of the Christian Church, for whom life pans out fairly well, who find they confront problems which their parents took to Church for solutions but which they themselves handle entirely differently.

There is the wide range of new problems which did not fall to their parents to experience; a reconciliation with drug-taking as a mode of life; a world where child-bearing is totally optional; a society where work is a routine group action controlled by one's Union and done for the 'lolly'. But their world is built on the pursuit of joy. They have no complaints except at anything which pulls them back from the search for joy, and within the search love, sex, possessions and world-wide freedom without codes are, to them, life. In the dire poverty of China within the last fifty years there was a catch-phrase among the ill-paid, or never paid, soldiery which symbolized a philosophy. 'Today I have had a glass of wine', so said the soldier and bedded down on the earth to sleep. Here in this country it is as though millions said, 'Every day has its glass of wine – why ask questions?'

It is this social situation, surely, which keeps Lord Soper at work when others of his generation have superannuated from responsible control. He of all ministers could have contracted out of the West London Mission with honour and given the rest of his time and energy to the important work in the Lords; surely a unique service to give to the Churches and his own Church. A handful of years ago there were those in Methodism who thought this could happen. It is possible for his friends and foes to imagine the aspect of his life involving charge of a church taken away and still leaving an intelligible Soper–national figure, veteran churchman, political idealist.

It could not be. Such thinking leaves out the thing which in spite of all the ramifications of an extraordinary life goes back to the beginnings and has never been absent even when opponents have wished that it were. This man is the boy of thirteen years who wanted to be a Wesleyan Minister and who survived academic training still wanting the same thing. A minister without a church is like a crab without claws.

Confronting the sort of world into which time has brought him he has to think of it in terms of the claws with which he has gripped his world from the beginning. He cannot be cured at his age of the will to be effective under all conditions. His tools have been the Mission. The Mission has shared the fate of the rest of the Church in Britain. Then the Mission must change.

So it comes about that Donald Soper still has far to go. The manner of his beginning his new journey crashed in on an astonished world in 1970 through the Press which announced the immanent sale of, in the words of the *Daily Telegraph* 'the Kingsway Hall, former Methodist stronghold' and the Methodist lovers of correspondence columns enjoyed an enormous excitement spending the popular dream figure of £3 million which would accrue from the sale. Seldom has a whole community of nearly 700,000 done the 'big win' trip!

Writing in the Mission magazine, *Kingsway*, of the changes which are everywhere Lord Soper puts his own perspective on the plans for the future. 'What does not change is the underlying purpose that has been responsible for the negotiations to dispose of the Kingsway Hall premises. I believe that the big hall is not suitable for our continuing worship, especially in the light of Methodist-Anglican movements towards unity, and that increasingly we must face the need to provide a place of worship which will beckon us to a relevant and acceptable churchmanship for the seventies and beyond.

'Then again I believe that the vast social work of the West London Mission must be safeguarded, and our resources, now locked up in bricks and mortar in Kingsway itself, can be better maintained by getting out of premises which are not vital for our needs, and therefore can be better turned into the sort of funds which are required for that social and rescue work.

'We shall, of course, need to find alternative accommodation for the crêche and the administrative needs of the West London Mission, but this is no insuperable task. I have shared these beliefs and intentions with the Trustees and with the Kingsway fellowship and they have caught the vision and we shall go forward with enthusiasm, but also with due regard for the risks which can reasonably be faced, and others which we ought not to accept and would not be faithful to our Methodist heritage if we did.

'One further word – the West London Mission has been a pioneer church in past days – we have blazed many a trail over the years. I hope that we in the Mission may be pioneers again, leading the way into the sort of institutional Christianity which is both apostolic and suitable to the conditions that face us in the years to come.'

If this call to his people is indicative of the plans which lie before the great Mission he inherited away back in 1936, then Lord Soper has, indeed, far to go. The plan is evidently a compromise between his view that the Church in its present institutional, gathered community form is due to disappear and the pressures which caring for the minority world of the churchmen of this very moment demand.

This is typical of the man whose life we have followed through so many hectic years. His technique has always been, if he will forgive the comparison, not unlike the structure of a modern automatic rifle. Click a switch and it fires single-shot rounds, and if necessary, through a telescopic sight. But tucked in neatly there is the magazine with 100 or more rounds for bursts of devastating fire when the moment demands them. So the great dreams of a non-violent world, the social establishment of the new society, the death and rising again of the whole universal Church, one and undivided and containing many fine people now outside its compass, lies like the magazine beneath his attack or defence.

Meanwhile there it is, the company for whose souls God has given him pastoral responsibility in this moment. They are face to face with today's problems of living out an intelligent Christian life just for today. 'Then feed my sheep.' The call of Jesus to the repentant Peter still confronts his present-day disciple. For this it all began for Donald Soper those long years ago and he does not need to be told three times.

To step into the Kingsway Centre in a business day lunch hour and find the cheerful, all-age group having lunch there and to talk with them, is to discover a very live Christian fellowship and also to know that the reconstructed place of the future is no dream but already here in embryo. But any one of the folk there will tell the visitor that the great thing about 'this place' is the intense depth of its spiritual encouragement. Someone will instance the power of, say, a Good Friday Three Hour Vigil when 'The Doctor' conducts it.

He still roams the world, if not so frequently; dashes off to take a T.V. appointment in the Regions; holds the fort in the Park and adds his word to the national debate in the House. But, he himself has said it, the ministry of the Word and Sacraments is his integrating salvation. He usually has the last word; let him have it in a sermon on the Sacred Ministry, a charge to Methodism's young ordinands.

'It is your duty, as it is the duty of all who profess the Christian Faith, to adorn that faith with every quality you possess and with every gift God has bestowed upon you. You will remember to dress with simple elegance bearing in mind the relation that must always exist between that elegance and the stipend you receive. You will be physically fastidious especially when holding out your hands to the sick person or when giving bread to your people at the table of the Lord.

'You will set your life within the pattern of such discipline as will carry you over the days that are hard and times that are weary. This is the competence that is required of all good workmen.

'I believe that if you will really put yourselves alongside the people God gave you to care for, you will love them. Baron von Hugel has said "I don't kiss my little boy because I love him; I kiss him that I may love him." It is only in the physical and mental contact that you and I can make with the people that we come to love them.

'I bid you in the name of Christ take the situation in which you will be put down and learn it and know it, and by a strange alchemy God will give you all the love and understanding you require.

'It is easy to talk of the Prophetic Ministry but, in one sense, unless you are a prophet you have nothing of value to bring to the ordinary daily occasion of your ministry. I beg you to see this ministry in the light of eternity, against the background of the Kingdom of God. Jesus Christ requires of us earnestly and continuously to imagine and work out what his Kingdom would be and what are the ultimate objectives to which you are moving. Such an enterprise is a very salutary thing because it unifies in you the little corners of the vineyard with the Master of the vineyard and his widest purposes. It keeps the ministry clean and wholesome because it keeps us free from malice, petty envy and immediate disappointment.'

Somewhere in the far-flung Methodist Connexion, on a fronded Caribbean Island, in the lanes of Hong Kong, where the giant waves of the South Atlantic pound the coastlands of West Africa, or driving through East Anglian fenlands on a winter's night, are men who will remember the man who did what he taught when, unlike the naval carriers, they do see the year 2000.

INDEX